Evaluating Leisure Services:
Making Enlightened Decisions

Evaluating Leisure Services:
Making Enlightened Decisions

Karla A. Henderson, Ph.D., Professor

University of North Carolina—Chapel Hill

with assistance from

M. Deborah Bialeschki, Ph.D., Associate Professor

University of North Carolina—Chapel Hill

Venture Publishing, Inc.
State College, PA

Production: Richard Yocum
Cover Design: Sandra Sikorski
Manuscript Editing: Michele L. Barbin

Library of Congress Catalogue Card Number 95-60641
ISBN 0-910251-72-X

To D.J.—

she knew how to evaluate intuitively!

Table of Contents

Unit One—Criteria:
Introduction to Foundations for Evaluation

Unit Two—Evidence: Data Collection

UNIT THREE—EVIDENCE: DATA ANALYSIS

UNIT FOUR—JUDGMENT: DATA REPORTING

LIST OF TABLES AND FIGURES

PREFACE

We live in an "information" society. Professionals in any field of human services must have means to assess and evaluate information about participants and organizations. To organize and manage leisure services, we need information about people's preferences, needs, and behaviors and the programs, administrative structures, and resources that frame the organizations. Evaluation can provide information that will enable us to make "enlightened decisions."

Evaluation is a process that each of us uses many times a day. You probably made a judgment about what you liked or didn't like as you saw the cover of this book and began to thumb through its pages. Although this type of intuitive evaluation is important, this book is about systematic evaluation that focuses specifically on identifying explicit evaluation criteria, collecting evidence or data, and making judgments about the value or the worth of something.

Unfortunately, evaluation strikes terror in the hearts of many students and professionals. You will find that evaluation does not consist of any magic formula. Nor can learning to do evaluations be done overnight. The more you learn about evaluation procedures, however, the easier they become. We hope to counter through this book the defeatist attitudes prevalent among students and some professionals that assessment, evaluation, and statistics are beyond their grasp.

This text will not make you an expert. It is intended, however, to provide an awareness and understanding of the need for evaluation research in the delivery of leisure and human services. We attempt to show how programming and management are linked to evaluation. We have made the assumption that the reader understands the leisure and human service delivery field and has some background about the value of leisure and recreation involvement. This book is intended to provide a basic overview and working knowledge of evaluation procedures. Knowing basic steps and having some familiarity with evaluation research tools, however, can help you to begin a process of lifelong learning about evaluation and how it can be used in organizations as well as to help you understand more about the research process in general. Each time you do an evaluation you will learn something that will be helpful for next time. Thus, this book will provide a primer that will enable you to use evaluation and become more experienced as you practice and apply the concepts and techniques.

This textbook is designed for upper level undergraduates, beginning graduate students, and practitioners who wish to apply evaluation research in their work.

It is written for students, but students are defined to be anyone who is in a learning situation. Many professionals find that learning makes the most sense once they are in the "real world" where they need to apply text material immediately to their situations.

This book consists of three main parts that are divided into four logical units. The three parts are the theses or the "trilogy" of the evaluation process—criteria, evidence (data), and judgment. Since the evidence section is mainly oriented to techniques, strategies, and research methods, we have divided it into two units on collecting data and analyzing data. Because evaluation uses a number of conceptual ideas and specific research applications, we have organized the chapters around specific topics. Sometimes it is useful to read about a particular concept and technique and reflect upon it before moving on to the next idea. Other times you may want to turn to a particular chapter that will give information on how to address a specific evaluation project.

We have taken the *USA Today* approach to writing this text. *USA Today* uses short articles that can be read and comprehended fairly quickly. Unlike *USA Today,* we have tried not to oversimplify the ideas but rather create chapters that can be easily read. The number of chapters in this book may seem a bit overwhelming, but none of them is particularly long, and we have tried to organize the reading by outlining key points and providing examples as much as possible.

We have also made the assumption that we are all in this recreation, park, leisure, and tourism field together. We have tried to use examples related to therapeutic recreation, youth agencies, community recreation, commercial businesses, camping and outdoor recreation. Although not all of these examples will be directly applicable to your interest, we believe that in a field that shares the common goals of enhancing the quality of life for people through leisure, that we can all learn from each other. In most cases the implications of evaluation to any one area of recreation can apply to other applied situations as well.

A number of people have influenced the writing of this textbook. We are most indebted to Herberta Lundegren and Pat Farrell (Pennsylvania State University) for the excellent evaluation book, *Evaluation for Leisure Service Managers,* that they wrote several years ago. We have used their model in writing this book and have tried to build upon their framework with the inclusion of more examples of evaluation based on qualitative data. The education we received about evaluation has come largely from our formal coursework in education and particularly adult education. Individuals who have affected those ideas greatly are Pat Boyle (University of Minnesota) and Sara Steele (University of Wisconsin-Madison). Other individuals in the field of parks, recreation, and leisure studies who have contributed to our understanding of evaluation are too numerous to mention here but are acknowledged throughout this book. We also want to thank the colleagues who provided an initial review of an early draft of the book: Stephen Anderson from University of North Carolina at Greensboro, Marcia Carter and Teresa Beck from Baylor University, Candace Goode from North Carolina State University, and Suz Welch from Camp Hantesa in Boone, Iowa.

This book evolved through teaching evaluation and research methods over the past fifteen years. Although we are indebted to all students who have helped us learn about how to teach these topics, we particularly want to thank the students in the LSRA 150, "Evaluation of Recreational Services," at the University of North Carolina at Chapel Hill who used a draft of the book during a semester and provided valuable written, as well as verbal, feedback that enabled a number of constructive changes to be made in the book before it went to press: Paula Anderson, Kimberley Boyette, Amy Bryan, Tonya Bryan, Brent Burnette, Laura Elliot, Andrew Fisher, Sandi Goode, Charlene Hardin, Victoria Huff, Jenny Long, Felicia Lucas, Ginna Millard, Cathy Mitchell, Cindy Newton, Lara Pietrafesa, Tonya Sampson, Sara Shope, Demetria Smith, Amanda Swaney, and Gretchen Walker. A special thanks is also extended to Yu-Ying Chu who served as graduate assistant for the class.

The writing of any book would not be possible without the personal and professional support of friends, family, and colleagues. You know who you are and you are probably delighted that this book has come to a conclusion, at least for the time being. A big thanks to all of you, especially Leandra, Joyce, Neta, Jeanette, Doug, Lee, Charlie, Sharon, and the Women's Center Nonfiction Writing Group.

We hope that you as students and readers will evaluate this book favorably because you set criteria that valued a readable, understandable, and useful text and that you found evidence that supported those criteria.

Unit One—Criteria:
Introduction to Foundations for Evaluation

Introduction to Criteria

Beginning a text is not easy. Because your anxiety may already be high, we dislike beginning on a theoretical note. Yet a certain framework needs to be presented to provide a foundation for evaluation. When discussing evaluation, we want to be systematic with the procedures that are outlined. It is sometimes more tempting to start in the middle of the process than at the beginning. To explore evaluation, however, we as authors and you as readers must communicate at the same level. Therefore, we will start at the beginning by providing a conceptual background. As a reader, of course, you can start wherever you would like, but we encourage you to ground yourself in a basic understanding of evaluation and research processes before beginning to collect data.

Evaluating Leisure Services is an attempt to provide the student or the professional with the tools to conduct evaluation research. The goal of systematic evaluation is to make reliable, valid, useful, and enlightened decisions. Of course, everyone is continually involved in a process of evaluation. How many times has someone stuck his or her toe in a swimming pool to test its temperature before jumping in? Crude as it may be, dipping your toes is a form of evaluation that will lead to a judgment or a decision about whether and how to enter the water. If only formal evaluations were as easy as sticking one's toes into the water and making a decision! Unfortunately, most evaluations in leisure services are more systematic and complicated than this intuitive example. In this book, we will provide a useful process of systematic evaluation.

This first unit will set a framework for evaluation and explore the aspects of **determining criteria**. It is probably the least "action-packed" unit of all, but certainly one of the most critical. One major problem with evaluations is that sometimes evaluators do not take time to plan and ascertain the appropriate criteria to use. For example, by putting your toes into the swimming pool, you determined the temperature criterion, but many other criteria could have been measured by using some other process, such as water quality or depth. Perhaps the pH level in a swimming pool is a more appropriate criterion to measure than temperature before you go swimming. Measuring the pH level with one's toes would not be appropriate if the criterion included a chemical balance check. Thus, an essential dimension of any evaluation is making sure you are collecting evidence about the appropriate criteria or research questions.

In this book we will refer to the individual or individuals conducting evaluations as the evaluator. Evaluation will refer to making decisions based on identified criteria and supporting evidence. Evaluation research will refer to the processes that are used to collect and analyze data or evidence. Leisure services refer to the human service organizations and enterprises related to parks, recreation, tourism, commercial recreation, outdoors, education, and therapeutic recreation. Other specific terms will be defined throughout this book. In addition, a glossary of terms is included to assist you as you read the text.

In this first unit, we will examine what evaluation is, its purposes, its relationship to research, and how the aspects of criteria, evidence, and judgment are defined. We will explore areas of evaluation within leisure services and the types of evaluation that might be done. Within these types we will examine various approaches and models that can be applied. Further, we will consider how evaluation systems as well as evaluation projects are designed. Finally, we will address legal and ethical issues that may be encountered in conducting evaluations.

1.01 The Basics: What is Evaluation?

Goals for Chapter 1.01:

—To write a definition for evaluation;
—To describe the importance of systematic formal evaluations; and,
—To identify the characteristics of evaluation for making enlightened decisions.

All of us would like to live in a perfect world. We want to get all *A's* because our school work is of the highest quality. In work situations, we want our participants to experience many benefits from recreation and leisure programs. We want staff to perform their duties enthusiastically and appropriately, our budgets to reflect cost-effectiveness, and people to flock to our programs. We don't want people to complain or to doubt our abilities as professionals.

In reality, however, our lives and our student or professional situations don't run perfectly all the time. We need to use the tools we continually have to strive to improve ourselves and make our organizations more effective. None of us will ever be perfect, but we can use the processes and techniques of evaluation to help us make enlightened decisions to improve what we do.

This text will define evaluation as the systematic collection and analysis of data to address criteria and make judgments about the worth or improvement of something. Many other definitions exist that have slightly different interpretations. Generally, however, the goal of evaluation is to determine "what is" compared to "what should be."

As indicated, we are all continually engaged in a process of intuitive evaluation. We say things to ourselves like, "The room is too hot," or "I'm too tired to think," or "I wish I hadn't eaten so much for lunch." The evaluation we do in leisure service agencies, although it may be intuitive on an everyday basis, can also be more trustworthy when it is systematically designed. A camp director told us once, "I don't use evaluations. I just watch, listen and talk to campers and staff, and I find out all that I need to know." We acknowledge these important means for evaluation, but we also believe that formal systematic evaluations need to be conducted from time to time.

A systematic evaluation process takes a greater effort (in time and money) than informal evaluations that rely on intuition or expert judgment. Systematic or formal evaluation, however, provides a rigor when outcomes are complex, the decisions are important, and evidence is needed to make reliable, valid, and useful, or, as we call them, "enlightened" decisions.

The major purpose of evaluation is, therefore, to make decisions. We want to make the best possible decisions based on systematically gathering evidence related to a particular purpose or standard for decision making. Evaluation provides information that can lead to decisions *and* action. Through evaluation, we try to improve, or show the value of, various aspects of leisure services. We generate this information through the application of evaluation research methods and techniques. Research and evaluation share common methods and a similar framework for making decisions. The differences between evaluation projects and research studies will be described in more detail in Chapter 1.05 but for now, it is important to keep in mind that the methods and tools for evaluation and research are the same. Methods and tools of scientific research are used to make the judgment process for making decisions more reliable, valid, and useful.

Thus evaluation, as well as research, requires the systematic use of a framework of procedures and methods that include: **criteria** (also known as hypotheses, research questions, guiding questions, working hypotheses, or objectives), **evidence** or data that are collected using some standard descriptive or experimental design and methods, and **judgment** as evidenced in conclusions and recommendations.

Criteria + Evidence + Judgment = Evaluation
A Brief History

Theobald (1987) provided a brief historical background on evaluation in leisure services that may be useful to consider. When many recreation programs and other social service programs began to emerge in the 1960s, a need to determine clear objectives and the meaning of "success" became evident. For many programs, the need for accountability increased faster than many organizations' ability to respond through evaluation. Some of the early recreation literature mentioned evaluation but provided little guidance for how it was to be done.

The earliest approach to evaluation dealt with measuring the amount of something like the number of staff, budget size, type and value of facilities, number and characteristics of participants, and/or the acreage of park land. These numbers were compared according to some preestablished standard. These standards were written, tested, and rewritten; many of these standards are still commonly used today. When it became necessary to measure program effectiveness or program success beyond numbers of participants, a type of goal-attainment model was used. A goal-attainment model means that objectives are determined and then measured to see how close an organization came to meeting the objectives. Depending upon whether program, staff, administration, or facilities were being evaluated, if a discrepancy existed, the evaluator could either revise the goal, end the activity, or control or improve the activity. Today a variety of models and approaches are possible within the field of leisure services. These approaches will be discussed in more detail in Chapter 1.07.

Evaluation Today

Evaluation today can be thought of as ranging from intuitive everyday evaluation to formal systematic experimental studies, all of which help to assess where we are, where we want to be, and how we can reach our desired goals. Thus evaluation might entail everyday evaluation, self-checks, expert judgments, descriptive designs, quasi-experimental designs, to experimental designs. Figure 1.1 provides a pictorial example of how evaluation might look as a continuum ranging from intuitive to formal systems. Each of these methods on the continuum for doing evaluations will be discussed in more detail in Unit Two.

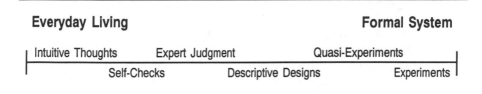

Figure 1.1 A Continuum of Evaluation

Developing a system for evaluation, gathering resources, and conducting periodic formal evaluations may be the basis for more efficient and effective operations, staff, and leisure programs that result in increased recreation, educational, and personal benefits for children, youth, and adults. To focus on evaluation for improving effectiveness and efficiency in the conduct of all aspects of leisure services, several important characteristics of evaluation should be kept in mind:

1. Evaluation is a process. It consists of the three dimensions of determining criteria, getting evidence, and making judgments. We must be sure decisions are based on sound judgments and not just on personal biases.
2. The goal of evaluation is to make decisions by ascertaining value or worth.

3. The most common way to evaluate is to measure and judge how well objectives are met. As you will see later in this text, however, the goal attainment model is only one approach that might be used.
4. The results of evaluation should lead to decision making about and for a specific situation or context.
5. Evaluation may be informal or formal. Systematically and formally gathering data, however, are necessary for making enlightened decisions for most leisure services organizations.
6. Evaluation within an organization should be ongoing with evaluation systems in place to address aspects of personnel, program, policy/administration, places (or areas and facilities), and participant outcomes. Evaluation takes place wherever services are delivered and organizational structures are used. Within these evaluations systems, particular evaluation projects may be undertaken.
7. Evaluation is continuous and does not necessarily occur only at the end of an event or activity. Evaluation may occur as an assessment to determine what is versus what should be, formatively throughout a program and to examine processes, or summatively, at the end, to ascertain outcomes.
8. Responsive evaluation is based on the premise that evaluation should respond to the issues and concerns of the various people who are interested in a particular leisure services program such as participants, staff, upper level management, or Board of Directors. In other words, evaluation should have relevance to an organization and those people who make decisions in the organization.
9. No magic formulas for evaluation exist. It is rarely a cut-and-dried thing. Each evaluation project undertaken will be different from the last and ought to reflect the particular uniqueness of the situation of an organization. Therefore, revision and modification is always ongoing as one plans, as well as implements, an evaluation project.

Each of these ideas will be revisited throughout this unit and will be applied in the process of doing evaluations by using criteria, evidence (data), and judgment.

From Ideas to Reality

In any professional situation, you have the choice to evaluate or not. Most of us are continually engaged in a process of intuitive evaluation about staff, programs, facilities, policies, and procedures whether or not we are consciously aware of it. Many times this intuitive evaluation is enough. Other times, however, colleagues, participants, or other stakeholders in an organization want some type of systematic proof that a situation exists. Thus, we need to have formal systematic information that documents the happenings in an organization. It may be documented information concerning the performance of a staff member, or it might be numbers that describe the average rating of satisfaction concerning a certain activity. Thus, it is necessary to collect these data based on criteria that will provide information to make judgments about what is happening within an organization.

1.02 Why Evaluate? Who Cares?

Goals for Chapter 1.02:

—To list the reasons why an evaluation might be undertaken given a particular situation;

—To describe the concerns and fears that some people have regarding undertaking evaluations; and,

—To determine when it is best to undertake an evaluation project and when evaluation may not be to the advantage of an organization.

The goal of evaluation is to determine the value or worth of something so that good decisions can be made. Information or feedback is obtained by developing criteria to be used to measure or gather data to make decisions. In other words, feedback is used for proactive or enlightened decisions.

Staff in any organization will have their own reasons for developing an evaluation system to aid in decision making. Each conducted evaluation project will likely have different purposes associated with the project. Regardless of the purpose, formal systematic evaluations must be done with predetermined criteria, reliable and valid evidence or data, and an open perspective for examining how programs, facilities, staff, and administrative procedures in leisure services can be improved. In other words, as Theobald (1987) suggested, you must first be aware that a decision needs to be made, then design the decision situation, choose from alternatives, and take action.

Some professionals are afraid of evaluation because they may not like what they find. If everything appears to be going smoothly, evaluation seems like more work on an already overburdened schedule just to find that everything isn't 100 percent right. The adage "don't fix it if it ain't broke" comes to mind. But evaluation is not meant only for crisis situations when changes *have* to be made. When evaluation is done systematically, crisis situations can often be avoided.

We live in an era of opportunities for decision making. Some societal trends are making evaluation imperative. For example, staff in many organizations need to justify how resources are being used to achieve realistic results from their programming and management efforts. Calls for good decision making and accountability are coming from participants including clients and consumers, from the professionals' desire to improve services, an awareness of good management practices, a recognition of society's limited fiscal and human services, and legislative mandates such as requirements of the Americans with Disabilities Act.

In the broadest sense, many professionals evaluate for several reasons: because it's compulsory; better for defense and/or offense to determine the worth, or lack of worth, of an aspect of the organization (e.g., program, a staff member, area/facility), or to improve or validate an aspect of the organization. More specifically we believe the major reasons for evaluation can be divided into eight broad reasons:

1. to determine accountability;
2. to assess or establish a baseline;
3. to assess the attainment of goals and objectives;
4. to ascertain outcomes and impact;
5. to determine the keys to successes and failures;
6. to improve and promote quality control;
7. to set future directions; and,
8. to comply with external standards.

These reasons are not mutually exclusive and often overlap one another a great deal. Evaluation usually does not occur for only one reason but occurs for a combination of reasons that enable decision making.

Accountability

Accountability, as one dimension of decision making, is often mentioned as a primary purpose of evaluation. We might think of accountability as being more of a reactive form of evaluation than proactive, although it can be used for proactive decisions. If an organization or program is not showing accountability, a decision may be made about whether that organization or program should continue to operate.

Accountability is a relative term that describes the capability of a leisure service delivery system to justify or explain the activities and services provided. According to Connolly (1982), accountability reflects the extent to which expenditures, activities, and processes effectively and efficiently accomplish the purposes for which an organization or a program was developed. Often projects are evaluated for accountability when some external unit, such as a city manager or a hospital administrator, requests the evaluation. Accountability, however, should be an ongoing concern of staff in any organization regardless of who is "watching."

Accountability results in determining legitimacy. It is also applied to see if a recreation program is meeting the needs and desires of people in the community. A by-product of the evaluation is that the agency may be seen in a better light, but the bottom line is that accountability should result in avoiding unnecessary expenditures of money.

Establishing a Baseline

Evaluation may be done to set a baseline. This usually results in an assessment or a needs assessment depending upon the context being evaluated. An assessment is the gathering of data or the measurement of a phenomena that is then put into an understandable form to compare results with objectives. Assessing a baseline can also provide a plan for future action. Community needs assessments, as well as clinical assessments of people with disabilities, are examples of evaluations used to establish a baseline in leisure services.

Assessing Goals and Objectives

One reason for doing evaluation is to assess goals and objectives. As indicated earlier, goals and objectives have been the backbone of evaluation efforts, although some approaches to evaluation do not take goals and objectives directly into account. Assessment of goals and objectives, for example, may help to determine how programs and area facilities contribute to leisure satisfaction for individuals or how to improve the quality of life in communities. Judgments from assessing goals and objectives result in determining if stated objectives are operating and/or whether other objectives are more appropriate. Thus, evaluation also can allow us to redefine the means for setting objectives and to determine exactly what goals the organizations ought to be setting and striving to accomplish.

Ascertaining Outcomes and Impacts

Determining the impact, effects, outcomes, and results of a program, area or facility, or administrative procedure is the bottom line of evaluation. By ascertaining the outcomes of a staff member's efforts, the expenditure of money, or the changes that occur in participants as a result of a program, value decisions can often be made. Impact evaluation asks what differences a program has made and how it affects people both now and in the future. Outcomes and impact are not always easy to measure, but are the essence of program planning, in particular, within leisure service organizations. If what we do does not have an affect on people, then it may not be worth doing whether the activity is done through therapeutic recreation, sports programming, or park planning.

Explaining Keys to Success or Failure

Some evaluations are undertaken to document processes that are used to obtain certain objectives. In other words, evaluation is done to see what works and what does not. In addition, determining what contributes to a successful program, as well as what might happen to create problems or failures, is useful. For example, weighing benefits against costs is one way to describe success. Other aspects of whether a program has worth relate to determining the input of staff effort, expertise, or leadership that might affect a program. Evaluation allows professionals to increase the utility and probability for successful programs that they conduct in the future and also allows individuals to share procedures and processes that might be useful with other professionals in similar situations.

Organizational Improvement and Quality Control

Organizational improvement and quality control are probably the most practical reasons for evaluation. Professionals evaluate personnel, programs, policies, or participants to make revisions in their existing programs. Sometimes the evaluation of staff, for example, results in promoting professional growth and education by appraising personnel quality and qualifications. The organization can also be improved by gauging public sentiment, attitudes, and awareness that provide information to enable professionals to improve and/or maintain high quality in the organization. Further, evaluation for improvement provides a way for two-way communication with the public.

Improvement might be sought by appraising existing facilities and physical property as to adequacy, accessibility, safety features, attractiveness, appropriateness, availability, and utilization. The evaluator tries to seek out and eliminate any detrimental features that could create risk or prevent the best recreation experience. Evaluation for improvement might also result in replacing outmoded concepts and invalid ideas about how a leisure service program ought to be run.

Rationalizing for Future Action

Evaluation can be a rationale for future action. In the starkest way, one might decide whether to keep programs or staff members or whether to let them go—a "go/no go" proposition. Rationale for putting money into future programs needs to be considered. Further, summative evaluations can lay a basis for further projects and can point a professional toward how to program more effectively in the future. When we know what worked and did not work and how people liked a particular program, it is easier to set objectives and implement plans in the future.

Complying with External Standards

Some organizations are required to do evaluations to comply with external standards set by the government or by some other professional body. These evaluations often are done for other purposes that directly aid the organization, but this evaluation may be done simply to meet accreditation or licensing requirements. The current procedures done by organizations like the American Camping Association (ACA) and the National Recreation and Park Association (NRPA) use a standard evaluation whereby a camp or a recreation organization can become accredited by showing that they have complied with certain standards. The accreditation process of these organizations is meant to be a guideline for helping organizations evaluate themselves by using the external standards as a starting point.

Many Reasons to Evaluate

As you can see, reasons for evaluation are numerous and overlapping; seldom would a professional only have one specific reason for evaluating. In fact, a problem may exist when the evaluation is so single-focused that the evaluator does not see all the possibilities for learning that can result from doing an evaluation project.

Evaluation experts such as Weiss (1972) have suggested some other reasons for evaluating that may not be as positive as the previous examples and may be detrimental to an organization if they are the sole reason for evaluating. Examples of these "not so good" reasons to evaluate include: to postpone decisions or avoid responsibility, to further public relations, to meet funding requirements, to justify programs, and to eliminate staff.

Occasionally, professionals use evaluations to postpone decisions or to avoid responsibility. Also, evaluation will "buy time" until something else can be figured out that has no relationship to the evaluation. If a supervisor or a manager has a tough decision to make, for example, she or he might decide to evaluate in hopes that some magic solution will occur. Sometimes this happens, but usually not. Evaluation still requires that necessary third element of judgment. Ultimately, the supervisor or manager will have to "bite the bullet" and take responsibility.

Evaluating solely for the public relations impact may not help to improve a program. It looks good to see an organization doing evaluations, but if nothing ever changes or the evaluation is not used, the public will not stay impressed for long. Related to this idea is doing evaluations just to increase prestige either within departments, in an organization, or with one's peers. Doing good evaluations will only increase prestige when they are appropriately used.

Evaluations done solely because of grant or funding requirements are often not as effective as those in which the stakeholders or the participants really care about how the feedback can be used for decision making. When funding sources require an evaluation, the evaluator ought to consider carefully what can be learned that may be helpful. A required evaluation is a wonderful opportunity to explore other reasons for evaluation that can assist in decision making.

Evaluation done only for the purpose of program justification or to eliminate staff may not be appropriate. An evaluation may result in program justification, but a great deal of bias may be built into something that has program justification as its only purpose. Further, an evaluation may give some ideas about what needs to be done to improve an organization, but using it solely for the purpose of getting rid of people is probably not going to be beneficial to the morale of the organization or the way that employees view the value of evaluation in the long run.

Fear of Evaluation

Many professionals fear evaluation for a number of reasons. Some people associate it with statistics, which is often a scary subject. If good objectives have not been written, evaluations are frequently difficult to do. In other cases, people do not know how to measure the information that they would like to know. Some professionals disregard evaluations because their prior experiences did not tell much more than they already knew. Others have done evaluations but then have not used the data so the evaluations were seen as simply a "waste of time." Still others are apprehensive of what they might find out if they evaluate—negative results are not always easy to take. Finally, some professionals shy from evaluations because they can be very time-consuming and most professionals are already too busy. Each of these fears, however, can be countered by paying attention to planning evaluation projects based on carefully determined and appropriate reasons for undertaking them.

When *Not* To Evaluate

Although evaluation is important and can be extremely useful, Theobald (1987) suggested that a professional must also know when *not* to evaluate. The first rule is to not evaluate unless you are sincere about making decisions to improve your program. Second, you may not want to evaluate if you know your program has serious organizational problems. The wise plan would be to try to fix those problems rather than think that evaluation is going to provide the magic answer.

Along with these concerns, make sure that you have goals and objectives that can be measured. You do not always need to have specific objectives, but you need to be clear about what you think your program ought to be doing. If you do not have any goals and objectives, it is best to get those written and then do the evaluation. Usually it is best not to evaluate when something is just getting started—give the program or staff member a chance to go for awhile or use a formative approach to make the evaluation more useful. Further, do not evaluate if you already know the outcome—it will be a waste of time, unless of course some stakeholder needs to see written documentation of the results. Finally, do not evaluate if you know the disadvantages will outweigh the advantages. If you know that an evaluation will be too time-consuming for what you will get, then do not do it, or do not use that particular evaluation design.

Knowing How to Evaluate

Although many excuses are valid for not evaluating, we suspect the major reasons that evaluations are not systematically conducted are because professionals do not know how to set up an effective evaluation process, how to analyze the data, and/ or how to interpret the data in ways to assist in making useful decisions.

The bottom line is that evaluations must be used for decision making. If the conclusions and recommendations are not used, the evaluation is useless. Evaluation is not necessarily a panacea for solving the problems in an organization, but the process can provide important information. We will address more specific ways to implement and use evaluation results in an organization in Chapter 4.05, but you should consider the whys of evaluation before you begin to evaluate any aspect of a leisure service system.

The best evaluation in the world cannot provide a definitive picture of the future, reduce the costs of goods and services, or determine the most desirable course of action. Those decisions are still up to you as a professional. You make the decision, however, based on the data you obtain from evaluations. Hopefully, as an evaluator you will make good decisions because you have the best possible data collected for the most appropriate reasons.

From Ideas to Reality

Suppose someone on your Park and Recreation Advisory Board suggests that she or he is not sure that the summer playground program is really meeting the needs of youth in your community. You believe that a systematic examination of that program may be useful to determine if the program is meeting children's needs. A number of reasons might be examined for doing this systematic evaluation: to determine if funds are being appropriately spent (accountability), to see if the goals and objectives for the program are being met, to determine if the input of staff and leadership are adequate to meet the program goals, to improve the program so that it meets the needs of children, and to determine exactly what is happening to children because of the program. All of these reasons will result in determining future action concerning the program. As you can see in this situation, the reasons for undertaking the evaluation are multiple. These reasons are important to consider before an evaluation is undertaken. Further, it is important to make sure that staff, board members, and participants are in agreement concerning why an evaluation should be undertaken and how the results will be used.

1.03 Developing an Evaluation System: The Five Ps of Evaluation

Goals for Chapter 1.03:

—To describe the five Ps and what components of each might be evaluated; and,

—To make a plan to determine what aspects of the five Ps might be evaluated in an organization over a five-year period.

Every aspect of leisure services has the potential for being evaluated. As indicated earlier, some of this evaluation may be done intuitively, but in other cases a systematic evaluation is needed. Whenever a new program is initiated or a new staff member is hired, some plan for evaluation ought to be considered. The purpose of this chapter is to provide a discussion of the areas of evaluation in leisure services and the systems that can be developed for evaluating within an organization.

Classifications can be used to determine broad areas of evaluation in leisure services organizations. Kraus and Allen (1987) suggested that there are program-oriented and people-oriented areas to evaluate. Lundegren and Farrell (1985) described the four major areas as personnel, program (including people), administration/policies, and areas and facilities. For purposes of our discussion and to help you remember the areas of evaluation, we would like to discuss the five Ps of evaluation: program, personnel, participants, places, and policies/administration. You should realize, however, that these five areas are not discrete and tend to overlap. For example, a recreation *program* is of little use unless some kind of impact is made on a *participant*. The *policies* of an organization may affect the *program*. The nature of a *place* in terms of the area or facility will affect the job of the staff person or *personnel*. Seldom do we evaluate any one of these aspects alone without also acknowledging how they relate to one another. We will use these five Ps to describe the areas of evaluation within leisure services.

Participants

The ultimate goal of most leisure service providers is to satisfy the participant in terms of her or his needs, wants, or interests. We will use the term participant throughout this book to refer to the people who receive leisure services. In applied cases, these participants might have other names such as consumers, clients, patients, guests, tourists, or campers; no matter what they are called, they all share common characteristics related to what recreation experiences may mean.

The common goal of all recreation and human service programs is to make life better and more rewarding for people. For example, if the consumer in a commercial or fee-based organization is not satisfied, she or he will not spend money in that organization. In other types of leisure service organizations we may be interested in evaluating the acquisition of a certain skill level or the improvement in attitudes toward recreation or toward oneself. Outcomes or impacts in terms of knowledge gained or changes made in one's life are also essential in evaluating leisure services. For purposes of marketing, we might examine the motivations and characteristics of participants. For example, in Table 1.3(1) participant motivations are measured with an evaluation instrument. In general, there are numerous possibilities for evaluating aspects of participants concerning their needs, interests, motivations, satisfactions, knowledge, skills level, abilities, attitudes, and many other personal dimensions.

Personnel

The benefits of staff evaluation include improving job performance and providing feedback for the personal development of staff regardless of whether they are young and in paid positions of responsibility for the first time or have been a professional for thirty years. Since evaluation is so important in the personnel process, mid-year or formative evaluations as well as end-of-the-year, or summative, evaluations are frequently used.

The formalities of personnel evaluations are up to the organization, but generally staff personnel files are kept that provide documented evidence of the performance of staff. Staff performance evaluations are generally based on a combination of the goals and objectives as found in the job descriptions and on the performance outcomes that result from doing the assigned jobs. Ideally, the evaluation should consist of an examination of the relationship between the criteria as stated in the job description and the performance of the staff member. Thus, a well-written, accurate job description is the basis for an individual staff evaluation. The staff member ought to know from the very beginning the criteria upon which she or he will be evaluated. The staff member must also receive feedback concerning the judgment that is made by the evaluator. The feedback to staff ideally occurs on an everyday informal basis, as well as during the formal process that is scheduled as part of a yearly performance appraisal.

Personnel evaluation is often called performance appraisal or performance evaluation. Most administration textbooks go into detail about this form of evaluation, but we would like to provide a bit of background so that the principles

Table 1.3(1)

Example of Motivations for Participating in Any Type of Leisure Activity
(adapted from Crompton, 1985)

	Very Important	*Moderately Important*	*Slightly Important*	*Not At All Important*
To be in a natural setting	_____	_____	_____	_____
To participate with friends	_____	_____	_____	_____
To develop my skills and abilities	_____	_____	_____	_____
To develop my general knowledge	_____	_____	_____	_____
To feel my independence	_____	_____	_____	_____
To share my skill and knowledge with others	_____	_____	_____	_____
To enjoy competing against others	_____	_____	_____	_____
To give my mind a rest	_____	_____	_____	_____
To improve my physical health	_____	_____	_____	_____
To build or create something	_____	_____	_____	_____
To have a sense of adventure and challenge	_____	_____	_____	_____
To enjoy quietness and serenity	_____	_____	_____	_____

of evaluation can be applied to personnel. Personnel evaluations are generally necessary for making decisions about compensation, promotion, training, and employee development. These personnel evaluations are formal, structured, systematic ways to measure an employee's job-related behavior.

Employees at all levels ought to be evaluated on at least an annual review pattern and preferably more often. This evaluation, however, is not just a single activity but takes into account evaluations made throughout the year. The criteria for personnel evaluation may vary greatly depending on the organization, but usually it is best to address aspects of the job and not an individual's personality. Ideally, the job description is the criteria. The purpose of the evaluation ought to focus on improvement and not necessarily on whether to keep or fire an employee.

The procedure used in employee evaluation is to assign duties, determine criteria for evaluation based on those duties, gather information about how the employee performs, appraise the performance, provide feedback to the employee, and make decisions and adjustments about the employee's performance. These decisions may relate to letting the employee know her or his relative value in the organization; identifying people for promotion; enhancing communication among supervisors, staff, and participants; providing directions for further continuing education and on-the-job training; and helping to establish and implement career goals.

Glover and Glover (1981) offered four recommendations necessary for effective personnel evaluation. First, the appraisal for development or improvement purposes should be separated from appraisal for administration that results in such decisions as determining job raises. Second, the evaluation system should provide "coaching" for the employees on a regular basis. Third, professionals who do the evaluating need training in how to be most effective not only in devising measurement criteria but also in how personnel evaluation is an ongoing process. Finally, the evaluation should be behavior-specific concerning the job the employee performs. A concrete plan to address deficiencies should exist. No matter what data are collected, the supervisor must ultimately make decisions about the employee's behavior on the job and will need to help the employee to improve upon her or his behavior.

Data for personnel evaluations can be obtained from administrators, other employees, or participants. Table 1.3(2) shows an example of a generic evaluation form that might be used with an employee. The supervisor would use this information in providing feedback to the employee along with other information obtained about the specific job duties that might be performed.

Policies/Administration

Evaluation is used for a number of policies, procedures, and administrative issues. Administrative aspects that may be evaluated include how the organization is organized and operated. Budget analysis is another way to examine policies and administration.

A professional might do public policy and community surveys to ascertain support for a particular activity, to measure the diversity of opinions, and gain

Table 1.3(2)

Example of a General Personnel Evaluation Form
(source unknown)

	Outstanding	Above Average	Average	Needs Improvement	Poor
1. Demonstrates insight and vision regarding objectives and long-range plans.	____	____	____	____	____
2. Possesses the physical stamina and drive to handle the rigors of the position.	____	____	____	____	____
3. Demonstrates pleasant personality and good communication skills.	____	____	____	____	____
4. Is consistent and fair; does not play favorites.	____	____	____	____	____
5. Solves problems rationally; can come to the heart of things.	____	____	____	____	____
6. Gets along well with other people.	____	____	____	____	____
7. Demonstrates ability to work together as a team.	____	____	____	____	____
8. Is approachable and willing to make changes.	____	____	____	____	____
9. Takes personal interest in each participant.	____	____	____	____	____
10. Welcomes and respects the opinions of others.	____	____	____	____	____
11. Is continuously alert to new ideas.	____	____	____	____	____
12. Is well-informed at all times regarding the total operation and how she or he contributes to it.	____	____	____	____	____

information from the public at large. Evaluations and needs assessments can allow an organization to gain a more comprehensive knowledge of the community, its people, their needs, their opinions, and special problems. Policy and administrative decisions may be made based on community dissatisfaction, perceived lack of opportunity, the need to equalize services or upgrade services, and to meet new demands.

Cost-benefit and cost-effectiveness are econometric models that are used as a means for evaluation in leisure services. Cost-benefit analysis is relating the costs of a program or an operation to the benefits realized from it which are expressed in dollar figures. Benefits other than dollars, however, are often hard to quantify. Cost-effectiveness is easier because it is the ratio of costs to revenue generated. A program that generated enough income to pay the expenses would have a cost-effectiveness of 1:1. Per capita costs may be related to amount of cost per person. For example, we might have a Little League program that cost $20,000 for 150 children. The cost-effectiveness would then be $133 per child. The cost-effectiveness of one program could then be related to other programs sponsored by the organization.

Economic impact is a specific example of a policy/administrative area that might be measured. Economic impact relates to the amount of revenue activity generated in an area due to a particular event such as a festival or other tourist activities. For example, we might determine that for every dollar spent on tourism promotion in a community, five dollars of income might be generated from tourist spending. Economic impact also expands beyond primary initial spending to secondary spending which results in a multiplier effect in the community.

Places (Areas and Facilities)

The level of use of leisure services, such as numbers of participants, is a common way to measure how well an organization is doing. When we evaluate places, we may examine many aspects including use, as well as safety and legal mandates. Preestablished standards are often helpful in evaluating risk management and safety concerns in the facilities, equipment, and landscape of an organization. Routine checks of facilities and equipment in the form of "walk-thrus" as well as scheduled maintenance procedures and the keeping of maintenance logs, can serve as a formal system of evaluation.

Master plans done for long-range planning are a form of assessment and evaluation. In these plans, one might examine the distribution of areas and facilities. Table 1.3(3) shows an example of such a checklist that might be used for evaluating what exists or does not exist in a community. Carrying capacity, defined as the amount of use an area can take before recreation experiences become diminished, is another example of evaluation applied to places.

Table 1.3(3)

Example of a Neighborhood Evaluation Checklist
for Facilities for the State of Pennsylvania
(adapted from Lundegren and Farrell, 1985, p. 191)

Recommended Component	*Yes*	*No*
1. Turf for field sports	——	——
2. Multipurpose, hard surface, all-weather court area	——	——
3. Space for recreation sports	——	——
4. Individual and dual sports	——	——
5. Water facility—Outdoor pool	——	——
6. Winter activity area	——	——
a. Ice area	——	——
b. Sledding slope	——	——
7. Outdoor education area	——	——
8. Natural area for nonmotorized travel	——	——
9. Communication space for dance, drama, music	——	——
10. Building	——	——
a. Multipurpose meeting rooms	——	——
b. Assembly area	——	——
c. Specialized activity area	——	——
d. Physical recreation area	——	——

A frequent way of evaluating places is through the application of standards. Many examples of standards exist in parks and recreation. The American Camping Association, for example, offers standards for camping that relate to property risks and safety equipment, as well as standards that also relate to personnel and program. The Joint Commission on Accreditation of Healthcare Organizations (JCAHO) has standards for hospitals. A new set of standards being proposed for evaluation of public park and recreation departments is now being devised with standards that relate to aspects of facilities and areas.

Program

Last but not least, and accompanying many dimensions of the Ps previously listed, is program evaluation. Program evaluation is sometimes referred to as impact evaluation. In the field of leisure services, however, we usually call it program evaluation. For many leisure service providers, the program is the primary concern when evaluations are discussed.

Evaluation is seen as one of the prime components of a program system when it is examined along with the phases of assessment, objectives, implementation, and evaluation. Evaluation, however, may occur not only at the end of a program, but also throughout it—even at the beginning. Thus, as Howe and Carpenter (1985) illustrated in Figure 1.3(1), evaluation may be done at all stages of the program.

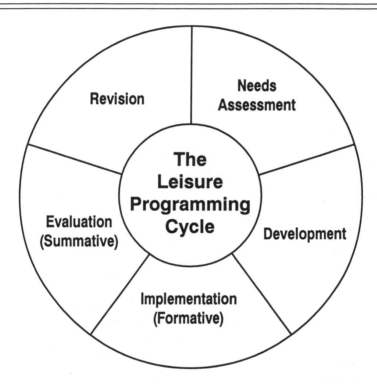

Figure 1.3(1)   The Relationship Between Program and Evaluation
(adapted from Howe and Carpenter, 1985)

Crompton (1979) suggested that it may be important to evaluate programs at all stages of their development. He further suggested the use of a program audit or evaluation to examine the total mix of programs. One might use attendance figures from the beginning, check trends with competitors or similar programs, and project program participation. Priorities then can be assigned for elimination or development of new programs. If programs are declining, you may have to look for new program ideas.

Many possibilities exist for developing program evaluations. An examination of levels of program evaluation adapted from the work of Bennett (1982) may be useful in further understanding program evaluation. See Figure 1.3(2). Seven levels of program evaluation are suggested:

1. **Input**—resources available and expended—time, costs, staff;
2. **Activities**—type and organization, publicity, delivery of program;
3. **People involvement**—number of people, characteristics of people, frequency and intensity;
4. **Reactions**—degree of interest, like or dislike for activities, satisfaction, expectations, appeal, immediate benefits;
5. **KASA objectives and changes**:
    Knowledge—awareness, understanding, problem-solving ability;
    Attitudes—feeling, change of interest, ideas, beliefs;
    Skills—verbal or physical abilities, new skills, improved performance, abilities;
    Aspirations—desires, courses of action, new decisions;
6. **Practice change**—adoption and application of knowledge, attitudes, skills, or aspirations to leisure or lifestyle; and,
7. **Long-term impact on quality of life**—social, economic, environmental, and individual consequences, how people are helped, hindered, or harmed as a result of this program.

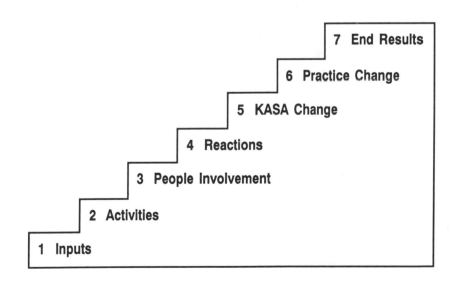

Figure 1.3(2) Levels of Program Evaluation

One of the challenges in program evaluation is to make sure that one is not trying to evaluate too many criteria at once. The seven levels identified provide a framework for making decisions about what aspects of a program may be most important to evaluate. Two examples of program evaluation forms are illustrated in Tables 1.3(4) and 1.3(5). Table 1.3(4) is an example of camper reactions (level 4) and Table 1.3(5) shows how to measure inputs (level 1).

Table 1.3(4)

Camper Program Evaluation
(source unknown)

Scoring:
Awesome!=5
Good=4
Fair=3
Yawn=2
Boring=1

Activities		*Score*
Archery		____
Battlefield Tour		____
Bible Classes		____
Camp Fires		____
Canoeing		____
Crafts		____
Cycling		____
Hiking		____
Meals		____
Music		____
Nature		____
Physical Fitness		____
Sports		____
	Basketball	____
	Softball	____
	Soccer	____
Swimming		____

Table 1.3(5)

Example of Parks and Recreation Department Program Evaluation
(adapted from Durham Parks and Recreation)

How are we serving you? Please take a minute to complete this brief questionnaire and return it directly to our staff. We value your participation and want to serve you better. Thank you.

Location _____   Date _____

Activity _____

Please check Yes or No: Yes   No

    1. Was the staff courteous?   _____ _____

    2. Was the facility clean and attractive?   _____ _____

    3. Was the activity well-organized?   _____ _____

    4. Was the area in a good state of repair?   _____ _____

    5. Did the activity start on time?   _____ _____

    6. Did you feel safe and comfortable at the facility? _____ _____

    7. Would you return to this facility for another activity? _____ _____

    8. Was the activity interesting?   _____ _____

    9. Overall, how would you rate this activity (please check one):

        _____Excellent _____Good _____Fair _____Poor

10. What other activities would you like us to provide?

11. How did you hear about our classes/programs. Check one/or any that apply.

____Mailed brochure	____Yellow pages	____TV
____Picked up brochure	____Flyer/poster	____Newspaper
____Friend	____Radio	____Referral
____Called P & R office	____Called facility	____Other

Developing an Evaluation System

Few park and recreation departments submit themselves to a continuous and systematic program of evaluation (Twardzik, 1987). Those organizations that use standards for accreditation have a system in place for evaluation, but more evaluation may be needed than once every three or five years. Many organizations use evaluation for various aspects of their program like staff performance appraisal, but few organizations have a clear system for how evaluation fits into their overall organization.

Not every aspect of an organization needs to be evaluated every year. In fact, for the time and money, it may be more useful to determine what and when evaluations ought to be done. Rather than doing piecemeal evaluations, the development of a way that the entire organization or system can be evaluated over a period of time (e.g., three years) may be more beneficial. A system can enable you, as a professional, to make sure that all five Ps are covered from time to time. A system in place can enable you to make enlightened decisions concerning the entire organization. Let's examine how this system of evaluation might look.

To develop a system, you must know which of the five Ps will be evaluated and how often this process should be done. As you read further into this book, the types of evaluation that are to be done, as well as the models that best serve to answer the evaluation criteria, will be determined. A systematic plan might be developed by establishing goals and objectives, examining conclusions from previous evaluations, examining strategic plans or long-range plans that exist in the organization before setting a schedule. Figure 1.3(3) illustrates how an evaluation system might be organized. You would determine what (what area of the five Ps), why (reasons for evaluation), when (timing related to how often and when during the year), and who will be evaluated, who will be in charge of the evaluation, and who will use this information. In developing the plan you might want to consider more specifically the type of evaluation needed and the resources needed to carry out the evaluation such as personnel, facilities, funds, and supplies. These components will be discussed in more detail in designing specific projects in Chapter 1.08.

You cannot evaluate everything at once. To try to assess everything usually results in poor conceptualizations of projects or failure to think about the issues involved. Further, the amount of data that you would generate would be overwhelming to those participating unless a system is established.

Theobald (1979) has offered several practical considerations as you set up the system for your organization. First, keep in mind the time and financial constraints of evaluation. On one hand, evaluation ought to be considered an investment. "Quick and dirty" evaluations, however, are usually not nearly as helpful as well-planned evaluation projects. On the other hand, the more money and time that is spent on evaluation will result in less available for program, staff, and the development and maintenance of areas and facilities.

Second, in developing a system, keep in mind that evaluations have political overtones. In determining the worth or value of something, you want to be sure that the criteria and measurements are appropriate. You also must consider the

What	Why	When	Who
Program			
Participants			
Personnel			
Physical Place			
Policy			

Figure 1.3(3) A System for Evaluation

scope of evaluation and what it will cover, the size of program, duration, program input, complexity, and span of goals.

Third, to have a system in place means that you will have established appropriate reasons for evaluating based on whether staff want the information, the funding organization requires it, or you have the need to make decisions to continue or terminate a program.

Developing an evaluation system will not be easy. As you work through this book, however, certain aspects of how the five Ps can be systematically analyzed within any organization over a period of time should become evident. Table 1.3(6) summarizes a number of examples of ways that the five Ps might be used in leisure service organization evaluations.

Table 1.3(6) Summary of Components of the Five Ps of Evaluation

Participants
- Motivations/Satisfaction
- Changes in attitudes as outcomes
- Changes in knowledge as outcomes
- Changes in skills and abilities as outcomes
- Carry-over into other situations
- How individuals interact?
- Demographic characteristics

Program
- Effective leadership
- Promotion of program
- Did participants gain anything?
- Risk management

Place
- Safety concerns
- Master planning
- Adequate facilities

Policies/Administration
- Accountability of budget
- Cost-benefit analysis
- Cost-effectiveness analysis
- Equitable provision of services

Personnel
- Performance appraisal
- Assess training needs
- Provide feedback for improvement

From Ideas to Reality

Obviously many aspects of organizations can be evaluated. An evaluator, however, must be able to make decisions about what can be feasibly and systematically evaluated at any given time. This chapter has provided a number of examples of the infinite variety of aspects that might be evaluated in leisure service organizations. It is best to choose one or two aspects each year on which to put evaluation emphasis. Over time, a system of evaluation will develop. For example, many organizations have good staff evaluation systems in place that simply will need to be maintained. The professional might then determine if all areas are being adequately evaluated. Program evaluation is a large undertaking, and the evaluator might want to focus on particular programs during different years. For example, the aquatics program might be evaluated one year, the adult and youth sports program the next, the senior adults program the next, and then the cycle would begin again. When evaluating participants, you might want to examine an outcome such as skill development in a number of programs and use that as an emphasis during a given year. The possibilities are endless and the evaluator must use a system to determine the most important aspects to evaluate, given the time, money, and expertise that may exist within an organization. All of the five Ps are important and all can be evaluated, but the immensity of the undertaking must be carefully considered so that appropriate and useful evaluations are conducted.

1.04 THE TRILOGY OF EVALUATION: CRITERIA, EVIDENCE, AND JUDGMENT

Goals for Chapter 1.04:

—To describe the value of using criteria, evidence, and judgment together in an evaluation project; and,
—To design a project showing how the trilogy of evaluation would be linked.

As has been suggested previously, the three components that must be present for evaluation and enlightened decision making to occur are criteria, evidence (data), and judgment. If any one of this trilogy is missing, successful evaluation will not occur. In other words, we might say:

Criteria + Evidence + Judgment = Evaluation

The purpose of this short chapter is to define this trilogy. It would be wonderful if a magic formula could be offered that showed how to use the evaluation trilogy for any given evaluation project, but that is not possible. Every evaluation project in every organization is going to be different. An infinite number of combinations exist for linking criteria, evidence, and judgment in an evaluation project. However, it is beneficial to borrow and learn from previous projects, from both internal and external sources. Regardless of the project, the importance of the trilogy for systematic evaluation lies in the ability to link and logically use the three elements of criteria, evidence, and judgment.

Criteria

Criteria refer to the standards or the ideals upon which something is being evaluated. Criteria are the basic organizing framework for evaluations just as hypotheses or research questions are used in research. Further, criteria will determine to a great extent what method would be best to use to address the criteria. To determine criteria is to determine the purpose of an evaluation, the models that might be applied, the levels of evaluation needed, and the specific evaluation questions that will be explored. In many ways, criteria are directly tied to planning because to develop criteria is to set a framework or a road map that the evaluator will follow from the beginning to the end of a project.

All of us have criteria in our heads, but they may not be appropriate in all situations. For example, when people disagree over how good a restaurant might be, care must be taken that the same criteria are being applied. If someone dislikes a restaurant because the servers are slow and rude, a different criterion is being applied than if the criterion is the price of the food or how it tasted. Of course when we eat at a restaurant we expect all criteria to be met or exceeded, but depending on the definition of criteria, our judgments might vary depending on what we were evaluating.

Developing criteria often appears to be the easiest aspect of the evaluation process, but in reality may be the most difficult. Depending upon the purpose of the evaluation, the criteria may be apparent. For example, if a program has a set of good goals and objectives to serve as the criteria, the evaluator can then decide how best to gather evidence. If, however, there is uncertainty concerning evaluation needs, determining criteria may be more difficult. Evaluators may not be able to measure everything with any degree of depth for every leisure services program or place.

One of the major pitfalls of evaluation is not stating the criteria specifically enough so that they can be measured. The evaluator must be able to articulate what is being measured. A great difference exists between determining how many people participated in a program and identifying their satisfaction with the program. Sometimes data are collected without a specific set of criteria in mind. If you are lucky, the data may answer the critical evaluation questions, but chances are they will not unless a plan was made. Sometimes data is collected with the intent to address one set of criteria only to find out this assumption was not the case. Sometimes the evaluator has one set of criteria that she or he thinks should be measured while stakeholders (e.g., Boards of Directors, parents) may have something else in mind. Thus, it is essential to identify clearly what questions you wish to address or what criteria to evaluate *before* data are collected for a project.

Many people struggle with how to design evaluation systems, as well as specific projects, because they do not have a sense of the criteria that need to be evaluated. To skip the step of identifying criteria, or to skip this unit of this book, will not be useful in the long run if we are to conduct useful evaluations that will lead to good decision making. The more time the evaluator spends determining what to evaluate, the more time will be saved later when collecting reliable and valid information and in making decisions about what the evaluation data mean.

Evidence

Evidence means data. Data are pieces of information that are collected to determine whether criteria are being met. In gathering evidence, the timing, type of data, sample size and composition, and techniques for handling data must be determined.

The two major types of data are qualitative and quantitative. Quantitative data in the simplest form refer to numbers from measurements that result in some type of statistics. Qualitative data refer to words used to describe or explain what is happening. Many evaluation designs and research methods can be used to collect these two types of data ranging from the two broad categories of experimental and descriptive designs to the more specific methods related to questionnaires, interviews, observations, and unobtrusive measures. All of these methods will be discussed in detail in Unit Two.

The aspect of evidence relates directly back to the criteria that were established. If poor criteria were set up, designing instruments that will measure what you really want to measure will be difficult. Applying data collection and analysis techniques and using research methods are not difficult to learn. Applying them appropriately based on criteria is what requires effort.

Judgment

Judgment is the determination of the value or worth of something based on the evidence collected from the previously determined criteria. Judgment is one aspect of evaluation that frequently gets left out. You can have excellent criteria and evidence laid out for an evaluation project; however, the final step of the evaluation process is lacking if judgments, in the form of conclusions and recommendations, are not made about what the data mean.

Judgment is not a matter of learning a process that can be applied each time. Each set of criteria and method of gathering evidence will result in a number of possible conclusions and recommendations. Conclusions should relate back to the hypotheses, objectives, and/or criteria of the project as well as the data. Recommendations are proposed courses of action to be followed based on the criteria, evidence, and conclusions. These conclusions and recommendations must be made obvious in the form of judgments before the evaluation is complete.

The Evaluation Process—Putting It All Together

The steps to evaluation involve more than just stating criteria, collecting evidence, and making judgments. Most evaluation projects use the trilogy as the framework for designing the entire process. Table 1.4 (page 36) provides a summary of how the trilogy relates to the process of evaluation. The use of the trilogy of evaluation is a simple way be sure that evaluation is being conceptualized appropriately. It is a useful and straightforward way of thinking about and moving through the evaluation process.

Table 1.4

Summary of How the Evaluation Trilogy Leads to the Evaluation Process

Criteria
- determining a problem and a reason for evaluation
- examining goals and objectives (if they exist)
- developing broad evaluation questions or a problem statement to be addressed (such as "what are the motivations for involvement in an activity" or "what job-related expectations should be used to evaluate a staff member")

Evidence
- method selection including instrument design and pretest
- sample selection
- actual data collection
- data analysis (e.g., coding and interpretation)

Judgment
- presentation of findings
- development of conclusions
- development of recommendations

From Ideas to Reality

Several brief examples may help to illustrate how the evaluation process works. If we wanted to examine what the outcomes to individuals were of participating in a particular kind of activity, we might decide to use satisfaction as the criteria. We would then find an instrument or develop one to measure satisfaction with an activity. We would select an audience or a sample, and collect evidence (data) by using that instrument. We would then analyze the data using descriptive statistics to develop conclusions and make recommendations about how satisfied people were with participation in a recreation activity.

Perhaps we were interested in determining if the riding area of a horseback program for children with disabilities was safe. We would have to determine the criteria that describe a safe riding area. Standards developed by other groups might provide the criteria to examine. Using those criteria and developing a checklist, we would observe the area where children with disabilities were riding. Based on the results we would then draw conclusions and make recommendations for how to improve an area so it will be safer for the participants.

We might be interested in whether the policy we have for refunds is appropriate. The criteria will be used to determine how often the policy has been implemented and what the situations are surrounding its use. The data would be collected from existing records that we would examine and tabulate. On the basis of those records, we would make judgments concerning how much and how often the policy was used and possible recommendations for how it might be improved in the future.

1.05 EVALUATION AND RESEARCH: VIVA LA DIFFERENCE

Goals for Chapter 1.05:

—To describe the differences between research and evaluation;
—To explain when a research study would be desirable and when an evaluation project would be more appropriate;
—To identify the major types of research that one might see in leisure studies journals; and,
—To define the meaning of theory.

This book is about evaluation and the evaluation research methods used to make decisions in leisure service organizations. Frequently, the words "research" and "evaluation" are used together. While many similarities exist in the processes of evaluation and research, differences exist in the outcomes of each.

As described in Chapter 1.01, evaluation is defined as the systematic collection and analysis of data to address some criteria to make judgments about the worth or improvement of something. Evaluation research is defined as the use of scientific principles and methods to examine something. Evaluation research is characterized by the use of a clearly delineated protocol in collecting, processing, and analyzing data. It is a specific form of applied research that results in the application of information for decision making.

Therefore, for our purposes, evaluation and research use the same methods but have different purposes and outcomes. Further we will suggest that although both research and evaluation can be classified as studies or projects, studies will refer to research and projects will refer to evaluation.

Differences in Objectives or Purposes

The scientific method, or the way that systematic data collection is done, is not bound by either subject matter or object, so it can be applied in both evaluation projects and research studies. Evaluation projects use research methods, but they do not have a specific method of their own. Most models of evaluation apply the basic rules of the scientific method. Thus, evaluation and research differ in their objectives or purposes rather than in designs or execution.

The objectives or purposes of evaluation projects and research studies need to be discussed because they constitute one of the major differences between evaluation and research. First, research tries to prove or disprove hypotheses whereas evaluation focuses on improvement in some area related to the five Ps. Researchers are usually concerned with increasing understanding, satisfying an inquiring mind, or finding scientific truth. Evaluators are concerned with problem solving and decision making. The aim of research is new knowledge that may or may not be applicable immediately. This aim does not mean that research studies do not address problems and offer data for application, but these direct applications are not necessarily the outcome of the research study undertaken as they would be for evaluation projects.

Second, evaluation projects compare the results with objectives to see how well the latter have been met. Research, by definition, applies scientific techniques to hypotheses testing focused on outcomes that are related to theory. Evaluators usually focus at the applied level for a particular situation and usually do not get into theory questions. Research involves inquiry based on a desire to know something in a theoretical and generalized sense. Thus, research is theoretically grounded whereas evaluation is problem based.

Third, evaluators are not interested in generalizing results to other situations, although sometimes that is a relevant outcome. Research, by using theory and random samples, should be generalizable to other situations whereas evaluation uses specific information for making decisions about a particular situation. Similarly, in evaluation, the evaluation questions or criteria emerge from the decision maker who will be using the information and not from the evaluator. In research, the hypotheses come from the researcher's interests and goals.

Fourth, evaluation projects are undertaken when there is a decision to make, and the relative worth of something is not known. Research studies are conducted to develop new knowledge. In other words, research leads to theoretical conclusions whereas evaluation leads to decisions for solving problems. As was discussed in the previous chapter, evaluation must lead to judgment about the worth of something; the value of evaluation lies in making valid judgments that result in enlightened decision making.

Fifth, research studies are usually published because their purpose is to add to the body of knowledge; publications and presentations are the way this purpose is accomplished. Although evaluation reports are generally written and presented formally to decision makers, the information is not necessarily shared broadly. We find some exceptions when we look at the applied research in some of the major journals of the leisure services field such as *Journal of Park and Recreation Administration* and the *Therapeutic Recreation Journal*. Editors of these journals often publish evaluation studies that serve as models for research methods or provide insights for other professionals to use in their organizations.

Sharing of Common Methods

In the broadest sense, research includes elements of evaluation and evaluation requires the use of research techniques. Frequently, we see separate chapters in research texts (e.g., Babbie, 1992) that focus on evaluation research. Evaluation projects make use of research procedures, but as indicated above, the purposes are different. Both research studies and evaluation projects share common methods. If you have a good grasp of the repertoire of methods as well as data collection and analysis techniques available for evaluation, you will have a sound methodological foundation for conducting research. The use of methods may be applied differently, however, because research relies on theory as its building blocks and evaluation relies on application and decision making. Figure 1.5 shows how evaluation and research share common methods but have different applications.

Remember that evaluation is not sloppy research. The same protocols and rules of methodology that apply to research apply to evaluation. Good evaluations rely on sound research methods. The process for evaluation is similar and even the first two aspects of the trilogy are necessary, but the major difference lies in the purpose of the research and how the evaluation or research results are used.

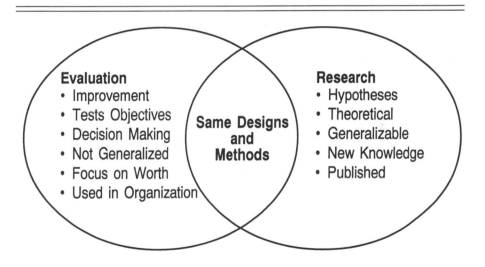

Figure 1.5 A Comparison of Evaluation and Research

A Word About Theory

The major difference between research and evaluation lies in the use of theory related to criteria and judgment. Whether one is doing an evaluation project or a research study, the evidence or data that are collected and analyzed are basically the same. For those individuals who may want to have a further introduction to research as a basis for understanding methods, we will briefly discuss theory and research. Keep in mind, however, many excellent books have been written about research, theory, and leisure sciences that a student or practitioner may wish to consult.

As indicated previously, it is most useful to think of research and evaluation as two separate approaches to finding answers. Although some researchers classify "evaluation research" as a form of research, we like to set it along side research and to acknowledge the importance of the common methods and techniques that are shared. Regardless of whether one is doing a research study that uses theory or an evaluation project, methods such as surveys, observations, unobtrusive measures (that might include historical research), or experiments are possible. Similarly, both researchers and evaluators will need to be concerned about sampling, measurement, and analysis. The major difference is the way that theory is used as a framework for planning and for drawing conclusions within a research study.

Two of the major aims of research are either to fit data to a theory or to generate a theory from data. Theory gives order and insight to what can be, is, or has been observed (Henderson and Zabielski, 1992). In other words, theory provides a "road map" (Tinsley, 1984). Research is sometimes criticized in the field of leisure services/studies because it lacks theory or has poor theoretical quality. Although not all research that lacks theory may be classified as evaluative, it is generally more like the evaluation process when theory is missing.

The use of theory ranges from theory testing and confirmation to theory development within research projects. In theory testing, a known theory is stated prior to beginning a research study. The study is then conducted to see whether or not that theory does help to explain what is related to the topic. In theory development, a theory is generated after the research to aid in explaining what happened. This theory emerges from the data and is frequently tied to other similar or related theories. Closely related to theory is the use of models for confirmation or development which occurs in the leisure research literature.

Conceptual frameworks are the basis of all research regardless of whether theory is being confirmed or tested. Conceptual frameworks precede theories and describe the assumptions from which the researcher is operating. In evaluation projects, concepts are often key dimensions that also provide direction for the evaluator in understanding the relationship among variables. In evaluation, however, the focus is not necessarily on linking the concepts together into a framework but in using the concepts to collect data and ultimately to make decisions. Concepts are always used in evaluation projects but they are not necessarily linked into conceptual frameworks.

A number of theories in the field of leisure research are used. Some of these theories are borrowed from other fields such as business and psychology. For example, marginality theory has been used to explain the lack of participation by people of color in recreation programs. Social exchange theory has been used to analyze the reasons why people choose or do not choose to become involved in Advisory Boards. Carrying capacity has been used to determine how much use an outdoor area can take before the resources and recreational experiences of participants are diminished. Conceptual frameworks and theory specifically related to leisure sciences have also been developed. For example, travel cost models are used to examine why and how people make vacation choices. Conceptual constraints models have provided a plethora of information about why people do not participate in recreation activities to the full extent they would like. Journals such as *Leisure Sciences* and the *Journal of Leisure Research* contain numerous examples of how theory and conceptual frameworks have been applied in the field of leisure research.

Some of you reading this book may be more interested in research and theoretical applications than in evaluation. If you read this book and study Units Two and Three, as well as portions of Unit Four, you will have a solid background in research methods. If you want to do research, however, we suggest you read additional material from texts designed specifically to address research issues and from journals that report the most recent research in our field. Doing evaluation projects does not mean that you shouldn't also know this research literature, but doing evaluation requires a different point of beginning and a different point of application in the end.

From Ideas to Reality

Evaluation and research are closely linked because they share common methods. The assumption has been made in this book that an individual is interested in conducting evaluation projects. Sometimes a fine line exists between evaluation and research but it is important that you know the difference since criteria and judgment are where the differences lie. In most cases, unless a theory is being tested, you will be interested in doing an evaluation project to determine the worth or value of something.

In some cases, either an evaluation project or a research study could be undertaken depending upon your purpose for using the data. For example, suppose you wanted to know what adolescent girls gained from a recreation experience. In an evaluation project, criteria might be developed to determine how self-esteem changed as a result of participating in an activity. You could measure these changes using a pre- and posttest to see what the girls experienced. From a research study perspective you might do the same thing, but the interest would be in examining a theory such as learned helplessness as a theoretical framework for understanding the changes. The difference between evaluation and research also relates to how you explain what the changes or lack of changes mean. In the judgment phase, the evaluator would be concerned with ways to make sure that these positive changes continued to happen in the program. The researcher would be interested in tying the findings to theory and building the body of knowledge about girls and learned helplessness that may or may not be directly applied to a particular recreation program.

It is possible to do evaluation and research at the same time, but the criteria phase will need to include theory and the judgment phase will need to include a discussion of how the body of knowledge can be enhanced with this information. Evaluation is generally, but not always, easier to do because it relates to addressing specific criteria for making decisions about programs, places, people, policies, or personnel. Most people who develop evaluation skills can also develop research skills, but it must be kept in mind that the reasons and applications are the major differences between evaluation and research.

1.06 TIMING OF EVALUATION

Goals for Chapter 1.06:

—To describe the differences between formative, summative, and assessment evaluations; and,

—To list some possible applications for each of the timing types of evaluation.

The five Ps of leisure services (i.e., program, participants, personnel, places, and policy/administration) can be evaluated in different sequences and ways. For example, Crompton and Lamb (1986) suggested that public parks and recreation agencies evaluate their services in three ways: effectiveness or the end results, outcomes, and impacts of service on the participants; efficiency or the relationship between inputs and outputs and the amount of effort, expense, or waste involved in delivering a service; and equity or the fairness of service delivery. The well-known evaluation specialists Rossi and Freeman (1993) say that possible components to evaluations usually address assessment, process, outcomes, and/or efficiency.

In addition to the ways evaluations are done, most evaluators discuss evaluation as occurring in some temporal or time sequence. It may be done at the beginning (assessment), during the process of a program/course of a year (formative) or at the end of the program/year (summative). These three approaches can be illustrated through a classroom example. Some professors may want to know how much students know about a particular topic at the beginning of a semester. They may give a quiz or exam on the first day of class to assess the knowledge level or attitudes that students have about a subject. Many professors are required to give final exams which are summative evaluations. They tell the instructor what happened at the end of the course but at that point, little can be done to change the learning or lack of learning that occurred. For this reason, many instructors give mid-term exams that might be thought of as formative evaluations. When these mid-terms are given, the instructor then has the opportunity to immediately improve upon the class if the learning has not occurred as planned. Three different timings of the evaluations or exams result in differing outcomes for those people who are using the exam evaluations. Assessment, formative, or summative evaluations may occur within any of the five Ps.

Formative and summative evaluation can be described as two ways of doing evaluation along with a third form of evaluation, known as assessment that occurs before any program takes place. Thus, evaluations may occur as assessment, formative, or summative depending upon the sequencing, timing, and the use of the evaluations. These three ways of doing evaluation are based on criteria that must be determined before an evaluation project is undertaken.

Although not completely congruent, we might say that assessment always examines some type of need and is the foundation for further *planning*; formative utilizes an examination of the *process*, and summative measures the *product* referred to as outcomes, impacts, effectiveness, and/or overall efficiency. Thus, the criteria developed for an evaluation project will depend on its timing and whether the use of the evaluation will be for planning, improving the process, or measuring the product.

Assessments and Planning

Assessment is a process of determining and making specific what a program, a facility, a staff member, a participant's behavior, or administrative procedure is. In community recreation programs, we often conduct needs assessments. These assessments identify the differences between "what is" and "what should be." The needs assessment often results in a process of prioritizing results to use in planning programs, places, policies, or the use of personnel. Therapeutic recreation specialists use assessment as the initial evaluation necessary to plan intervention strategies and serve as a baseline for measuring client outcomes (Stumbo, 1991).

The assessment thus serves as a set of outcomes or judgments that focus on gaps between current aspects of the five Ps and desired results; assessments provide the direction for reducing those gaps. Assessments may determine answers to such questions as what is socioeconomic profile of a community? What are unmet needs? What forms of recreation services are needed? Needs are complex and often hard to understand so an assessment evaluation can help to address such aspects as the context of need, dealing with denial of need, and how needs can be used in program planning.

Assessment evaluation assumes that you want to find out where to begin. Where to begin applies to whether you are assessing a participant, the resources available in a community, or the needs for training a new staff member. To collect data for a needs assessment, for example, a plan must be devised. The plan usually includes defining what needs to be known, developing a plan of action, generating goals, collecting data about "what is," analyzing data for discrepancies between "what is" and "what should be," and then developing a plan of action for the desired intervention or for the programs to be initiated. The assessment is based on determining criteria, collecting evidence, and making judgments about where any of the five Ps of your organization are now, where to go in the future, and how to get there.

The only time an assessment need not be conducted is when the goals and objectives for the organization, program, clients, or staff are sure and when that information is complete, correct, valid, and useful. An assessment may be done internally or externally depending on the particular situation.

Formative and Process Evaluation

Formative and summative evaluations may not be measuring different aspects of leisure services, but the timing is such that the results often are used in different ways. In general, formative evaluation is concerned more with organizational objectives, while summative evaluation is concerned with the overall behavior objectives.

When we are interested in examining the processes associated with an organization, formative evaluation is often used. Formative evaluation is defined as the systematic examination of steps in the development and implementation of a program, organizational structure, policy, or staff person. Formative evaluation occurs while a program or administrative procedure is in progress and is used to examine the process as it is occurring within the organization. Feedback is provided early so that revisions can be made and weaknesses pointed out while there is still time to correct them. The value of formative evaluation lies in the changes that can be made while a staff member is working, when a budget is being used, or when a program is going on. Examples of process evaluation questions that might be asked are: Is the program attracting a sufficient number? How are staff contacting participants? Are some media methods working better than others? Are the participants making progress toward their individual goals?

Evaluation using standards of practice developed by professional organizations is a good example of formative evaluation. For example, in therapeutic recreation, the concept of quality assurance (QA) is frequently cited. This concept pertains to providing quality healthcare and determining what constitutes quality care within therapeutic recreation (Riley and Wright, 1990). QA is a mechanism employed to systematically monitor and evaluate the appropriateness and quality indicators of patient care activities. This system uses written criteria that directly contain structure, outcome, indicator, and process measures that can be evaluated formatively to aid in ongoing patient care.

Another example of a formative process might refer to the concept of quality of service (MacKay and Crompton, 1990). Professionals in tourism and other areas of recreation have a growing interest in service quality. The intent is to use any number of methods to examine how services are provided. Tangibles, such as physical facilities, equipment, appearance of personnel, reliability including the ability to perform the promised service dependably and accurately, are measured. Responsiveness, or the willingness to help users and to provide prompt attention, assurance which indicates courteous and knowledgeable employees who convey trust and confidence, and empathy that includes offering caring and individualized attention to users, are also evaluated. By comparing what customers expect and what they experience, an organization can make formative changes to provide better services for present, as well as future, participants.

Another common formative evaluation is done with seasonal staff. In this process, staff are evaluated after the first two weeks or midway through a summer to see how they are doing. At this point changes can be made in duties, or needed training can be provided to address whatever potential problems are uncovered. Rather than waiting until the end of the season to give a staff member an evaluation, the formative evaluation allows one to receive feedback that can be used to improve or to change immediately.

Summative and Product Evaluation

When most people think of evaluation, they tend to think of the final evaluation, the evaluation that occurs at the end of something that measures the outcomes or the results. A grade at the end of the semester or the bonus/pay raise at the end of the year are examples of a summative evaluation. Summative evaluation uses an overall examination of impact and effectiveness that is completed at the end of a program or the end of the year. A decision to continue or discontinue the aspect evaluated is imminent although the material gained in a summative evaluation can be applied to subsequent programs. Formative evaluation can occur within any stage of organization process whereas summative only occurs at the end. Summative evaluation is particularly important for accountability purposes, but it should not be used exclusively for that purpose.

A common form of summative evaluation is impact evaluation that ascertains if a program produced the intended effects. The evaluator is interested in determining the net effects of a program, policy, or place/facility. The results are comparative in that you examine what happened based on where an organization began. For example, experimental designs often are used for the purpose of summative evaluation. A pretest is given before a program and a posttest after it is over to determine the impact and change that was a result of a program. In another example, the bottom line of impact analysis relates to a comparison of what did happen after implementing the program with what would have happened had the program not been implemented (Mohr, 1988).

Iso-Ahola (1982) described one illustration of impact evaluation. He suggested that intrinsic leisure motivation should be the main concern of evaluation. If leisure is a state of mind, then those aspects in participants such as an outcome goal of leisure satisfaction ought to be evaluated. He defined leisure satisfaction as having feelings of freedom and control and suggested measures whereby we could determine how leisure helps people receive a degree of balance in their lives, promotes social interaction, and gives feedback about their competence. Different people prefer different leisure activities/programs for different intrinsic rewards at different times. Rossman (1982) suggested that the notion of leisure satisfaction is best measured by investigating underlying satisfaction dimensions rather than a single, all-encompassing measure of "overall satisfaction." Table 1.6 shows examples of some of the impacts that could be measured through a summative evaluation.

Table 1.6

Examples of Measures of Leisure Satisfaction
(adapted from Rossman, 1981)

Achievement
- I learned more about the activity.
- It was a new and different experience.
- My skills and ability developed.
- I became better at it.

Family Escape
- I was able to be away from my family for awhile.

Autonomy
- I was in control of things that happened.
- It gave me a chance to be on my own.

Social Enjoyment
- I enjoyed the companionship.

Environment
- The area was physically attractive.
- The area is fresh and clean.
- I liked the open space.
- The facility design is pleasing.

Risk
- I liked the risks involved.
- I liked the chance for danger.

Physical Fitness
- I enjoyed the exercise.
- It keeps me physically fit.

Impact evaluation, however, can become a very complicated aspect when one starts to evaluate what really happens to people. Halle, Boyer, and Ashton-Shaeffer (1991) suggested two types of impact criteria that ought to be examined: experimental and therapeutic. Experimental criteria implies that a program causes a desired effect or has a definite outcome. We also need to consider, however, the therapeutic criterion which refers to the importance and meaning of the change produced. In other words, does a particular leisure program make a difference in people's lives? Halle, Boyer, and Ashton-Shaeffer (1991) did a study of ten ambulatory students with moderate intellectual disabilities participating in aerobic exercise who were paired with fourteen exercise buddies. They collected data on weight, percent body fat, graded exercise, and the frequency and quality of social interaction between those individuals with and without disabilities. They found that the social value of the program was just as important as any physical change that had occurred in fitness levels. Thus, summative impact was broader than just an experimental design.

Summative evaluation using impacts may be measured related to different hierarchies of change, as well as timing. For example, we might look at impacts immediately after a program or may examine what is occurring six months later or ten years later. Similarly, changes may be specific to a situation or may influence an individual to change his or her life. Summative impact evaluation can become very complicated as we seek to determine what criteria or levels of evidence ought to be measured.

Efficiency, as another aspect of summative evaluation, relates to a bottom line in terms of numbers and costs to organizations. We are often concerned with examining costs in comparison to benefits. Are funds spent for intended purposes? Does a program achieve its success at a reasonable cost? Can dollar values be assigned to outcomes? Efficiency assessments, including cost-benefit and cost-effectiveness, provide a frame of reference for relating costs to program results. Inputs and outputs are measured in numerical terms. To calculate efficiency, costs to and benefit for whom must be examined. Further, costs and benefits may refer to individuals, program sponsors, or society at large.

We need to use a proper amount of caution in determining benefits. Not all benefits can be converted to monetary terms. Cost-benefit and cost-effectiveness often are viewed more conceptually than they are technically because the required technical procedures of converting benefits to dollar amounts may be beyond expertise and resources of most evaluators. Political and moral controversies also exist about whether value can be put on some outcomes. For example, what is the value of a child's life if she or he is given swimming lessons so that someday she or he will not drown? These dilemmas about dollar figures may obscure the relevancy of evaluations if one gets too caught up in the numbers. Measuring benefits, however, as a form of summative evaluation is a useful and popular activity as evidenced by the use of the benefits-based management approach now undertaken by the USDA Forest Service (Driver, Brown, and Peterson, 1991).

Efficiency evaluation might also relate to the concept of a program audit, an accountability term to refer to the process of quantifying the amount of services rendered and the identity of program participants. Program audits provide a year-end descriptive summary of what happened within an organization during a given year.

From Ideas to Reality

As indicated previously, timing can relate to all aspects of evaluation. Assessment involves getting potential baseline information about available inputs, what needs and interests people have, current involvement, attitudes and reactions to leisure or a particular situation, and an assessment of what knowledge, skills, aspirations, and attitudes now exist. A formative evaluation would be concerned with various aspects of efficiency as leisure services are delivered. The summative evaluation would be concerned with impact or effectiveness. Clearly the timing of evaluations will be closely linked to the reasons for conducting an evaluation project.

All aspects of timing are needed within organizations but not all programs, participants, places, policies, or personnel need to be evaluated within each timing sequence. Decisions will need to be made concerning the most appropriate timing to be used for a particular evaluation system and project. Sometimes in the case of personnel, you may be doing assessments, formative, and summative evaluations whereas in other situations such as evaluating safety procedures on a camping trip, only formative evaluation might be used. As an evaluator, you will need to decide when and how evaluations are most appropriate and most useful to aid you in making the most enlightened decisions.

1.07 FIVE MODELS FOR EVALUATION

Goals for Chapter 1.07:

—To describe the differences between the five models presented; and,
—To choose an appropriate model given a particular situation that requires an evaluation.

We can become easily overwhelmed when we examine evaluation literature and try to make sense of the process of evaluation. Numerous models for evaluation exist that provide a framework for conceptualizing and planning evaluation projects. No one model is specific to leisure services, however, because professionals in the field have borrowed heavily from education evaluation principles as well as from business management and operations.

This lack of specific models for leisure services creates both problems and opportunities. It is a problem in that there are many choices that have to be made based on the models designed in other fields. On the other hand, it is an opportunity in that we can choose the best model for the specific criteria to be measured for one of the five Ps.

In determining how various aspects of leisure services might be evaluated, we will discuss five models that may provide helpful frameworks. Intuitive judgment is a pseudo-model with the other four systematic models being: professional (expert) judgment, goal-attainment, goal-free, and systems approaches. Remember that no one model of evaluation will work everywhere. We simply cannot apply a standardized model across organizations or even across the five Ps within leisure organizations. The value and applicability of any of these models lie in diversity and adaptability, not in uniformity and rigidity (Patton, 1978). All of these models have some relation to one another and offer a framework for organizing evaluation systems and planning projects.

A Pseudo-Model: Intuitive Judgment

A traditional component of evaluation is gut-level judgment. After you have conducted some type of program, you have a sense of whether or not it went well. With the development of the scientific method applied to evaluation, however, more systematic models have evolved beyond these intuitive feelings.

The pseudo-model, intuitive judgment, has importance but is not necessarily a systematic approach. This form of evaluation relates to the day-to-day observations that we make that provide information for decision making. For example, if staff sensed that potential participants had not heard about a special event to be held even though a promotional plan had been implemented, something would need to be done. Even without a systematic evaluation, changes could be made immediately to better promote the event. Many changes and improvements occur in organizations based primarily on intuitive judgment and experience. The intuitive judgment model is useful, but reliable and valid evaluations that use systematic approaches to determine criteria, collect evidence, and make enlightened decisions are also necessary.

Professional (Expert) Judgment

Evaluation by professional judgment or expert opinion is commonly used in leisure services. It often relates to two common approaches that might be used: hiring an external evaluator or using a set of external standards. Even if an external evaluator is hired, she or he may use one of the other models to obtain information in addition to her or his expert judgment.

Howe (1980) talked about evaluation by professional judgment as being like an art criticism model where someone other than the artist critiques the artwork. The pros and cons of using a consultant or an external evaluator will be discussed in more depth in Chapter 1.09. Using the professional judgment of an external person may be a good idea when a high degree of objectivity is required, money is available, and an expert is available.

A more common way that professional judgment is used is in evaluation by standards, generally through some type of accreditation process. Essentially, evaluation by standards involves a critical review by an individual or individuals who are experts because they have had training in judging established predetermined minimum criteria.

A standard is a statement of desirable practice or a level of performance for a given situation. Standards are an indirect measurement of effectiveness. People evaluating by using standards assume that if stated desirable practices are followed, the program will be effective. These judgments about standards enable evaluation by comparison through ascertaining what is actually happening within an organization compared with what the accepted standard of desirability is. They are not maximal goals but minimal goals and should be used as a guide, not necessarily a quality rating.

Standards change and must be reviewed regularly and revised as conditions change. Standards ought to reflect the needs of the patients, clients, participants, or campers in the specific area being served, must be reasonably attainable, and must be acceptable and usable to the leisure services professional. These standards are based on sound principles and the best information available about practice. They should stand the test of time, although they also should be revised to reflect changing societal conditions.

The process used for evaluation by standards is generally to have an organization (e.g., a hospital, public recreation department, camp) do a self-evaluation, make changes and improvements to comply with the minimum expectations or guidelines established by the accrediting body, and have trained outside experts confirm that particular situations exist that meet the standards. The process of evaluation by standards is well-known in the recreation field. Most people are aware of van der Smissen's *Evaluation and Self-Study of Public Recreation and Park Agencies* (1978). An example of a standard from this publication would be the use of a population ratio method like ten acres of park land per one thousand people in a community.

The American Camping Association has *Standards for Day and Resident Camps* (1992) as well as *Standards for Conference and Retreat Centers* (1993). Table 1.7(1) (page 56) shows some examples from the camping accreditation process. The National Recreation and Park Association (NRPA) and the American Association for Leisure and Recreation (AALR) have been accrediting recreation and leisure curricula in universities for the past fifteen years. New standards are currently being developed for public recreation programs (Twardzik, 1987). Quality assurance standards within therapeutic recreation are related to the Commission on Accreditation of Rehabilitation Facilities (CARF) and the Joint Commission on Accreditation of Healthcare Organizations (JCAHO).

The standards used for accreditation are usually criterion referenced. That is, evaluations are based on some standard level of performance. They also may assess whether standard objectives have been met. Criterion referenced evaluation is not compared to any other organization but simply is used as a standard for measurement. In the case of the above examples, the standards usually exist in a checklist to which the evaluator responds yes/no, or fully met/partially met/not met. In some situations such as the NRPA/AALR accreditation of universities, qualitative comments are made for standards that are not met to indicate where a problem exists and how it might be corrected.

Table 1.7(1)

Sample of Standards
(*adapted from* Standards for Day and Resident Camps, *1992, p. 70*)

D-24 (Standards for adventure/challenge activities)

Are procedures in practice that require all spotters and belayers be:

A. Instructed in proper procedures and directly supervised until competency is demonstrated? Yes No

B. Located in positions from which they can continuously observe (spot) and/or quickly assist any participant? Yes No

Interpretation: All adventure/challenge activities (as defined for these standards) require some level of spotting or belaying. The level of instruction and competency required will vary, depending on the type of activity, the area, and the abilities of participants.

Compliance Demonstration: Visitor observation of activities when possible; director/staff description of procedures.

D-25

Is there a policy in practice that requires the use of protective head gear by all participants when climbing, rappelling, or spelunking?
Yes No

Compliance demonstration: Visitor observation of activities when possible; director/staff explanation of policy's implementation.

D-26

Are procedures in practice to control access to activity areas such as ropes courses, rappelling towers, ziplines, etc? Yes No

Interpretation: The intent is to prevent use by unauthorized or unsupervised persons, as well as to avoid potentially hazardous situations when the area is in use. Procedures may include such things as education, posted regulations, scheduling, dismantling equipment, and/or a physical barrier.

Compliance demonstration: Visitor observation of activities when possible; director/staff explanation of policy's implementation.

Norm-referenced standards might also be applied in some situations. These measures tell the relative position of a person or thing in reference to another person or thing, using the same measuring tool. Persons compared to a norm of performance such as physical fitness tests would show the relationship of an individual to others in her or his age group. For example, if an individual is in the top quartile, she or he would be among the top 25 percent of those who took a particular test. The meaning of the score lies in the comparison to others. Professional judgment is used in these measures to determine the meaning of the rank of one person in relation to others.

Although evaluating by professional judgment is an important means of evaluation for recreation and leisure agencies, several precautions should be noted. A great deal can be learned from professional judgment about the administrative procedures, areas and facilities, and programs. The model is less useful for people dimensions such as measuring personnel performance or participant impacts. According to Howe (1980), the implied association of standards to performance is a problem; high scores on standards do not necessarily reflect high quality or effectiveness. Another criticism of the professional judgment model related to standards is that the standards often become the maximum rather than the minimum guidelines. Last, evaluation based on standards assumes that all recreation and leisure programs operate in the same context when this may not be the case at all. We must be careful that the use of standards does not result in homogenized programs that are the same everywhere regardless of the context and resources of an organization.

Goal-Attainment Model

The goal-attainment model, also known as evaluation or management by objectives, is probably the backbone of educational evaluation applied to recreation and leisure programs. Goal-attainment is a preordinate model because preestablished goals and objectives are used to measure outcomes. The model works best when goals are discrete and/or objectives are measurable. Within this model, an evaluator can measure broad goals or specific objectives. Generally a focus on specific objectives when using the model is easiest and best.

A goal is a clear general statement about where the organization and its programs are going related to the purpose or mission. Goals may be expressed in broad general terms or may be readily quantifiable and measurable in objective terms which are usually then called objectives. Objectives may be defined as written or expressed intentions about intended outcomes. Goal-attainment evaluation is based on measuring the congruence between performance and objectives. For this model to work, you must have well-written objectives and good criteria. Writing objectives may not always be the most fun activity, but they are necessary if the goal-attainment model is to be applied. Goal-attainment can be used in any area of recreation and applied to any system. It may also be used in assessment, formative, or summative evaluations. Therapeutic recreation specialists, for example, have used the model effectively in setting goals and objectives during the assessment phase of treatment (Touchstone, 1984).

The prerequisite for using the goal-attainment model of evaluation is to have appropriate and measurable goals and objectives. This process requires the setting of goals at the outset preferably before a program is initiated, before an employee begins work, or before an administrative procedure or policy is implemented. Goals and objectives can be set prior to beginning the actual evaluation, although this timing is not as desirable as prior to the beginning of delivering services.

Objectives, then, are specific operational statements related to the desired goals and accomplishments of the organization, staff, participant or program. Many objectives may exist for an organization depending on who is setting them. Objectives may be written for participants as well as for staff and for the organization. Objectives are the criteria when using the goal-attainment model. Thus, determining the appropriate measurement of objectives is critical.

For purposes of this discussion on the goal-attainment model, we will refer to behavioral and organizational objectives. Organizational objectives address the process that will be used to achieve the goals of the organization. For example, an organizational objective might be to recruit, train, and supervise ten volunteers to assist with the youth athletic program. Another organizational objective might be for a staff member to obtain a good or better rating on 75 percent of the evaluations completed by her or his tennis class.

Behavior or performance objectives are a description of the performance you want participants or staff to be able to exhibit when they have achieved the stated objectives. For example, a behavioral objective might be that a participant would pass half of the skills in the swimming test. An objective for a staff member might be that she or he would oversee the publishing of a program brochure three times each year.

A quick review of how to write objectives may be helpful. The essential components include describing a task, who will do it, identifying the action that should be taken and the conditions, and stating the criteria for an acceptable minimal level of performance for the task (Lundegren and Farrell, 1985). In writing these objectives, consider using strong verbs, stating only one purpose or aim per objective, specifying a single end product or result, and specifying the expected time for achievement. Examples of action verbs that might be used in writing objectives include: to enjoy, to assume responsibility, to engage in, to accept responsibility, to examine, to identify characteristics, to change, to develop, to define, to prepare, to compile, to visualize, and to understand.

Within the behavior objectives, several domains have been identified:
1. cognitive (thinking, knowledge);
2. affective (feeling, attitudes);
3. psychomotor (movement, acting); and,
4. social (how people relate to each other).

When writing objectives for a participant or a program, it is necessary to keep in mind the area where change in performance or behavior is desired. As indicated previously, these objectives then become the criteria for evaluation. Objectives are often written for KASA (i.e., knowledge, attitudes, skills, and aspirations) as were identified in the program evaluation previously discussed. In measuring the impact of a program, objectives often provide the foundation for collecting data and making judgments about the success of a program.

In summary, the goal-attainment model is a useful model for leisure service professionals. It requires well-written and measurable goals and objectives. Make sure that you don't get so focused on evaluating the goals that other evidence that suggests good things came out of an organization, a program, or a staff member's work is ignored. Measuring objectives does not mean that unplanned objectives cannot be measured, so the goal-attainment model must be kept flexible enough to accommodate unplanned measurement. The information received may result in more appropriate goals and objectives written to be used for evaluation next time.

Goal-Free (Black Box) Model

A model of evaluation that is receiving more support in the field of recreation and leisure services is what is referred to as goal-free or the black box model (Scriven, 1967). The model has been around for a long time, but its value is only beginning to be realized. The basis of the model is the examination of an organization, group of participants, or program irrespective of the goals. In other words, the intent of goal-free evaluation is to discover and judge actual effects, outcomes, or impacts without considering what the effects were supposed to be. The evaluator begins with no preconceived idea about what she or he might find. The value lies in discovering descriptions or explanations that may have unintended side effects. Scriven argues that if the main objective of an evaluation is to assess the worth of outcomes, you should not make any distinction at all between those outcomes that were intended as opposed to those that were not.

To be completely goal-free is impossible because an evaluation always involves some type of question or comparison. Further, the evaluator must select only certain information out of the total information pool that she or he could collect. Data are collected in relation to recognized concerns or guiding questions. Otherwise collecting data could go on forever. Often evaluation concerns emerge, however, from the issues identified by participants, citizens, or staff. The proponents of the model argue that the evaluator should be free to choose the range of concerns to use for an evaluation and should be able to recognize concerns and issues as they arise.

The data collected in the goal-free model may be either qualitative or quantitative, although the model lends itself very well to qualitative approaches as you will see when we get into the chapter that discusses data collection methods. In the goal-free model, the evaluator will usually talk to people, identify program elements, overview the program, discover purposes and concerns, conceptualize issues and problems, identify qualitative and/or quantitative data that need to be collected, select methods and techniques to use including the possibility of case studies, collect the data, match data and the issues of audiences, and prepare and deliver the report. The evaluator is a detective, in a way, as she or he tries to identify the important relationships and outcomes that exist within an organization or a program. Unlike the goal-attainment model, however, the evaluator does not start out with a specific plan for what criteria will be measured.

The goal-free evaluator uses logical analysis and observation as well as any other needed data collection methods. The drawback to this model of evaluation is that it may be very time consuming and some outcomes may be difficult to measure. The results, however, can be helpful in understanding in depth aspects of the five Ps of evaluation in leisure services.

Systems Approach

The systems approach, as an important model of evaluation, has been mentioned by recreation evaluation experts such as Lundegren and Farrell (1985), Theobald, (1979) and Howe (1980). This model is process-oriented in general and does not use goals specifically. The model is used to establish a working understanding of an organization that is capable of achieving end products such as the provision of leisure services. The focus is on determining the degree to which an organization realizes its goals under a given set of conditions. The type and timing of data collected depends on the structure of the system or the organization.

The systems approach is often used in management planning and has specific designs that are developed. Examples include Program Evaluation and Review Technique (PERT), Critical Path Method (CPM), Program Planning and Budgeting System (PPBS), Management by Objectives (MBO), and Total Performance Measurement (TPM). Data related to inputs, process, and outputs result in feedback that is used for decision making. If you were to develop an evaluation system for a recreation, park, or leisure services organization, you would likely use a systems approach in determining how evaluating the five Ps fit into the overall operation of an organization. Fiscal evaluations also are frequently used within a systems context.

Within leisure service organizations, program planning is often based on a systems approach with evaluation being just one part of it. The strategy and goals are input, the program design is the process, the implementation yields outcomes, and evaluation produces feedback. Planning, delivery, and evaluation are related to one another. An evaluator can examine how an organization is operating to determine how effective it is. Within the systems model, an entire system, or just pieces of it, can be examined using the approach that objectives are determined and programs, facilities, and staff then are examined and monitored. An evaluation through the systems approach results in the determination of impacts and outcomes as well as an assessment of the processes used by an organization. The model assumes that different decisions require different types of information inputs. Decisions are based on continuation, modification, or termination of the program or staff or whatever is being measured.

These five models provide a way to frame evaluation. They offer a context for assumptions for determining how to set criteria and collect data. They are applied in varying degrees when conducting evaluation projects. In undertaking an evaluation project, it is essential to set the stage by determining which model best sets the framework for the evaluation. Table 1.7(2) provides a summary of the strengths and weaknesses of each of the models.

Table 1.7(2)

Summary of the Strengths and Weaknesses of Evaluation Models

Model	Strengths	Weaknesses
Intuitive	Relatively easy Day-to-day analysis	Not scientific Lacks reliability
Professional Judgment	Uses expert opinions Standards based Easy for organization Less time required	Must have an expert Expensive

Goal-Attainment	Most commonly used
	Uses preestablished goals
	  and objectives
	Objectivity
		Need good goals and objectives
		Requires measurement
		  instrument
		Too much focus on goals
		  possible

Goal-Free	Allows for qualitative data Examines actual effects Uses logical analysis Allows depth analysis	Goal-free impossible Possible bias Time-consuming Evaluator driven
Systems Approach	Process-oriented Useful in management	Broad-based Complicated to use

From Ideas to Reality

Choosing evaluation models is not the most exciting task that an evaluator undertakes. Yet it is important to consider from which model you are operating so that appropriate decisions can be made about criteria and methods. The five models outlined here might be used for any of the five Ps. Further, depending upon how the organization is set up, any one of the models might be applied to a particular situation. For example, say you wanted to find out if an older adult program was contributing to the life satisfaction of the individuals who participated, the intuitive judgment model could be used while informally observing the older adults and drawing conclusions. External evaluators (experts) might be invited to help you determine the contribution that the program is making to the lives of older adults. Goals and objectives set for the program (goal-attainment) could be used as the basis for collecting data to determine how the program affects life satisfaction. Or, using a goal-free approach in-depth interviews to find out how the older adult programs affect the individuals who participate could be done. The exact model is not as important as the framework decided on for the evaluation. The models simply provide a road map for making decisions about how an actual project might best be conducted by helping to determine criteria and ways to collect data.

1.08 Designing an Evaluation Project: When Push Comes to Shove

Goals for Chapter 1.08:

—To write an evaluation project plan including why, who, what, when, where, and how;
—To determine the considerations that should be made in planning any type of evaluation project; and,
—To analyze whether an evaluation plan is feasible and has the potential for producing usable results.

Once you have determined what to include in your organization's evaluation system, you can then plan specific evaluation projects. Planning a project includes choosing a model as a guide, determining the timing of evaluation and the area (five Ps) within leisure services that will be evaluated, and selecting specific methods to use. Sometimes the design for a project, such as a performance appraisal of staff development, is a tool that will be used over and over again. Other times, each individual project will be designed anew. Generally small scale, highly focused, and manageable evaluations are more useful than large, broad evaluations. Sometimes more complex projects will be necessary, and cutting a major project into manageable portions may be needed to complete it successfully. Regardless of the magnitude of the project, keeping it focused and on target is essential. The purpose of this chapter is to describe the details that must be considered when designing an evaluation project.

A design is a plan for allocating resources. The design must be carefully considered for each project depending on the specific context of the evaluation situation. There are always many choices. Various constraints, however, are associated with every plan, and you must do your best given the financial, time, and human resources constraints that may exist. In addition, for any evaluation, many designs may be proposed, but no single plan is necessarily going to be perfect. Thus, decisions will have to be made.

Taking time to plan is important in any project. Lead time will be needed to plan the entire process of evaluation. Unfortunately, when an evaluation system is not in place, evaluations often are done as a result of crisis rather than as a part of the overall organization's plan for improvement and accountability.

Developing Plans for a Specific Evaluation Project

Planning guidelines provide a most useful framework in developing individual evaluation projects. In general, when planning an evaluation project you will be examining several basic questions:

Why (e.g., for what reason is this evaluation project being done, is it worth the effort, and what use will the results have);

What (e.g., which of the aspects of a place, participants, program, personnel, or policy will be evaluated; what issues need to be addressed; and what criteria are to be measured);

Who (e.g., who wants the information and in what form, who will actually conduct the evaluation, and who is the sample to ask for information);

When (e.g., timelines and timing);

Where (e.g., sample size and composition); and

How (e.g., how to collect and analyze data, methods, techniques, ethics, how the final report with be presented, and resources needed).

These questions resemble what was asked in setting up the evaluation system, but in an evaluation project design you will get more specific about how a project will actually be conducted from the beginning to the end. The design of the actual project is the "nitty gritty" of evaluation.

Theoretically, the *why, what, who, when, where* and *how* will be considered together, but practically, each will build upon the other. Smith (1989) suggested that two types of error must be avoided in the initial planning: measuring something that does not exist, and measuring something that is of no interest to management and policy makers. Thus, the first three steps of determining *why, what,* and *who* are essential.

The *why* of doing evaluations was discussed extensively in Chapter 1.02, but the evaluator must always keep in mind the purpose of the project so that it will stay focused and on track. The *why* has implications for *what* and *who.*

The *who* often refers to the stakeholders or who wants the information. Stakeholders are those individuals who are personally involved in the organization, who derive income from the organization, whose future status or career might be affected by the quality of the organization, and/or who are the clients or potential recipients of the organization's services. Arranging a meeting of the stakeholders for a proposed evaluation project is often useful before beginning. Staff are usually more involved in the organization than either sponsors or clients, so they need to have input about how an evaluation will be conducted. Many aspects of the evaluation plan such as the type of evaluation, the availability of resources, and the reasons for evaluating can be determined early in the project by talking to stakeholders. Further, clarifications should be made specific about *why* a project is being undertaken, and *what* the project is.

A second part of the *who* question is to determine who has the information needed. In some cases, documents may already exist that can help to address the evaluation criteria. Existing research/evaluation literature may be used as well as organizational records. You may want to find out what has been done elsewhere, if possible, and borrow or adapt their approach and/or instruments whenever possible and appropriate.

A third part of *who* is to determine who will be in charge of the evaluation. Although an evaluation project may be done by one person, a team approach is often desirable. The more people involved in an evaluation project, the more likely they are to have ideas that can help to make the evaluation recommendations usable when completed. A citizen advisory committee, for example, may be used depending on the type of project undertaken.

What relates to the criteria to be measured. Is it possible to measure the criteria desired? Do the resources exist to do an appropriate evaluation project? Is the level of evaluation and the timing of the evaluation consistent with what the stakeholders want and need? These answers represent a critical aspect in developing the evaluation plan because now is the point that an initial decision should be made about whether to attempt a particular evaluation project or not. If the goal-attainment model is to provide the framework, for example, you must be certain that measurable goals and objectives exist or can be written. This is the time to determine which model is going to be best to use.

When refers to the timing and timelines. Should the evaluation be assessment, summative, or formative? If the evaluation is summative, when is the best time to collect information: immediately or after several weeks have passed after a program? How long will the project take to complete? When are the results of the evaluation needed? When is the best time during the program or the year to do the evaluation? To some extent, these answers will depend on the criteria being used. The evaluator must try to be realistic about how long a project may take to complete. It takes time for proper pretesting of instruments, training of data collectors, getting related material from other books and journals, analyzing the data to draw conclusions and make recommendations, and writing the report. It is possible, but very unlikely, that someone could do a survey in two or three weeks if it is brief and done on a telephone. A survey of several hundred or a few thousand, however, may take a few months or more than a year to complete. Also think about the unintended consequences that might be encountered such as an inadequate sample size, that could slow down the data collection. All of these issues will be discussed further in Unit Two, but the conscientious evaluator will consider the possible problems in the planning phase to try to prevent them from happening when the evaluation is actually implemented.

Where the evaluation is conducted will depend upon the leisure service area being examined, the sample to be used, and the timing. The particular aspect of the five Ps will also determine the *where*. Usually the *where* question is not difficult to answer once the other components of the planning have been carefully considered.

The final task is to determine *how* to do a project. *How* relates primarily to data collection and analysis. Such decisions include sampling, evaluation research design, data collection administration, choice of statistics, and a report of the findings. Once the preceding questions are answered, these *how* questions will likely fall into place, although other decisions will still need to be made. The problem with some evaluations is that the decision is made to use a particular technique, like mailed questionnaires, before any of the other aspects of designing the evaluation project plan are determined. The *how* aspect of the plan, however, has to be realistic because one must also assess the resources available for the project. The evaluator must be careful to avoid "data addiction." That is, you should plan to collect only the data that are needed, not everything that would be interesting to ask. If criteria are appropriately delimited, data addiction should not be a problem.

The *how* also includes considering costs such as:
- staff time for planning;
- labor and material costs for pretesting;
- copying costs;
- supervisory costs for hiring, training, and supervising interviewer staff or volunteers;
- cost of preparing codes and mailing;
- labor and material costs for coding and entering data;
- cost of cleaning up the data if mistakes are made in entering it;
- computer programming or software costs;
- computer time;
- labor time and material costs for analysis and report preparation; and,
- telephone charges, postage, reproduction, and printing.

A good evaluation is not always inexpensive, although some projects are more economical than others. The costs will obviously increase with the complexity of the project and amount of analyses needed.

After these *why, what, who, when, where,* and *how* decisions are considered, a brief proposal or written plan will be useful to make sure that all people involved in your organization agree with what will be done in the evaluation project. Sometimes when things are written down on paper, possible mistakes or problems are easier to see. The following planning framework outline (Table 1.8) is offered as an example and a model that can be used in doing evaluation project planning.

Table 1.8

Example Evaluation Project Planning Framework

(adapted from the work of students: Ginna Millard, Sara Shope, and Amy Bryan)

Agency—University of North Carolina Hospitals (Pediatric Play Room)

Why?

Background—problems exist trying to keep track of the toys, videos, and other resources that are available to use and check out in the Pediatric Play Room

Purpose—to describe the process (success and failures) in the present system, set a baseline, and to provide for organizational improvement in the future

Cost-effectiveness—the administration of the project can be done by volunteer under-graduate students who will provide a report to the C.T.R.S. responsible for the play room

What?

Model—goal-free

Criteria—what are the problems, what policies currently exist, how are they enforced, how willing are staff and volunteers to enforce policies

Data Type—a combination of qualitative (field observations) and quantitative data (questionnaires to staff and volunteers who supervise the play room)

Who?

Who Wants the Information—Director of Therapeutic Recreation Services at UNC Hospitals and C.T.R.S. in charge of playroom

Who Will Do the Project—undergraduate TR students in an evaluation class

Who Will Provide Data—the evaluators will observe the playroom and survey all individuals who have responsibilities for supervising the playroom

When?

Timing—formative evaluation

Timeliness—March (observation) and April (surveys and analysis) 1994

Where?

Sample Size and Composition—random sample of observations during various hours that the play room is open; a population sample will be done of supervisors in the play room

How?

Method(s) to Use—field observations and quantitative questionnaires

Time and Money Resources Needed—time to plan, conduct, and write report is volunteer time from students; supplies for printing from hospital budget=$10; computer analysis free

Special Considerations—gaining cooperation of supervisors in the play room

(*Note:* More detail will be added to each of these as the specific plans for data collection are solidified.)

Other Considerations

Several other items might be considered in designing an evaluation project. First of all, baseline data about a program, participant, staff member, or place may be needed before the data collection begins. It may be of use to know the current state of affairs that existed up to the present time. This information might provide a standard of comparison against which the outcomes of the evaluation are measured.

Second, evaluators also need to be aware of their agendas and biases for any evaluation study as well as those of the stakeholders or audience. Possible conflicts should be discussed ahead of time and negotiated. The goals of the project should be agreed upon and the possibility of unexpected consequences, such as what happens if undesirable effects are found, should be anticipated. All parties in the evaluation should be aware of how the evaluation is to be conducted and how the data will be presented.

Finally, usefulness for enlightened decision making is the primarily focus of evaluation. As Patton (1978) suggested, evaluations are not a panacea for problems. For an evaluation project to be used, criteria must be addressed to answer questions for decision makers. Questions that decision makers do not want answered should be avoided as should questions that already have known answers. Unless a lack of knowledge and information is a part of the problem, evaluation research will not help an organization. If the problem is a disorganized organization, one should organize it rather than try to evaluate it. Further, as Hudson (1988) suggested concerning community needs assessments, evaluation projects must be comprehensive, customized, versatile, flexible, and efficient, Evaluations take a commitment of time and resources and often have limitations. They must be designed, however, to provide the greatest potential to get useful information for making the best possible decisions.

From Ideas to Reality

Planning evaluation projects beyond the idea stage is often not the most exciting part of doing evaluation projects. Some evaluators, particularly when they are novices, have a tendency to want to begin to collect data and later work out the "bugs" of a study. It is best to consider drafting an outline for each phase of the evaluation plan before beginning to collect data. It will set a course that can provide direction as you move through the project. The plan provides a foundation to use. The plan does not need to be elaborate at this stage, but it at least can give you some direction. It may be modified slightly as the project develops. Once more information about the methods, such as questionnaires or observations, and techniques, such as sampling and analysis, are available, a more sophisticated plan to follow can be developed to implement the evaluation project and to write the final report.

1.09 COMPETENCIES AND THE ART OF EVALUATION

Goals for Chapter 1.09:

—To describe the advantages and disadvantages of using internal versus external evaluators;
—To determine when it is best to hire an outside evaluator or use an internal evaluator; and,
—To list the competencies needed to become a successful evaluator.

Most people are pretty good intuitive evaluators, but education, training, and practical experience are necessary to become confident and competent at systematic formal evaluation. As indicated in the preface, reading this book is not necessarily going to make you an expert evaluator. That learning will take years of experience. It is necessary, however, to have some basic skills and background to conduct and evaluate your own projects and improve your abilities.

A critical aspect of learning is that when acquiring knowledge about a few things, we often discover all the things that we *don't* know. We have learned as professors over the years that sometimes the value of a college education is not in what you learn, but how a person comes to appreciate what she or he does not know. Thus, one important aspect of developing competencies for evaluation in leisure services is to learn the limitations of one's own skills, as well as the limitations of what evaluation can do for an organization.

Sometimes understanding how to evaluate evaluations is just as important as being able to actually conduct them. Some organizations rely on external evaluators who come from outside the organization to conduct an evaluation. Other organizations use only internal evaluators who are professionals within the organization who have job responsibilities that include evaluation. Therapeutic recreation specialists, for example, spend a great deal of their time doing individual assessments and evaluations for their clients. Whether you are actually the internal professional who conducts the evaluation, or whether you use the information obtained from an external evaluator, it is still necessary to know the terminology and the components that must be considered in the evaluation process.

Internal Versus External Evaluations

The ideal situation for a leisure service organization is to have both internal and external evaluations conducted appropriately within the evaluation system. The decision whether to use internal or external evaluators may depend on a variety of factors. Table 1.9 provides a summary of the advantages and disadvantages of internal or external evaluators.

Certainly many advantages exist with using internal evaluators. The professional who is a member of the organization ought to know a lot about the organization. Less time will be needed for the evaluator to become familiar with the intricacies of the organization. An internal evaluator will also be more accessible to colleagues and will likely not be as obtrusive as an external evaluator. Once the evaluation is complete, the internal evaluator may be in a better position to make changes and to use the results of the evaluation for decision making. When internal evaluators are used, they receive their regular salary so the costs would likely be lower. Further, because the internal evaluator knows the organization, realistic recommendations that can enhance the efficiency and effectiveness of the organization might be more easily offered.

Obvious advantages also exist to using external evaluators. These individuals, often called consultants, may have more objectivity due to their distance from the situation, and the freedom from responsibility to the organization or the services. Their objectivity is also based on a professional commitment to the field and not to the individual organization. Further, they have credibility based on their professional experience and competency. With more experience, they may have access to a greater variety of methods and techniques. They may also know more about how other organizations address some of their evaluation concerns. They may have resources such as sample measurement instruments or computer programs for data analysis that may not be available to internal evaluators in an organization. Since external evaluators have less investment in a program, they may feel less pressure to make compromises in their recommendations. In addition, if staff conflicts are a problem in an organization, outside evaluators may be able to mediate them more effectively than someone who is involved within the organization. Their objectivity will likely be unencumbered by a knowledge of personal issues and conflicts. A further advantage is that they may have data from other organizations that would make for comparative evaluations.

A down side exists to using only internal or external evaluators. The internal evaluator may feel pressure to have positive results, or her or his job or the jobs of colleagues, may change. It is generally easier for an internal evaluator to focus on strengths rather than weaknesses. An internal evaluator may find difficulty to criticize certain aspects of a program. Further, an internal evaluator that does not have extensive training in evaluation may not be as competent as someone who has evaluation as a specialty.

Table 1.9

Advantages and Disadvantages of External and Internal Evaluators

Internal

Advantages
Knows the organization
Accessible to colleagues
Realistic recommendations
Can make changes

Disadvantages
Pressure to have positive results
Difficult to criticize
May lack training

External

Advantages
More objectivity
Competence
Experience
More resources
Less pressure to compromise

Disadvantages
Threat to employees
Must get to know organization
May disrupt organization
May impose values
Expensive

The external evaluator may also have disadvantages. This outside individual may be seen as a threat to employees; they will be on their best behavior, and the organization may not appear as it really is. The external evaluator must spend a great deal of time just getting to know an organization and may miss some of the nuances that go on within a particular organization. The outside evaluator may take valuable time away from staff or may disrupt the normal functioning of an organization. As is true in any situation, the external evaluator may impose her or his value system on an organization that may not hold the same values. Further, to hire an external evaluator often is expensive, and many leisure service agencies do not have those resources.

Decisions will have to be made about who is the best person to conduct an evaluation. Some decisions are obvious. For example, personnel evaluations are usually conducted by one's immediate supervisor, an internal evaluator. To bring someone from the outside would not make sense. On the other hand, when standards are applied through an accreditation process, external reviewers are required. Some programs may be evaluated easily "in-house" whereas hiring someone to conduct a more thorough evaluation may be useful every once in awhile.

Developing Competencies

Regardless of who conducts the evaluation, every recreation, park, tourism, and leisure services professional ought to have some training in systematic evaluation that can be used in an organization. The more individuals who have evaluation training, the better off the organization will be. Even if an external evaluator is hired, the professionals in the organization have to know how to formulate criteria for the project and will need to determine the reliability and validity of the judgments made by external evaluators.

In hiring an external reviewer or conducting an evaluation with organizational staff, several specific competencies ought to be required:

1. The individual conducting the evaluation should have some knowledge about the topical area being evaluated. If the adult sports league is being evaluated, for example, the evaluator ought to know something about recreation programming for adults and about sports programming. In addition the basic terminology of evaluation should be understood.

2. An evaluator ought to know something about designing evaluation systems, developing planning frameworks for individual projects, and writing goals and objectives. Knowing why and what to evaluate are necessary prerequisites for writing different types of objectives. The evaluator must be able to judge how measurement can be conducted in relation to these goals and objectives.

3. The evaluator ought to know all the possible evaluation research methods. She or he should know how to determine the best way to collect data, how to choose a sample, and the appropriate techniques for analysis.

4. The evaluator should be able to interpret the data and relate those results to the criteria. An understanding of the trilogy of evaluation and how the parts fit together is essential.

5. The evaluator should know how to analyze both qualitative and quantitative data using the most appropriate strategies or statistics. As you will see later, evaluators may be partial to qualitative or quantitative data. These preferences, however, do not preclude knowing the basic assumptions about each type of data so that sound evaluation judgments can be made.

6. An evaluator must understand how to use evaluation results in decision making regardless of what area of the five Ps are being evaluated. This competency will involve knowing how to organize, write, and present evaluation reports so that the information can be communicated effectively to those individuals (e.g., staff, Board or Commission members, parents) who want and/or need information.

7. An evaluator needs to be able to address the political, legal, and ethical issues that may be encountered in doing an evaluation. Certain legal and ethical concerns must be addressed as well as how evaluators can be politically responsive to those users of the evaluation information. More detail will be given about these issues in Chapter 1.10.

8. Although most of the above competencies relate to conceptual and technical skills, certain personal skills are an additional aspect needed to be a successful evaluator. Personal qualities are necessary such as an interest in improving programs, places, policies, participant experiences, and/or personnel. The evaluator must be worthy of trust of her or his colleagues as well as of the administrators and the decision makers of organizations. She or he must be as objective as possible, although one's personal biases cannot help but enter into any undertaking. The effective evaluator must be able to see and respond to sensitive issues and situations as they relate to the uniqueness of organizations.

When one begins to examine the competencies needed to conduct evaluation projects, they may appear to be a bit overwhelming. These competencies are not that rigorous if the evaluator sees evaluation as a system of linking criteria, evidence, and judgment. Conducting evaluation or using evaluation information need not be anything to fear. The best way to learn is to "just do it," and the only way to get started is to begin. Some aspects of evaluation are technical, but not so difficult that they can't be used by an enthusiastic and committed leisure services professional.

From Ideas to Reality

As indicated earlier, to become a good evaluator requires a combination of education, training, and practical experience. All leisure services professionals ought to have a basic background in evaluation that will enable them to do projects and judge the merit of evaluation projects done by others. No magic formulas exist to learn how to be a competent evaluator but by learning the basics and trying them out, evaluating your own work, and practicing, you can become effective and successful as an evaluator.

Whether to use internal or external evaluators is a decision left up to an organization. Both have advantages and disadvantages. Many times organizations do not have the funding necessary to hire outside consultants so they rely on internal evaluators. In some situations, it is better to go outside the organization regarding some types of criteria that may need to be measured. The professional will need to determine when it is most appropriate to do internal or external evaluations and how that relates to the entire evaluation system.

1.10 POLITICAL, LEGAL, ETHICAL, AND MORAL ISSUES IN EVALUATION: DOING THE RIGHT THING

Goals for Chapter 1.10:

—To identify possible political, legal, ethical, and moral dilemmas that you might face in doing an evaluation; and,

—To avoid possible problems by being honest with all involved in an evaluation project.

Most research and evaluation books include a chapter or a section on legal and ethical issues late in the text. You may not have enough information about data collection at this point to fully comprehend this chapter placed toward the beginning, but the legal, ethical, moral, and political questions surrounding evaluations ought to be put in the forefront. Chances are that many of these issues will not need to be addressed negatively if the design of the project has been carefully considered. On the other hand, decisions about planning an evaluation project based on some of these concerns will likely have to be made.

Regardless of the project, the bottom line is to consider how subjects and organizations will be treated with dignity. This belief is easy to articulate but often hard to implement into practice because of the many issues that may arise when conducting evaluation projects.

Political Issues

Politics deal with practical wisdom related to the beliefs and biases that individuals and groups hold. Evaluation systems and projects can be political in that they may support or refute the views that people hold. The simple fact that people are involved in evaluation projects makes them political.

Politics encompass personal contacts, value-laden definitions, controversial recommendations, subtle pressures to please, and advocacy for certain results or outcomes. According to Patton (1978), to be innocent of politics in evaluation is to become a pawn. Value orientations and the collection of empirical (observable) data make evaluation projects political whether we like it or not. The fact that criteria, evidence, and judgment are used makes evaluation political. Further, politics effect the utilization process. By their nature, evaluations are political when the information is used to "manipulate" other people even though the manipulation may be positive.

As an evaluator, you may want to be aware of several considerations that can make the evaluation process less political. An evaluator must first understand the organization well before an evaluation project is undertaken. This suggestion means understanding the strengths and the limitations of an organization. Second, before claiming anything in the evaluation, evidence must be provided. Thus, the judgments must be directly linked to the criteria and the evidence. Sometimes generalizations and recommendations are easy to make without paying attention to the data. An evaluator must be careful not to go beyond the actual findings in drawing conclusions. Third, the purpose of the evaluation must be made clear to all involved *before* it is undertaken. That purpose must also be kept clear throughout the process.

Essentially, the only way that evaluations are not political is if they are not used, and even nonuse may make a political statement. Not understanding the political ramifications may be a reason why evaluations do not get used. What a waste of time, however, if the recommendations of an evaluation project are never even considered. If we acknowledge that evaluations are often political, then those politics can be used to our advantage by not resisting or ignoring them.

Legal Issues

In the vast majority of evaluation projects, you will probably encounter few legal concerns. If you were collecting information about illegal behavior and its cessation due to a recreation program, however, you might run into legal issues. For example, if someone admits during an evaluation interview that they are drinking at the recreation center is the evaluator obliged to "turn them in?" The answer is probably "no," but you must be careful that names are not associated directly with your data in the event that some legality must be addressed.

Ethical Issues

Ethics have to do with what is right and wrong and how you conform to the standards of a given profession. In this case, certain "rules" must be considered when doing evaluation projects. Ethics involve primarily being as open as possible about a project within the constraints of privacy. This statement means that people (participants or personnel) have the right to know that they or their programs are being evaluated. In addition, they also have some right to privacy and confidentiality concerning the information that they wish to divulge.

An evaluator has ethical obligations to the people with whom she or he works. First of all, an evaluator must be careful not to promise too much from an evaluation. An evaluation project's value and limitations should be presented realistically. The evaluator must assure loyalties to the profession and to the public above the program evaluated.

Privacy is a second ethical issue. The evaluator also has the responsibility to assure anonymity and confidentiality if that is needed in the evaluation. Anonymity means that no one, including the evaluators, will know the names of the participants in an evaluation project, such as the individuals who complete a survey. Confidentiality says that the evaluator will know who participated, but no one else will. Some projects do not require this assurance, but others may require confidentiality or anonymity. For example, the evaluator may want to use only code numbers to identify respondents instead of people's names. Those codes must be kept separate from questionnaires, and the codes should be destroyed once all data are tabulated so even the evaluator does not know who provided information. The evaluator may also want to present statistics by broad enough categories so that no one can figure out how a particular individual might have responded. People answer differently sometimes depending on whether their name goes on the survey. Sometimes using the person's name makes a difference, but that person *must* give you permission to do so.

Coercion is a third ethical concern in some evaluation projects. People should never be forced into participation unless involvement is a necessary prerequisite that is understood. For example, staff evaluations are required in most organizations. A staff member knows when she or he takes a job that a performance evaluation is required, so she or he should not feel any coercion. In other evaluation situations, however, participation should be optional. Evaluators need to make a project interesting and important enough that people *want* to participate.

Related to coercion is a fourth area of written consent. Written, informed consent is not necessarily required in most evaluation projects, but evaluators need to be aware of its potential use. Written consent is a way to assure anonymity or confidentially to individuals by having them sign a form indicating that they are aware of how data will be collected and used. For some types of extensive evaluation involving children in particular, informed consent may need to be obtained from parents or guardians as well as from children.

A fifth ethical question raised in evaluation relates to how someone may be harmed by evaluation. If any harm is possible as a result of an evaluation, care must be taken to make sure that the harm does not occur. This ethical concern refers to physical or psychological harm in doing an evaluation or in *not* getting a treatment. For example, if we want to find out if some new activity in therapeutic recreation really works, we may design an experiment where half of the clients will get the treatment and half will not. In this situation, we have to ask what possible harm could be incurred to the group not getting the treatment. After considering the possible negative physical and psychological effects, the ideal experimental design may not be possible, if harm would be caused. Most recreation professionals will not be in situations where these concerns of possible harm will arise, but one must always be aware of them.

A final ethical aspect that might be considered relates to how much participants have the right to know about the results of a project. Most agree that they have the right to know the results of an evaluation project. Sharing results with participants as well as other professionals is the best way to assure that good evaluation and programs are developed. You may want to offer to send the results to participants or have a meeting to explain what was learned from an evaluation project. Sometimes this procedure is referred to as "debriefing," but it need not be that formal. People, however, who have been involved in giving you information should have access to that information.

Moral Issues

Moral issues are closely related to ethical issues. We will address them separately, however, as they relate to what the evaluator himself or herself might do that could be construed as right or wrong in conducting an evaluation. Moral concerns relate to biases and mistakes that might be unintentionally made in conducting an evaluation project thereby affecting the outcome of the project. For example, the choice of an inappropriate or inadequate sample may affect the outcomes of a study. If the evaluator is aware of a concern such as this and does nothing to compensate for it, she or he has acted in a morally inappropriate manner.

Cultural and procedural biases may also cause evaluation problems. The careless collection of data by using an inappropriate instrument for the respondents or poorly written questions are moral concerns. An evaluator must be honest about her or his skills, and either get help or do an evaluation project that is appropriate to her or his competence and skill level.

Allowing bias, prejudice, preconceived perceptions, or friendship to influence the evaluation outcomes, or being a patsy to the stakeholders, are further moral issues to avoid. The evaluator must also be careful not to be predisposed to any particular outcome.

When the evaluator actually gets to the judgment phase and writes the report, several aspects must be considered. For example, not publishing negative results is a problem as is discounting some findings or not disclosing all the information. All the details of the study need to be reported including procedures that may not have gone particularly well. The possibilities of negative results should be discussed and addressed ahead of time with the stakeholders of an evaluation to avoid moral conflicts and embarrassment arising from the evaluation situation.

Taking too long to get results out also has moral implications. Since evaluation is oriented toward problem solving and enlightened decision making, most people need that information just as soon as possible. Although not morally wrong, an evaluator has a responsibility to get an evaluation project completed in a timely manner.

Morally the evaluator is bound to do the best possible evaluation. Thus, shortcuts must be avoided. Improper sampling procedures and the use of a convenience sample rather than a probability sample may not be appropriate and may effect the results of a study. Further, procedures need to be pretested to assure that they are appropriate.

Quality control must be instituted throughout the project. The evaluator must also be able to address the possibility of what are called in research, Type I and Type II errors. Type I are false positive errors or the finding that a program really makes a difference when it does not. These errors may be compared to Type II errors which are false negative and assume that a program makes no beneficial difference when it really does. In evaluation, Type I errors are more likely, but the possibility of both and what they mean from a moral perspective have to be considered.

Avoiding Problems in Evaluation

Posavac and Carey (1992) have offered several key ideas to consider in addressing legal, ethical, political, and moral issues in evaluation. First, humility won't hurt. You must realize what can and cannot be done, be able to admit your limitations, and adjust. Second, evaluation is not easy and it is not a "slam-bang" proposition. Patience is necessary and impatience may lead to disappointment and problems. Planning is essential to avoid pitfalls. Third, the evaluator must focus on practical questions and feasible issues. The evaluation questions must be well-focused and the criteria clearly defined. Get other staff to support you, and make sure they know what is going on and are able to monitor the quality control of your project as well. Finally, adopt a self-evaluation orientation in the work. You as the evaluator are ultimately the one who knows whether the appropriate moral, political, ethical, and legal decisions have been made. You must continually monitor yourself to do the right thing.

From Ideas to Reality

Political, legal, ethical, and moral issues will be different in each study. Hopefully none of these will be a problem, but they are always a possibility. If you are honest with yourself, your colleagues, and the individuals associated with any aspect of the evaluation project, you will probably not face major dilemmas. If there are problems, it is best to face them squarely and try to adjust to overcome them. Covering up problems or deceiving people in any way is likely not to be the way to find success in conducting evaluations.

Unit Two—Evidence:
Data Collection

Introduction to Evidence

Now you should have a firm background in the way that criteria are identified and/or developed and how people plan evaluation projects. After the criteria are determined, the evaluator can begin to examine possible ways to gather evidence, usually referred to as data collection methods. Once the methods are determined, procedures and strategies for obtaining that data can be developed. As mentioned previously, the possible methods, techniques, and tools used for gathering evidence for evaluation projects are the same as those used in research studies. The ways that these methods are applied and the use of theory determine the differences between evaluation and research.

Unit Two will explore the differences between quantitative and qualitative data. In addition, we will examine the options available for method choices, and we will discuss the actual procedures used in developing questionnaires, conducting interviews, designing experiments, and doing observations. Further, the specific application of evaluation tools used in recreation and leisure services will be examined. Sampling, triangulation, and determining the trustworthiness of data will be discussed. These applications will tie to the second phase of evidence, data analysis, described in Unit Three. Evidence relates to both data collection and data analysis but considering them separately may be less overwhelming initially.

This unit moves into the technical part, the "how-tos," of doing evaluations. Methods have particular rules, guidelines, and protocols associated with them that will be explained. Hopefully, this unit will provide you with the tools needed to address most of the evaluation questions and criteria that you will encounter as a recreation, park, and leisure services professional. We also believe the second and third unit will provide you with a sound background that can be used in research projects or evaluation studies.

2.01 Qualitative and Quantitative Data: Choices To Make

Goals for Chapter 2.01:

—To describe the differences between qualitative and quantitative data;

—To state why one type of data might be preferable to another given a particular evaluation project;

—To make a decision, given evaluation criteria and a particular situation, about which type of data or combination of data is best to collect;

—To describe general differences between the interpretive and positivist paradigms; and,

—To explain the links between paradigm, methods, and data type.

Qualitative and quantitative data were mentioned along with designing evaluation projects. Before making method decisions, an evaluator must understand the differences and the similarities between qualitative and quantitative approaches to evaluation as well as how these data might be used.

Some individuals are purists in that they believe that evaluation can best be done using only qualitative or quantitative data. Different situations, however, may call for a particular type of data. It is possible to collect and use both qualitative and quantitative data in a single evaluation project if the criteria are such that this combination would be helpful. This chapter describes both types of data and why they might be used either separately or together in collecting evaluation evidence.

Evaluation World Views and Data

The differences between evaluation world views and data are important to clarify. World views or paradigms are foundations for how we might think about evaluation. Data are the evidence. Methods are the tools.

Because people see the world from different world views or paradigms, different methods of inquiry are typically used. Patton (1980a) has eloquently described how paradigms are related to methods. For example, he says that method-type is typically linked to paradigm so allegiance to a paradigm is usually the major, but not the only, reason for making methods decisions. If one's theory of evaluation is more closely related to the attributes of paradigm A than B, one will usually favor those research methods that are linked to A. Further, qualitative and quantitative data are ideal-types, and the real world choices usually vary. Most methods will typify more closely the attributes of one or the other paradigm. Methods will depend on measurement options including kinds of data, design options, personal involvement options, and analysis options such as inductive analysis (moving from specific to general) versus deductive analysis (moving from general to specific).

Most of the models of evaluation imply a positivist world view that purports facts and truth can be found; this view is most often associated with the scientific method and results in quantitative data. The goal-attainment evaluation model is usually closely related to the positivist paradigm. Positivist approaches to data usually result in the use of numbers to make decisions. Because evaluation requires that judgments be made, however, all quantitative data are always going to call for a certain amount of interpretation.

A second paradigm, the interpretive paradigm, suggests that not one, but many truths may exist within any evaluation project. The goal-free model is often used in this case to collect qualitative data. An interpretive approach to evaluation assumes that the realities of a program are multiple, and that different perceptions, descriptions, and interpretations can be found in the same program as data are collected. For example, programs sometimes have an impact opposite of the one intended. In an evaluation conducted of an exercise program, the gains made in cardiovascular fitness might be minimal compared to the positive social experience that older adults have as a result of an organized walking program.

Evaluation Data Types

This is not a debate as to whether one approach to data collection, qualitative or quantitative, is better than the other approach. One approach may be better given a particular evaluation situation and the criteria that are to be measured, but the evaluator must make that determination. Much has been written about qualitative and quantitative data in the past several years, but a discussion of which one is better is not useful as each has its place in research studies and evaluation projects. How to use the data is a more important question.

We also want to emphasize that no such thing as a qualitative and quantitative *method* exists. You can do an interview and collect either type of data, quantitative data or qualitative data, depending upon the design of the interview and the types of questions asked. The same is true of observations and even questionnaires. The nature of the data provides the framework for whether a project is qualitative or quantitative, not the methods that are used.

Either of the two types of data may be collected, quantitative and qualitative, depending on the questions asked and the way the data are collected. The simplest distinction between the two types of data is to suggest that quantitative data use numbers or easily convert words to numbers such as 1=yes and 2=no. Qualitative data use words almost exclusively. The meanings of these differences, however, are more complicated than this simple explanation would imply.

Qualitative data allow individuals to describe experiences in words. Open-ended questions that allow for elaboration on the part of the respondent result in qualitative data. These data are usually more useful in providing in-depth understanding about issues that may be impossible to acquire through quantitative procedures related to scales or yes/no questions. Ellis and Williams (1987) suggested that the increased interest in time and the context of experiences has resulted in changes in evaluation methods. Questions about change across time, the context within which change occurs, and the nature of the causes or conditions associated with change are being asked in evaluation projects. Questions about the context in which change occurs, and the use of goal-free models of evaluation make qualitative data useful. Rather than provide a list of preestablished responses to questions about a particular activity or program, the evaluator using qualitative data elicits responses in the actual words of the participants.

Depending upon the criteria being measured, either or both quantitative and qualitative data may be useful in measuring any of the five Ps. Further, although qualitative data may be most useful in evaluating recreation programs, they may be used in any area of leisure service evaluation. The evaluator will need to determine how best to collect the data to assist in decision making.

Describing Differences in Data

A number of contrasts can be made between evaluation projects that rely on collecting quantitative or qualitative data. Table 2.1(1) (page 88) gives an example of some of those differences, but it is also useful to explain them.

Quantitative data usually follow standard procedures of rigor related to instruments used and statistical data analysis. Quantitative data are deductive in that particular evaluation questions serve as the start, and data are reduced to measure those questions. Quantitative data are often the result of a goal-attainment or systems-oriented model with verification as the purpose. The instruments used for quantitative data collection are paper and pencil tests or surveys. Preordinate designs are used. Preordinate refers to having a specific plan laid out ahead of time concerning the data to be collected. Once the data collection begins, nothing changes with the preordinate design. The treatment of quantitative data is stable with specific statistical procedures. Variables or analytic units are used in analyzing quantitative data. Statistics are used to determine averages and relationships among variables. Quantitative data are generally highly controlled such as in experimental designs. Fixed procedures and specific rules for collecting data are common in the quantitative approach.

Table 2.1(1)

Making Choices about Quantitative and Qualitative Data
(adapted from Henderson, 1991)

Quantitative	Qualitative
Rigor in techniques	Relevance of techniques
Reductionist stance	Expansionist stance
Verification purpose	Discovery purpose
Paper/Physical instrument	Inquirer as instrument
Usually systems or goal-attainment	Goal-free model
Experimental	Natural setting
Stable treatment of data	Variable treatment of data
Variables as analytic unit	Patterns as analysis
Fixed methods	Dynamic methods
Product-oriented	Process-oriented
Reliability-based	Validity-based
Uniformity	Diversity
Deductive	Inductive
Results in facts	Results in understanding
Preordinate designs	Emerging designs

Qualitative data, on the other hand, are concerned with the relevance to the context or the situation. Qualitative data are often goal-free and concerned with discovery. Qualitative data are expansionist as we try to understand all the causes or reasons for something. The logic of generalization for qualitative data is to examine individual cases to determine a number of conclusions that fit the data. The inquirer or the evaluator is the instrument in the qualitative approach as she or he interprets the meaning of the words. Data collection and design are likely to emerge together as data are uncovered in projects using qualitative data. In an emerging design, the evaluator may follow ideas that flow from the data such that the questions and answers about a project are occurring simultaneously. The evaluator is the instrument used to find patterns within qualitative data. Dynamic and evolving procedures are used to collect these data.

In general, quantitative data usually measure the outcome of an intervention or a program, while qualitative data are used to describe what was done. In other words, quantitative data tend to be more focused on the outcome or products of an evaluation whereas qualitative data more often reflect the process. Reliability is paramount in quantitative data, and validity is more important for qualitative data. Finally, quantitative data are quantifiable and concerned with facts whereas qualitative data provide a means for understanding.

Choosing Qualitative and/or Quantitative Data

As indicated previously, one approach to data collection is not superior to another. The dominance of quantitative data, however, sometimes has severely limited the evaluation questions asked and the way that criteria are applied within evaluation projects in recreation, park, leisure, and tourism organizations.

Different situations and criteria may require different kinds of methods. Table 2.1(2) provides a checklist that may be useful in determining what type of data to collect. If, for example, we want to know how many people with and without disabilities attended a program, then counting them using quantitative data and using statistical procedures may be appropriate. If we want to understand whether the attitudes of people without disabilities have changed due to a recreation program offered, and what the interaction is between people with and without disabilities, then some form of qualitative data such as interviews or observations might better allow the evaluator to obtain that information.

Table 2.1(2)

Checklist for Considering Qualitative or Quantitative Data
(adapted from Patton, 1980a)

Is the evaluator interested in individualized outcomes?

Is the evaluator interested in examining the process of evaluation and the context in which it occurs?

Is detailed in-depth information needed in order to understand the phenomenon being evaluated?

Is the focus on quality and the meaning of the experiences being studied?

Does the evaluator desire to get close to the participants/staff and immersed in their experiences?

Do no measuring devices exist that will provide reliable and valid data for the project?

Is the evaluation question likely to change depending upon how the data emerge?

Is it possible that the answer to the evaluation question may yield unexpected results?

Does the evaluator wish to get personally involved in the evaluation?

Does the evaluator have a philosophical and methodological bias toward goal-free and qualitative data?

If the answer is *yes* to any of these questions, the evaluator ought to at least consider the qualitative methods as possible ways to approach the research question being addressed.

Qualitative data, however, have not been without critics (Patton, 1978). For example, qualitative data are often considered too subjective. Objectivity is traditionally thought to be the essence of the scientific method. Some people think that to be subjective means to be biased, unreliable, and nonrational. Subjectivity implies opinion rather than fact, intuition rather than logic, impression rather than confirmation. The scientific community tries to control subjectivity particularly with an emphasis on reliability.

This dichotomy between qualitative and quantitative data, however, is false. Quantitative data can be subjective and qualitative data can be objective. Subjectivity also refers to getting close to and involved with the data; it allows researchers to take into account their own insights and behavior (Patton, 1978). Subjectivity involves applying critical intelligence to important problems.

The evaluator who knows the advantages and disadvantages of qualitative and quantitative data is best equipped to do evaluation projects. Making decisions about what data to collect and how to collect it is not easy. You must look at the criteria and determine which type of data or combination is most appropriate.

Using Qualitative and Quantitative Data Together

Qualitative and quantitative data can be used together and may compliment each other. In Chapter 2.13 of this unit, triangulation and the use of more than one method or data set will be addressed. Purists say you cannot mix qualitative and quantitative data, but many evaluators agree that in some projects this mixing may be necessary and important. The pursuit of good evaluation should transcend personal preferences for numbers or words. Further, the evaluator must recognize that quantitative data may become qualitative when explanations are needed for unexpected results. Qualitative data can become more quantitative as evaluation criteria become more focused and specific within a particular project.

From Ideas to Reality

Choosing the type of data that will be used depends upon a combination of determining the criteria that need to be measured and personal preference. One type of data is no better than the other if the data provide the answers to the evaluation questions. A combination of the two may also be appropriate in some situations. Decisions about data will need to be carefully considered by the evaluator as a project is planned.

2.02 Choosing Designs and Methods: The Big Picture

Goals for Chapter 2.02:

—To describe what constitutes an experimental design and a descriptive design;

—To specify the methods most often associated with each design; and,

—To list some of the advantages and disadvantages of each of the methods that might be used to collect data.

If we were to try to classify the types of evaluation designs used in recreation and leisure services, we might classify them into two broad categories: experimental and descriptive designs. Within those two designs we could construct a continuum as was done in Chapter 1.01 that ranges from the most sophisticated double blind experiment on one end, to an intuitive judgment on the other end, with quasi-experimental and empirical descriptive studies in the middle. Within the descriptive studies the possibilities of collecting quantitative or qualitative data would be seen; experimental designs are concerned almost exclusively with quantitative data.

Some texts refer to experimental versus nonexperimental as the two major categories of evaluation or research design. This dichotomy puts more focus on the value of "experimental" by referring to its opposite as "non." Thus, this text will refer to experimental and descriptive designs to highlight the value of both. Descriptive designs include all empirically-focused projects that are conducted in real world situations. This description might also be appropriate for true experiments but they have the difference of having an associated control group that descriptive evaluation projects seldom have.

Experimental design is an empirical investigative technique employed to assure control so that the evaluator or researcher can feel confident that the results of the experiment conducted represent the true situation (Lundegren and Farrell, 1985). Experimental studies or projects that focus on a randomized sample and a controlled setting are probably the classic example of evaluation, but these designs are not common in leisure services. Within the category of experimental designs falls true randomized experiments. Experimental designs require that an independent variable be controlled and manipulated. Many important variables like skill development, aptitudes, integrity, and characteristics of recreation leaders, however, cannot be controlled and manipulated within experimental designs. Further, in the evaluation of personnel, places, and policies, experimental designs are frequently impossible to apply.

Descriptive designs are more commonly used in recreation, park, leisure and tourism organizations. They do not require matching or comparison, but are concerned with gathering empirical data. Empirical data are data that you can observe or see. Empirical data may be qualitative or quantitative. The purpose of descriptive designs is to determine existing conditions. The descriptive studies include nonrandomized quasi-experimental designs, cross-sectional and one-group surveys, judgmental assessments, and interpretive explanatory projects. The major methods that are employed might be surveys, observations, and unobtrusive measures. These designs can be further divided to include specific methods such as questionnaires and interviews as tools comprising the survey method, checklists and field observation tools used as observation methods, and document analysis and nonresearcher contact tools within unobtrusive measures.

An evaluator will need to determine how to make method choices based on the two broad categories of experiments and descriptive designs. You will further need to choose specific techniques to use depending upon whether surveys, observations, unobtrusive measures, or experimental designs are chosen. Each of the major evaluation methods will be discussed in more detail, but Table 2.2 is provided to help in making decisions when comparing the possible broad methods that might be chosen.

Table 2.2

The Advantages and Disadvantages of Selected Designs and Methods

	Method	Advantages	Disadvantages
Experimental Designs	*True Experiments*	Assure control Randomized sample Pretest used Represent what happened Generalizable	Manipulation required Lab setting sometimes best Control difficult Ethics concerns Sample sometimes difficult Guinea pig effect
	Quasi-Experiments	Some qualities of experiments Control some outside variables May be appropriate to situation	Nonrandomized Threats to validity Ethics concerns
Descriptive Designs	*Surveys*	Most commonly used Generally inexpensive and easy May allow face-to-face encounter Determine existing conditions Discovery of quan/qual relationships Useful for validity checks, triangulation Goal-attainment model applied Use methods protocols and statistics	Obtrusive and reactive Dependent on instrument Misinterpretation possible Require training Require respondent cooperation Evaluator affects Highly dependent on evaluator's abilities

	Observations	Face-to-face encounter or not
		Large amounts of data obtained quickly
		Low/High interaction with respondents
		Allow for a priori/emerging designs/data
		Wide range of data possible
		Many possibilities for sample
		Discovery of possible relationships
		Useful in triangulation
		Data on nonverbal, unconscious, and
		    communication behaviors
			Missed data
			Misinterpretation possible
			Lack of respondent's words
			Ethical dilemmas
			Success depends on evaluator
			Bias by evaluator possible
			Possible observer effects on
			    those observed
			Ethics concerns

	Unobtrusive Methods	Data easy to analyze Wide range of types of data Easy and efficient to administer Easily quantifiable Good for nonverbal behavior Measuring devices may exist Provide for flexibility Wide range of types of data Good for documenting major events Natural setting	Possible misinterpretations Ethical dilemmas May be expensive Depend on evaluation model Dependent on evaluator's investigative ability Minimal interaction

From Ideas to Reality

Having design options presents both opportunities as well as concerns for an evaluator. The advantages are that there is no one best way to do any project and the creativity of the evaluator can be exercised in developing evaluation projects. On the other hand, the options can also seem a bit daunting and overwhelming. With more experience and practice in doing evaluation projects, the options will make more sense and the best choices will become easier to make. Usually more than one way exists to do a project, and it will be necessary to choose the best design based upon the project and the resources available.

2.03 Trustworthiness: The Zen of Data Collection

> ## Goals for Chapter 2.03:
>
> —To describe the factors considered in determining whether an instrument used in an evaluation project is reliable, valid, and usable;
> —To design or select an instrument that has high reliability and validity;
> —To explain how the selection of evaluation criteria is related to validity; and,
> —To evaluate other projects to ascertain that they are reliable, valid, and usable.

A great evaluation project can have wonderful criteria, but if the tools you are using aren't appropriate, the project is likely doomed to failure. The evaluator should always be concerned that data collected for any evaluation project are trustworthy, or of high quality. An evaluator wants to make sure that measurement instruments possess characteristics of reliability and validity. Thus, trustworthiness is a foundational aspect of data collection. If a data collection instrument fails to do what it is supposed to do, everything else fails in an evaluation project.

Error can exist in any measurement device. To be completely reliable or valid would mean no sources of error, a feat which is next to impossible. But you try to minimize the errors as much as possible. Three areas of trustworthiness as they relate to aspects of data collection for any type of design or method—reliability, validity, and usability—will be examined. Reliability is concerned with the replicability, consistency, and dependability of scientific findings. Validity addresses meaning and meaningfulness of data, or "does the instrument do what it should" related to credibility and transferability. Usability refers to finding meaning within the results.

Reliability

Reliability is also known as dependability. Reliability relates to whether a measure consistently conveys the same meaning to readers; it addresses the degree of stability or consistency that a scale yields. A test is reliable to the extent that virtually the same scores result in retestings. In other words, a reliable measure of behavior will perform in the future the way it did in the past.

In collecting qualitative data, dependability is referred to as meaning something similar to reliability. To be dependable, the evaluator must keep a record of how data were collected. This process is referred to as an audit trail. Dependability "depends" on letting someone else know exactly how data were collected and how conclusions were drawn. This process will be clearer when in-depth interviews and field observations are discussed later in this unit.

For some quantitative instruments, a reliability correlation or coefficient is given as a statistic that tells just how likely the instrument is to measure consistently. Correlation refers to the similarity between two sets of scores for one person. In other words, when the score for one test remains in the same relative position on the second, the reliability will be high. Test-retest is one way to measure the stability with a comparison between the two test administrations. The length of time between the two tests will vary but is usually around a week or two.

The reliability coefficient ranges from 0.00 to 1.00 with the scores closest to 1.00 being the best because they indicate the test has less error variance. The level that one is willing to accept depends on the nature of the evaluation being done. Most instruments that have a reliability coefficient greater than 0.40 may be used with some confidence, although an evaluator would rather have coefficients higher than 0.60. The higher the reliability, the more consistently the instrument measures what it is supposed to measure. Reliability coefficients may be obtained by measuring internal consistency through correlation statistics, by giving alternative forms of the instrument, or by test-retest procedures.

Inter-rater reliability is another term which the evaluator may wish to address if more than one person is making observations. Inter-rater reliability is a measure of the consistency from rater to rater rather than from time to time. The reliability coefficient is produced by comparing the ratings generated by two or more observers who have observed the same event or behavior. The two are compared by correlation. High correlations indicate a high amount of agreement. This inter-rater reliability can be improved by observer training and a clear delineation of the behaviors being rated. The higher the correlation is (i.e., generally over 0.80), the more dependable the observations. With a low inter-rater reliability, too much error may be associated with an observation.

Without reliability or dependability a measurement's usefulness is in doubt. As questionnaire development is discussed in the next chapter, you will note a number of ways that reliability can be improved. For example, items that do not communicate effectively should be eliminated. Items should be clear, unambiguous, and appropriate in length and difficulty. To improve reliability, one can lengthen the test although extreme lengthening may produce a fatigue or boredom effect. Suppose we wanted to know what was good about a particular recreation program. A questionnaire with only one item would be highly unreliable. A participant might have liked a lot of aspects of a program but not have liked the one aspect that you asked in the questionnaire. A one-item test is subject to a number of chance factors and, therefore, is not usually reliable. To improve reliability, therefore, an evaluator has to try to reduce as much error as possible.

Validity

As defined in the introduction to this chapter, validity concerns whether or not the instrument measures the intended information or what it is supposed to measure. Other synonyms for validity might be accuracy, authenticity, genuineness, and soundness. In other words, the respondent must understand the question the way that the evaluator asked it and must provide the information in a manner that is consistent with criteria the evaluator had established. The validity refers to the results of the measurement, and not the test or questionnaire itself. An instrument is valid only if it is appropriate for the group and the evaluation criteria being measured.

Reliability is necessary for validity to occur. Data, however, can be reliable without being valid. People can be consistent in their responses but an instrument can be measuring the wrong information. Therefore, if an instrument is not valid, it does not make any difference how reliable it is. If an evaluator wanted to know the change in attitudes about art that result from a crafts program, but asks participants their reactions to the instructor's teaching techniques, she or he may get reliable responses but the measurement is not valid for the issues she or he is analyzing.

Several types of validity are frequently mentioned in evaluation research. Validity may refer broadly to internal and external validity depending upon how it is applied. Internal validity is how well the instrument measures what it is supposed to measure for a particular evaluation project. It also shows whether a difference exists in any given comparisons. Lincoln and Guba (1985) refer to credibility in qualitative approach as the equivalent to internal validity. One type of internal validity is known as concurrent, or criterion-related validity, which simply asks whether the scores on a particular instrument correlate with scores on another existing test. The most important type of internal validity for evaluation is content validity. Content validity reflects the contents or the theoretical expectations that one wishes to measure with an evaluation project. Subjective judgment, sometimes called face validity, is often used regarding whether the instrument measures the content intended. The evaluator must define the content and establish its relevance. Further, levels of evidence discussed in Chapter 1.07 play heavily into content validity. For example, it may appear that you are measuring how attitudes change toward a particular activity when you are actually measuring satisfaction with the process. Content validity requires a careful analysis of what you want to measure, and how the items you select and the data you collect actually contribute to that measurement. You must make sure the instrument you select or develop and the data collect do, in fact, measure the criteria identified.

External validity refers to how well the measures can be generalized to other situations. External validity is also called transferability in qualitative data collection. Predictive validity is associated with external validity and is used to examine the way an instrument can predict some behavior. A common example of predictive validity is the fact that the high performance on SAT tests usually predicts success in college.

Validity must be a concern early in the use or development of any instrument. An evaluator will be responsible for content validity, but frequently others can be involved in the process to confirm that validity exists. For example, expert panels may be used to confirm content validity. Experts are asked to judge the instrument's ability to measure the desired content. Or it might be desirable to involve colleagues or a supervisor to examine the instrument. They can then be asked if what you say you are evaluating is really coming across in the way the instrument is constructed.

The more adequate the planning time in designing an evaluation project, the more likely reliable and valid measures can be used. To improve reliability or validity, don't rush into developing an instrument. Care should be taken to make the instrument clear and to write it at an appropriate reading level for those respondents who will be using it. Items need to relate to constructs, enough items to measure the constructs must be presented, and no identifiable pattern or response should be evident. Further, the evaluator needs to keep in mind that she or he can't necessarily use the same instrument for every evaluation situation. Some instruments work better with some groups than do others. The evaluator must develop the reliability and validity of an instrument in a particular setting for the specific audience that is using the instrument.

In collecting qualitative data, credibility can be improved by prolonged engagement either in interviews or observations, persistent observation, and/or triangulating by using more than one data source or method. One can also pay attention to negative cases (e.g., cases that are not like the others) as well as use member checks (e.g., go back and talk to people) to see if the way the interview data or observations was interpreted in the way the participants intended. Transferability can be enhanced by using examples from the data and by using "thick description." Qualitative evaluators use "thick description" to mean using the direct quotes and words of respondents about what happened or how they felt in a given situation.

Usability

Usability relates closely to reliability and validity, but has particular significance for evaluation. If the instrument is not usable, and if the data collected are not used, the project is a waste of time. For example, although an instrument might be highly reliable and valid, if it can not be easily administered it may be of little use to an evaluator.

Several items must be considered in assessing the usability and quality of data. The administration of an instrument can affect reliability and validity. An instrument should be easy to administer whether as a self-administered test or as one given by a tester. The time required should be reasonable for the situation and for the population being studied. The instrument should be easy to score and should be able to be interpreted. Directions should be consistent. Provide a good atmosphere for testing. Dunn (1987) used the example of not giving program satisfaction surveys in a pool where people don't have a dry place to write. You need to always ask yourself if the evaluation procedure is appropriate for the setting and to be aware of the subject's situation and attitudes when administering any test or questionnaire. Further, the costs should not exceed the potential benefits that might come from using a selected measurement instrument.

Usability also relates to qualitative data, but it is assumed that these data would not be collected unless usable in some manner. Competent evaluators who have training in qualitative methods are needed. One becomes better at collecting qualitative data by practice. Further, to be usable the qualitative evaluator must devote adequate time to the data collection and analysis. As one looks for negative cases and attempts to explain the variance between individuals or situations, a time commitment is necessary. Finally, triangulation may make an evaluation project more useful because the data come from more than one source.

Table 2.3 (page 102) provides a summary of some suggested ways to improve the trustworthiness of your evaluation. After reading subsequent chapters, you may want to review this table again.

Trustworthiness is essential to the collection of data. To have a trustworthy evaluation project, the evaluator attempts to eliminate error as much as possible. This error may be from respondents, the investigator, or the sampling procedures. For example, the respondent may feel the guinea pig effect whereby she or he is aware of being tested. She or he may also demonstrate other kinds of behavior such as hostility or indifference that would also affect the results of some measurement instruments. Further, sometimes participants are aware of the social desirability associated with an instrument and will respond the way they think society would. Some of these errors are difficult to avoid, but an evaluator must be aware that they can exist and try to minimize them if the evaluation project is to be useful. If the data are not reliable and valid, they will have little use in the evaluation project.

Table 2.3

How to Improve Trustworthiness of Data Collected

	Quantitative	**Qualitative**
Reliability	Well-written items Lengthen the test Pilot test/planning Clear directions Appropriate to group	Use audit trail
Validity	Subjective evaluation Predictive Choose appropriate model Pilot test/planning and level of evidence Clear directions	Prolonged engagement Use negative cases Use examples Thick description Effect of evaluator used
Usability	Easily administered Reasonable time required Easy to score/interpret Appropriate cost	Competent evaluator Time commitment Triangulation Explain all variance

From Ideas to Reality

Unless the data and the design can be relied on, an evaluation project may not be useful. Reliability, validity and usability are the keys to conducting good evaluations. This chapter has presented a number of ways to make evaluation projects trustworthy. You will need to refer to these suggestions continuously while conducting an evaluation project. No magic formulas exist, but the all of the strategies suggested will help assure that you are undertaking the most trustworthy evaluation possible.

2.04 Choosing and Developing Measurement Instruments

Goals for Chapter 2.04:

—To determine the aspects to consider in evaluating and choosing an existing instrument;

—To state the basic procedures used to design questionnaires;

—To write questions representing the five question types using past, present, and future tenses where appropriate;

—To describe the differences between open-ended, closed-quantitative, and partially close-ended question structures;

—To evaluate the difference between a well-worded and formatted questionnaire and one that is not; and,

—To develop a questionnaire to measure criteria that uses different question types and structures.

Once the criteria to be measured is determined and a research design has been selected, you will need a measuring device. For most quantitative studies, an instrument or test of some type is developed. If a reliable and valid instrument that you can use already exists, you will save yourself time and effort by using that instrument. Unfortunately, not many evaluation instruments exist in leisure services that have been standardized and tested for reliability and validity. Further, evaluators must look at their particular situations to decide what type of instrument can best measure the criteria desired. Thus, an evaluator must be able to do two things well:

1. Evaluate existing instruments to see if they are reliable, valid and usable; and,

2. Develop instruments that are reliable, valid and usable to address evaluation criteria specific to a situation.

When we talk about measurement instruments, we are referring to tests, checklists or questionnaires that might be developed. Some measurements might refer to observation checklists, while others will refer to opinionnaires, attitude, or performance measures. When a set of questions is written specifically for an evaluation project with the assumption that respondents will answer honestly, the instrument is commonly called a questionnaire rather than a test. Instruments may be used to collect qualitative or quantitative data, but measurement instruments usually refer to quantitative surveys and observations.

Tests usually include standardized ways of asking for information. Tests have additional features such as scores and inferences from scores. They usually involve some questions about the respondent's ability and/or willingness to answer accurately, honestly, or completely.

Tests given to individuals are usually divided into four areas: ability, achievement, attitude, and personality tests. Ability tests are supposed to measure what a person is capable of doing. Achievement tests show what a person has learned. Attitude tests attempt to measure some opinions or beliefs of the test-taker about an object, person, or event; they refer to some internal state of mind or set of beliefs that is stable over time. Personality tests refer to most anything else that relates to characteristics of an individual.

Choosing Instruments

Assessment instruments are probably most abundant in the field of leisure services because many communities conduct needs assessments, and therapeutic recreation specialists use a number of assessment instruments in their work. Fewer "already developed" instruments exist for formative and summative evaluations.

Several resources exist for finding already existing instruments. In the field of therapeutic recreation, several researchers compiled lists of such instruments. One of the most recent was done by Norma Stumbo in 1991 in the *ATRA Annual*. She also describes what to look for in good instruments. The *Burros Mental Measurements Yearbook* is available in most libraries and tells about various personality and achievement instruments including their reliability and validity. Table 2.4(1) shows an example of some of the information that would be found in the *Burros Yearbook*.

Often instruments and tests are borrowed to use in various settings. Borrowing from another department or another organization may save time, but the evaluator must be careful to assure that the instrument is really a reliable and valid measurement.

A standardized test has been previously used for a relatively large group of subjects; many test results have provided information about the answers or scores to expect from similar subjects. These standardized tests usually come with elaborate and complete instructions about how to administer the test so that your results are comparable to results from other testers. Major question design problems have been resolved as these tests have been improved and standardized. If you want to compare the results you obtained from using a standardized test, however, the tests must be given exactly as the instructions suggest. Even additional explanations cannot be given. The standardized test may be reliable and valid in general, however as was discussed in the previous chapter, it must be valid for the particular audience involved and evaluation criteria that you are using. To develop standardized tests is difficult, complicated, and goes beyond

Table 2.4(1)

Example of Material Found in a Standardized Test Summary
(adapted from Burros Mental Measurements Yearbook)

Torrance Tests of Creative Thinking. Grades K through graduate school; 1966-84; TTCT; 2 forms; 2 tests; norms-technical manual ('74, 80 pages); scoring worksheet ('66, 1 page) for each test; 1983 price data: $12 per 20 sets of tests, 20 scoring worksheets, and 1 manual; $5.70 per norms-technical manual; $6.50 per specimen set; scoring service, $2.25 or less per booklet; E. Paul Torrance; Scholastic Testing Service, Inc.

(a) **Verbal test.** Test booklet title is *Thinking Creatively With Words*; 3 scores: fluency, flexibility, originality; individual in grades K-3; Forms A, B, ('66, 15 pages); directions manual ('74, 49-50 pages) for each form; $20 per examiner's kit of reusable toys and pictures; $3.40 per directions manual; 45(60) minutes.

(b) **Figural test.** Test booklet title is *Thinking Creatively With Pictures*; 4 scores: fluency, flexibility, originality, elaboration; Forms A ('66, 8 pages), B ('66, 7 pages); Form A directions manual ('66, 43 pages, minor revisions 1972), Form B directions manual ('74, 43 pages); streamlined scoring workbook figural A ('84, 39 pages); streamlined manual figural A and B ('84, 74 pages) ; $3.40 per directions manual; $3.40 per streamlined scoring manual; 30(45) minutes.

---

what can be discussed in this book. If available and appropriate, however, standardized tests developed by others may be used.

Dunn (1989) has suggested some guidelines for using published assessment evaluation procedures that might also include standardized tests. She suggests that locally developed assessments may be good, but confidence may not be as high in them as in previously published tests. All standardized instruments have specific instructions that include time limits, oral instructions, preliminary demonstrations, ways of handling inquiries, and other details for the testing situation. They also may have norm-references or averages established from previous testing done. The instrument chosen should provide evidence of validity and should have been validated on a representative sample of sufficient size. The relationship of subscores to total scores should be evident. Further, information about reliability should be provided. The manual and test materials should be complete and of appropriate quality. The assessment should be relevant to the participants served by the agency. Finally, the instrument should be relevant to the decisions made based on evaluation or assessment results.

Dunn (1989) further suggests that an assessment or evaluation instrument should be revalidated when any changes are made in procedures, materials, or when it is used for a purpose or with a population group for which it has not been validated. The instrument should be selected and used by qualified individuals and should be used in the intended way. The published instrument might be combined with other tests, but it should maintain its integrity. The administration and scoring should follow standardized procedures. During the administration, care should be taken in providing a comfortable environment with minimal distractions. The administrator of the instrument also must be aware of the importance and effect of rapport with respondents. Additionally, the security of materials must be protected if confidentiality is guaranteed. Specific test results should not be released without the informed consent of the test-taker. Data regarding patients' assessment in therapeutic recreation, for example, should be kept in a designated file.

Many advantages can be found in choosing existing instruments rather than developing your own measures. As is obvious from this discussion, however, many considerations must be weighed thoughtfully in choosing instruments. In summary, an evaluator might want to ask several questions about any instrument being examined:

- Do measures exist for reliability and validity?
- Does the instrument measure the factors or traits desired to be measured?
- Is the instrument appropriate to the participants who will be completing it?
- Is the instrument reasonable in time and cost to administer?
- Are the directions clear, concise, and unambiguous?
- Is the instrument easy to score or are specific scoring directions included?
- Does it provide the best way to measure the data?

If the answer to any of these questions is *NO*, then perhaps you should look for another instrument or consider developing your own.

Developing Measurement Instruments

It may be more appropriate to develop your own instrument for an evaluation project or research study rather than use one that already exists. Developing good measurement instruments and questionnaires is an art that requires care and practice. Fortunately, many guidelines exist to help you develop a good instrument. These guidelines can be applied to the development of checklists, survey questionnaires, or test items. Several basic steps are consistent in the development of any survey or test:

1. Define the problem;
2. Determine the contents including criteria to be evaluated and broad questions;
3. Identify and categorize the respondents;
4. Develop items, structure, and format;
5. Write directions; and,
6. Ensure response.

The remainder of this chapter will focus on determining the contents, developing items and structures, and writing directions. It will divide the development of instruments into several components: types of questions (determining the contents), question structures and wording tips (developing items), and instrument design (formats and directions). Sampling and identifying respondents will be covered in Chapter 2.05 on "Choosing a Sample" and how to ensure responses will be addressed in Chapter 2.06 on "Surveys: Choosing Perfect vs. Good-Enough Survey Methods."

First, however, a word about the overall development of questionnaires should be addressed. To develop a questionnaire, you must know what you want to find out or what criteria are to be evaluated. Orthner, Smith, and Wright (1986) gave an excellent example of a process used for developing a needs assessment questionnaire for the Navy. Figure 2.4 (page 110) shows the process used to develop the Navy questionnaire. Although most of the evaluation projects you undertake may not require such an elaborate plan, the diagram is helpful in understanding how a problem is defined and how a questionnaire is refined.

Orthner, Smith, and Wright (1986) first got a panel of Navy and recreation experts together and asked them to examine and review a list of possible issues and questions. From this procedure, prototype questionnaires were developed. The items were then revised, the questionnaire tested in a real situation, revisions to the questionnaire were made, a panel once again reviewed it, the questionnaire was pretested in a focus group and revised again, presented to headquarters for review, field-tested on eight bases, revised, field-tested for a final time, and the final questionnaire was then completed.

It is *not* necessary have to go through all of those stages unless the questionnaire is going to be standardized and/or completed by thousands of people. Several parts of this model, however, are particularly important to consider. First, the evaluator must make sure she or he knows what it is she or he wants to find out and that this information may be obtained from some source, whether it is participants, colleagues, or organizational leaders. Second, plan to go through several revisions of the questionnaire. Even people who have been designing questionnaires for years cannot write a perfect questionnaire the first time. Third, the questionnaire should be tested with a small sample to make sure that it is measuring what it is supposed to do. Fourth, even after the questionnaire is used, some flaws (hopefully, all minor) may be discovered that can be corrected if the questionnaire is administered again.

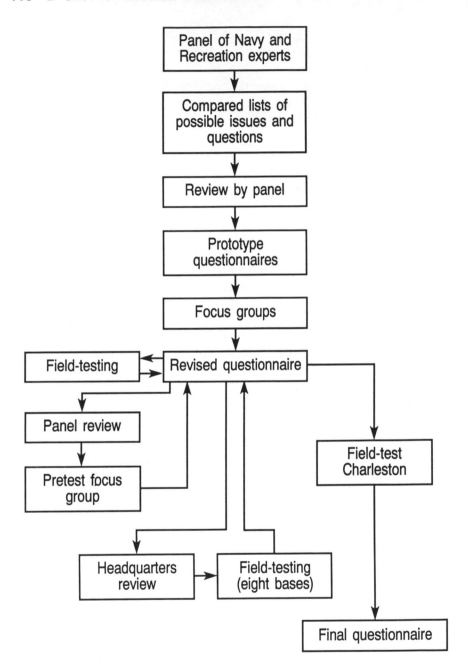

Figure 2.4 Navy Model of Instrument Development
(adapted from Orthner, Smith, and Wright, 1986)

Ask only necessary questions. Sometimes evaluators think that they can ask many questions and then determine later what information to use in the evaluation report. This endeavor is a waste of paper and a waste of the respondents' time. Know exactly what criteria are being measured at the start, and then develop questions to get that information.

Types of Contents

The questions asked will have great variability depending on the nature of the evaluation project, the design used, and the criteria to be measured. Specific questions may be addressed followed by peripheral questions to get in-depth information.

A result of designing good instruments is that people will respond honestly. Questions may be asked in the time frame of past, present, or future. For most recreation, park, and leisure service organizations, questions are likely to address one or all of these five areas: *experience/behavior, opinion/values* (needs and interests), *feelings* (emotional responses), *knowledge/facts*, and *background/ demographics*. The data may be qualitative or quantitative. The questions may be open-ended or close-ended, although most of this discussion will be based on writing objective, close-ended questions. No matter what type, good questions should be neutral, singular, and clear.

Let's talk about the information that you want to obtain from a questionnaire. The questions are going to pertain to the level of evidence to be addressed. For example, to determine the reactions that individuals had to a particular recreation activity, you would likely use opinion/value or feelings types of questions. On the other hand, if you wanted to find out what people learned as a result of an activity, questions about knowledge or facts might be asked.

A single questionnaire might ask several different content questions, and possibly in different time frames. It must be clear however, as to what criteria are to be measured. To know what people will do in the future, questions that pertain to the future must be written. Let us look at a few examples of possible questions to address the five categories above:

> **Experience/behavior questions**—What a person does or has done. For example:
> > *present:* If I were to follow you through a typical day like today, what would I see you doing?
> > *past:* How many times did you swim in the XYZ pool in 1994?
> > *future:* On the average, how many times do you anticipate any member of your family swimming at the XYZ pool in 1996?

Opinion/value/attitude questions—Cognitive and interpretive processes held by the individual. For example:

past: What did you like about last year's volleyball league?

present: When you call the recreation office, are the receptionists usually very helpful, helpful, or unhelpful?

future: Do you favor the development of both a recreational and a competitive volleyball league?

Feeling questions—Emotional responses (past or present) of people to their experiences. For example:

past: Did the trip make you feel happy?

present: How does volunteering with this youth group make you feel?

Knowledge Questions—What factual information the respondent has, usually at the present time. For example:

present: What is your target heartbeat during aerobics class?

present: How many fouls does a basketball player get before she or he fouls out?

Background/Demographics—*Present* personal characteristics. For example:

present: How old are you?

Question Structures

A number of structures can be used in question design. The structures used will depend to some extent on the content and criteria that is to be addressed and the statistical techniques to be used. Writing good questions takes practice.

Three major structures and the scales that can be used with each will be discussed:

1. Open-Ended;
2. Closed-Quantitative with Ordered (Forced) Choices and Unordered Response Choices; and,
3. Partially Close-Ended Quantitative.

Open-Ended

Open-ended questions are directed with no preformed answers. The respondent supplies her or his own answer with no restrictions on the content of the response. They often use lists or short essay responses. Open-ended questions are most often used when a variety of information is needed and the evaluator is unsure of possible responses. In this way, open-ended structures also provide diagnostic information. These structures are used to collect qualitative data and to develop specific questionnaires from broad information. As you develop questionnaires, it is necessary to ask yourself if all the information is currently available so that categories of responses can be written in advance or whether open-ended questions will provide responses not currently known. Open-ended questions are easy to ask, but tallying the results is not always as easy as you will see in the discussion of qualitative analysis in Chapter 3.07.

The advantages of the open-ended structure is evident when the population characteristics are not known and when the evaluator does not wish to overlook any possible answers to a question. From initial open-ended questions, it is possible to draft more specific close-ended questions, especially if the open-ended structure is used as the first step in developing a more quantitatively oriented questionnaire. A further advantage to open-ended structures is that the answers are less influenced by the evaluator writing the question; a wide variety of responses which include many that are unique to an individual's situation can be elicited. Open-ended structures can help to introduce new topics or allow respondents to summarize what is on their minds. These structures can provide valuable background for interpreting evaluation results and can add a "richness" to the data because of the potential for depth of response.

The disadvantages of open-ended responses include a lack of uniform responses that may not be easy to tabulate. Further, this structure is affected by a respondent's verbal ability and written communication skills. The data obtained are sometimes more useful when the respondents have a higher educational level. When using open-ended questions, problems of definition and vocabulary may occur, and fewer questions can be asked. Open-ended questions typically take longer to complete, and people may not take as much time with them if they require lengthy written or verbal responses. In addition, problems with coding or organizing the data for interpretation may emerge and some responses may be irrelevant based on the criteria the evaluator established.

In summary, open-ended structures are easy to write and are usually straightforward. An example of an open-ended question that measures attitudes about an activity in the past is: "What did you like best about camp this summer?" The evaluator, however, must also be prepared for the volume and variability of information that may be provided by respondents.

Closed-Quantitative Structures

In closed questions, specific responses are provided for the respondents to select. These responses may be of two types depending on the nature of the question: (1) ordered with a forced choice, or (2) unordered. Close-ended structures that use ordered responses include Likert scales, semantic differential scales, and rankings. Unordered close-ended questions are typically used as checklists and are unique to the specific evaluation criteria being measured.

Several concerns must be kept in mind in developing closed-quantitative question items. First of all, response categories should not overlap. The answer categories should be mutually exclusive so the answers fall into one category only. For example, in asking someone her or his age and giving choices, the categories should be listed as "younger than 19," "20-29," "30-39" and *not* "younger than 19," "19-29," "29-39." Second, the responses should be exhaustive and should cover the gamut of possible answers. Third, the responses also must be appropriate to the questions asked and consistent in focusing on the same dimension being measured. Finally, remember that the same question may be asked in many ways using a variety of close-ended choices. The evaluator has to choose what is best.

The advantages of close-ended responses are that they are uniform and can be easily coded for data entry and analysis in a computer. If you want a quick analysis, then close-ended question structures are the most useful. For example, the question, "Overall, how satisfied were you with the organization of the crafts fair?" might provide forced ordered choices of, "4=very satisfied, 3=satisfied, 2=dissatisfied, 1=very dissatisfied." Tallying the results to find out the percentage of people satisfied or the mean or average score for this question would be fairly easy to do.

The disadvantages of closed-ended structures occur if you do not provide the most appropriate choices for response. If the real responses are missing from the list of choices, only partially valid answers or no answers at all will be obtained. In the example concerning satisfaction with the organization of the crafts fair, an individual might have been satisfied with some aspects but not all aspects. A disadvantage to the close-ended response is that she or he does not have an opportunity to explain anything about the response.

As indicated, two types of closed-quantitative questions exist: unordered close-ended responses and ordered forced choices (commonly called scaling devices). Close-ended questions with unordered responses are structures used with items that have no particular value associated with them in the statistical analysis. The evaluator may want to know many answer possibilities for a question, or simply the one best answer. For example, someone could be asked to choose the best thing about an aerobics program, or could be asked to check all of the items that apply. An example of an unordered response would be the following question:

What did you like best about the aerobics class? Check one item.

_____Becoming more physically fit
_____Getting out of the house or job for awhile
_____Meeting other people
_____Having fun
_____Moving to the music

As indicated above, this same question could be asked in another unordered form by allowing individuals to check all of the items that applied about what they liked about an aerobics class.

"Yes/no" questions or "true/false" questions are another form of unordered close-ended question structures. These responses are appropriate to use and easy to write; however, the evaluator must keep in mind the limited amount of information that may be obtained from yes/no questions. Some people can clearly answer yes or no for a given situation particularly related to knowledge or experience/behavior questions. Many times, however, yes/no responses require qualification. In using close-ended yes/no questions, the evaluator must consider the information that is not evident in these responses.

Scaling is the major form of ordered close-ended questions used for measuring participation rates, attitudes, and opinions. An example would be, "how often do you compete in a road race?" A scaling technique would be to use the ordered responses: "0 = never," "1 = once a year," "2 = 3-4 times a year," "3 = monthly," "4 = weekly," and "5 = twice or more a week." Descriptive terms, or word anchors, should be used at each point on the scale so the respondent knows what the numbers mean. In other words, using a number may be useful later in data analysis, but the respondent must be clear about what the numbers mean. Common forms of other scaling devices include Likert scales, semantic differentials, rankings, and self-assessments.

Likert Scales

Likert scales, named for the man who developed them, are a particular kind of close-ended question structure that uses a scaling system. Likert scales are most often used for attitude measurement. Usually both negative and positive statements are used with four or six responses related to strongly agree, agree, disagree, or strongly disagree. These scale names are referred to as response anchors. Some people will make a three to seven response scale and will include a middle option of neutral or no opinion. It works better to use an even number of items so respondents are forced to "take a stand." Some respondents may see "no opinion" as the "easy way out," and evaluators generally want to force people to choose one response or another. Without a neutral option, however, respondents might skip a question which may result in unreliable data. An evaluator will need to decide the best way to design a Likert scale.

A Likert scale usually has a matrix type of design with questions on the left half and anchored responses on the right half. Each response is then scored in some way, usually with the most positive response receiving the highest point value. In a four-point scale, anything with a mean or average of 2.5 and above is usually considered positive; below that score would be negative. The Likert scale is easy to construct, has moderate reliability, explores attitudes, involves simple computations, and is easy to score. Table 2.4(2) shows an example of a Likert scale.

Table 2.4(2)

Example of a Likert Scale Used to Measure Satisfaction with a Campground

	Strongly Agree	Agree	Disagree	Strongly Disagree
1. The entrance to the campground was attractive.	SA	A	D	SD
2. Staff were friendly and courteous.	SA	A	D	SD
3. The campsites were large enough.	SA	A	D	SD
4. The distance between campsites was appropriate.	SA	A	D	SD
5. Restrooms and showers were clean.	SA	A	D	SD

Semantic Differentials

Semantic differentials, as another scaling structure for close-ended questions, includes a list of bipolar adjectives written in linear fashion. See Table 2.4(3). Semantic differentials, often used to assess attitudes and responses, are assigned numbers as done with Likert scales. The items to be measured are selected and then bipolar adjective pairs are chosen to anchor both ends of the scales. These words should be as near to opposite as possible (such as good/bad), and may or may not necessarily use the same baseword (such as familiar/unfamiliar). Points should be anchored with numbers on the scales between the two points so that scoring averages can be calculated later. In the listing down a page, the items should be put in opposite directions so not all the positive attributes are on one side of the scale. Semantic differentials are particularly good scales for examining the past and present attitudes and opinions about a particular phenomenon.

Ranking

Ranking is another form of a forced, close-ended structure that is used to get a sense of how individuals might evaluate certain items. Where items fall on a ranking scale does not indicate good or bad but simply an attempt to look at the

Table 2.4(3)

Example of a Semantic Differential for Analyzing a Youth Leader

Please indicate your perception of the leadership ability of your youth leader. Check where you believe she or he falls on the scale.

Dedicated	__	__	__	__	__	__	Could Care Less
	6	5	4	3	2	1	

Enthusiastic	__	__	__	__	__	__	Very Low Key
	6	5	4	3	2	1	

Organized	__	__	__	__	__	__	Disorganized
	6	5	4	3	2	1	

Strict	__	__	__	__	__	__	Lenient
	6	5	4	3	2	1	

Always Late	__	__	__	__	__	__	On Time
	6	5	4	3	2	1	

relative meaning of one item to another. These ranking scales are simple to use for descriptive data, but require less commonly used statistical techniques. The biggest problem ranking has is with validity. Too many items to rank is confusing to the respondent. Usually ten to eleven items is the maximum number to use. If there are more items to rank than that, it might be necessary to divide your scale into two questions.

One of the major disadvantages to ranking as a question structure is that respondents are often confused by the directions. Be clear and thorough in giving directions so the individual knows exactly what to do. The evaluator should say how the items are to be ranked, such as suggesting that a "1" is the *best* and "2" is *next best* and so on. The ranking is often useful but it has to be realized that it is difficult to say much about what the rankings mean. For example, in Table 2.4(4), it is not known for sure whether the camper liked any of the activities. Further, she or he may have liked them all and may have seen little difference among the ten items.

Self-Assessments

A further example of an ordered, close-ended structure is called a self-assessment. It is not uncommon in everyday language for someone to ask, "on a scale of one to ten, how would you rate XYZ?" In the self-assessment structure, a respondent is asked to describe where she or he is on a scale, usually done as a 1-10 scale. For example, you might ask a question such as "After taking this class, based on a scale of one to ten with 1 being lowest and 10 being highest, how would you rate your knowledge of the rules of tennis?" The response may be a ladder where the respondent places an "X" to show the position of the response, may be a mark on a line with "1" on the left and numbers written consecutively to "10" on the right, or you might simply ask the respondent to write down a number in a space after the question.

Table 2.4(4)

Example of Ranking Question about Camp Activities

Rank the following ten activities from what you like the best to what you liked the least. That is, choose the activity that you liked best and give it a 1. Choose the second best activity and give it a 2. Continue through all the activities until each has a number from 1 to 10. The number 10 ranked activity will be your least favorite.

_____ horseback riding
_____ swimming lessons
_____ free swimming
_____ evening programs
_____ free time in the afternoon
_____ arts and crafts
_____ overnight camp-out
_____ mealtimes
_____ cabin activities
_____ afternoon rest period

Partially Close-Ended Quantitative

A final type of closed-quantitative question structure is called partially close-ended. These questions provide some responses, but also leave room for people to write in their own answers or additional information. To assure that the response categories are exhaustive, "other" is sometimes included as an item response. Care should be taken to allow enough room to write what "other" means and that the respondent knows that "other" replies are acceptable. An example of a partially close-ended question is:

How did you hear about the Sunday hike at the Nature Center?
_____ Announcement on the radio
_____ Flyer at the recreation department
_____ From a friend
_____ Other (please explain)_____

Wording Issues

Writing questions seems fairly easy at first, but mistakes often are made. Many of these mistakes could be avoided by paying careful attention to the wording of each and every question. Here are some things to consider

1. **Use only one idea per question.** Make sure the question is straightforward and that you are asking an individual to respond to one construct or idea.
2. **Clear, brief and simple are the rules for good question writing.** Make questions as simple to answer as possible. Begin with a major question and then break it down into several additional questions, but the respondent must always know how to proceed. Two or three simple questions are better than one complex one.
3. **Avoid leading questions that suggest a particular kind of response.**
4. **Avoid asking people to make estimates.** Try to force them to answer as honestly as possible to assure reliability.
5. **Think about trying to formulate a question from the respondent's viewpoint.** Use words that are familiar to the respondent.
6. **Avoid advanced language and technical jargon that is familiar to a professional, but that the respondent may not understand.** Avoid the use of acronyms (e.g., abbreviations such as ADA that may be common to an evaluator, but meaningless to the general public). As leisure service professionals we use many words such as programming, multiple use, and therapy that may be misunderstood by the public. People are reluctant to admit they don't understand words, and this attitude may affect the validity of measurement instruments.
7. **Be clear about what is being asked.** Don't say, "Should the P & R Department be more active with environmental education?" Respondents may misunderstand the question because they do not know what the words "P & R" or "more active" mean. Every question should have a time frame. Phrases such as "more active" should be explained by saying what is already occurring.
8. **Avoid negative questions that may confuse the reader.** For example, don't say "Why would you not want the bond issue to be defeated?"

9. **Avoid the use of "iffy" words like often or seldom.** These words may mean different things to different people, so they need to be defined if used.

10. **Do a pilot study and look at every comment made in a pretest concerning wording.** Don't take anything for granted about a questionnaire and work to keep the wording as simple as possible.

11. **State the alternatives precisely.** "Should the government put more money into recreation or not?" is a poorly worded question. Clarify what you are asking. Put options into the question if asking for options or else explain what those options are going to be. For example, a good question might be, "The current green fee for eighteen holes of golf is twenty dollars. Should the green fees at the public golf course be higher, lower, or remain the same?" People unfortunately tend to choose the middle of the road if they are unsure about a response.

12. **Some questions may require several stages to get adequate information.** These staged questions require several questions to assure a valid answer. Shafer and Moeller (1987) suggest, for example, that a complex question might require up to five questions: first determine awareness by a free-answer question concerning knowledge, next develop uninfluenced attitudes on the subject with another open-ended question, record specific attitudes through multiple choice, then find out the reasons through another open-ended question, and finally determine the intensity with a multiple-choice question. An example of this process is the following:

    1. Have you visited Rivers Bend Park?

       ___ Yes (go to question 2) ___ No (go to next section)

    2. What did you like about Rivers Bend Park?

       _____

    3. How satisfied were you with your visit to Rivers Bend Park?

       _____ very satisfied
       _____ satisfied
       _____ somewhat satisfied
       _____ dissatisfied
       _____ very dissatisfied

    4. What do you look for when you visit a County Park?

       _____

    5. How likely are you to visit Rivers Bend Park in 1996?

       _____ very likely
       _____ somewhat likely
       _____ not likely

Formats and Instrument Design

Clearly worded questions and an aesthetically pleasing instrument will often invite a respondent to complete a survey. Too often, no more time is given to the layout of a questionnaire than to creating a grocery list. General appearance, however, may be critical to the success of a survey; all instrument developers should be concerned with overall effects and a motivational design. At first glance, a potential respondent will determine the importance, difficulty, and length of a questionnaire. From this first impression, she or he is likely to decide whether or not to complete the questionnaire.

The sequencing of the questions is important. Always begin with questions that have a direct relevance to the purpose of the evaluation. These questions may also provide a context for determining attitudes and knowledge. Choosing the very first question should be done carefully. Although demographic questions may be easy to answer, they are seldom directly related to the purpose of the evaluation. Save the demographic questions until last. If a respondent doesn't get to them you will still have the important information collected at the beginning. Put questions of less importance later in the questionnaire. Controversial items should be grouped with less controversial ones. If something is really controversial, put it at the end of the questionnaire. The evaluator may start with general questions and proceed to more specific or she or he may begin specific and proceed to more general questions. The choice depends upon the nature of the evaluation criteria.

Group the questions together according to content. Use the same types of question structures together as much as possible, if content is appropriate. It is easier to fill out an instrument when similar question structures are grouped. Also, build ties between the questions. If there is different content being collected in the instrument, it may be used to head sections such as (A) Attitudes, (B) Participation, and (C) Background (Demographics). This format may help divide a long questionnaire into manageable sections and allow the respondent to move through the questionnaire more easily.

Design the instrument layout so that respondents do not get confused and/or miss an item. It usually helps to maximize white space on the questionnaire so that an individual does not feel overwhelmed with questions. Design staged questions or questions that require the respondent to "go to" another item with easy follow-through. For example, if answering "yes" leads to another question, make sure the individual knows where to go in the questionnaire to answer the next question. Similarly, if "no" means that you skip questions, make that clear as well. Some questionnaires use exclusively verbal instructions such as "If *no*, then skip to Question ten. If *yes*, then go to the next question." Some questionnaires make use of heavy lines and directional arrows that indicate where to go next. Whichever technique is used, establishing a vertical flow through the instrument is essential to motivating a respondent to continue to the end.

Several other formatting issues might be considered. It is often useful to use lower case letters for questions, upper case letters for answers. Using numbers to identify answer categories rather than boxes to check or letters to circle will be easier when the coded responses are entered into a computer. Try to make sure the responses to a question all fit on one page or else move the whole question to the next page. When a series of Likert responses are used that move onto another page, put the scaling anchors at the top of the next page so that the respondent does not get confused about how to answer the questions. Layout should include enough space in-between questions and consistent spacing. Table 2.4(5) shows an example of a possible questionnaire layout. This example comes from Dillman (1978) who presents excellent information about mail and telephone surveys.

The way that the questionnaire is put together physically is important. Colored paper is often more interesting than plain white. A subdued color, such as yellow or light blue, is usually good for most instruments. The more professional an instrument looks, the more likely people will respond. Using a booklet with saddle stitching is desirable for lengthy surveys, although it is also more expensive. The front page should include the title of the questionnaire, some type of graphic (optional, but interesting), the time of year it is being administered (e.g., Fall 1996), directions, and the information (name, title, and address) of the sponsor or evaluator who is conducting the project. The back cover may include a "thank you" and designate space for individuals to write further comments.

Whatever is done, the instrument should look professional and have *no* typographical mistakes or anything else that might raise questions about the credibility of the instrument or the evaluator. Also, the items should be easy to read. Smaller print allows more text per page, but may be difficult to read for some people.

The length of an instrument also is important to consider. Instruments should be long enough to get the needed information, but not too long. Shorter questionnaires reduce fatigue and are more likely to be completed. An evaluator may get a higher response rate with a two-page than a six-page questionnaire; however, a well-designed six pager is better than a poorly designed one pager. People should know about how long it will take to complete an instrument so they can plan their time. As stated before, the better the layout and design, the easier the questionnaire will be to complete.

Clear directions throughout the instrument are essential, but are often over-looked. People should be told to check a response or circle numbers, and that the *best* response (or more than one) is wanted. Give complete directions, especially if there is a series of questions. Explain the directions for each scale each time it is encountered in a questionnaire. Most instruments have an introduction that tells the respondent what to do and how to do it. The instructions should be clear, concise, and adequate to explain what is expected, but it may be necessary to remind respondents as they proceed, particularly if the questionnaire is lengthy.

Table 2.4(5)

Example of Questionnaire Layout for Demographic Questions

Q1 Number of children you have in each age group (If none, write "0")
Number of Children
____ UNDER FIVE YEARS OF AGE
____ 5-13 YEARS
____ 14-18 YEARS
____ 19-24 YEARS
____ 25 AND OVER

Q2 Your present age: _____ YEARS

Q3 Do you own (or are you buying) your own home? (circle number)
    1. NO   2. YES

Q4 Are you presently: (circle number)
    1. EMPLOYED   3. RETIRED
    2. UNEMPLOYED   4. FULL-TIME HOMEMAKER

Q5 Please describe the usual occupation of the principal wage earner in your household. (If retired, describe the usual occupation before retirement).
    TITLE: _____
    KIND of work you do: _____
    KIND of company or business: _____

Q6 What was your approximate net family income from all sources, before taxes, in 1994? (circle number)
    1. LESS THAN $9,999   6. $50,000 to 59,999
    2. $10,000 to 19,999   7. $60,000 to 69,999
    3. $20,000 to 29,999   8. $70,000 to 79,999
    4. $30,000 to 39,999   9. $80,000 to 89,999
    5. $40,000 to 49,999   10. OVER $90,000

Q7 Which is the highest level of education that you have completed? (circle number)
    1. COMPLETED GRADE SCHOOL
    2. SOME HIGH SCHOOL
    3. COMPLETED HIGH SCHOOL
    4. SOME COLLEGE
    5. COMPLETED COLLEGE (SPECIFY MAJOR)_____
    6. SOME GRADUATE WORK
    7. COMPLETED GRADUATE DEGREE
       (SPECIFY DEGREE AND MAJOR)

From Ideas to Reality

This chapter is full of ideas for choosing and developing instruments. The first crossroads will be the decision about whether to use an existing instrument or to develop one. Using existing instruments often saves time, but they must be reliable and valid for the group with whom you wish to use them. Developing your own instrument can be a lot of fun, but it also can be time-consuming because of the myriad of details that needs to be addressed when constructing an instrument. Any instrument that is developed should be just as reliable, valid, and usable as any instrument chosen. The instruments must also be practical and simple—easy to use, easy to understand, and easy to summarize. Why make evaluation any harder than it already is? The choice to use existing instruments or to develop your own is up to the evaluator. As usual, the criteria that are set likely will determine the choices that are made.

2.05 CHOOSING A SAMPLE

Goals for Chapter 2.05:

—To describe the differences between probability, nonprobability, and theoretical sampling;

—To draw a sample from a population using one of the strategies for probability sampling;

—To calculate the standard error of measurement and explain what it means;

—To use the table of random numbers to draw a sample; and,

—To determine the appropriate sample size based on the population and the data that will be collected.

No matter how great the criteria or how reliable the instrument, an appropriate sample must be selected. Sampling procedures vary depending upon the methods used and the resources that are available. Sometimes an evaluator may not select a sample, but may use the entire population. For example, if we wanted to find out the attitudes toward a pottery class that had ten people in it, we would likely survey the entire population of ten people in that class. Other times, however, evaluators will choose a smaller group from a large population.

A population refers to all the people who might comprise a particular group. For example, when talking about the population of a city, we refer to all the people that reside there. When talking about the population of intramural sports participants, we are referring to all who played during a given period of time. Many times, however, an evaluator does not have the ability and the resources to have all individuals, the entire population, participate in an evaluation project, so it is necessary to select the sample carefully. A sample should represent the population so the results of the evaluation can be generalized to the total population.

Sampling can be simplified into three categories: probability, nonprobability, and theoretical sampling. Probability refers to everyone within a population having the same potential of being selected as part of a sample. Nonprobability samples are selected in some other way where not everyone has an equal chance and the likelihood of selecting any one member from a population is unknown. Theoretical sampling is used primarily with qualitative data and refers to sampling until the evaluator reaches a point of data saturation. Each of these will be discussed in some detail in this chapter.

Keys to Appropriate Sampling

Several key points can be emphasized regarding sampling. First, do not confuse the size of a sample with representativeness. The sample size required for a survey will depend on the reliability needed, which depends on how the results will be used. A large (several thousand participant) sample is not necessarily better than several hundred and often does not make economical sense. No simple rule for sample size, however, can be applied to all evaluations. A moderate sample size is sufficient for most needs. For example, national polls usually use samples of 1,500, which is fine for a representative sample of a country with over 250 million people. A properly selected sample of only 1,500 individuals can reflect various characteristics of the total population with a small margin of error.

Second, the sample size can be selected in various ways. Table 2.5(1) shows an example of the sample size needed for various populations. For example, for 500 campers, you would need to select a sample size of at least 217 people. It is also possible to calculate the approximate sample size by using statistical procedures, but this text will not get into that detail. (For more information see most any statistics book or the article by Krejcie and Morgan, 1970). Generally the statistical dividing line between large and small samples is 30. Further, data are usually considered fragile if you get less than 60 to 70 percent of a sample to respond.

Third, methods of sampling are grounded in statistical theory and theories of probability. The sample used depends on the objective and scope of the method used, including the overall budget, the method of data collection, the subject matter, and the kind of respondent needed.

Fourth, the relevant population must be clearly identified. From there, a sample can be selected based upon the method used and the data desired. In other words, the evaluator must decide whether she or he will sample participants, parents, staff members, or board members depending upon the program that is to be evaluated.

Fifth, in sampling, as few people as necessary should be surveyed to get an accurate probability representation. Crompton (1985) uses the example of having a barrel with 10,000 red and white marbles from which you take 400. According to probability, the proportion of red and white marbles would be the same as if you took 400 from a barrel of 100,000 marbles.

Two sources of sampling errors must be addressed related to sampling and nonsampling. Sampling error is the difference between the characteristics of a sample and the characteristics of the population from which the sample was selected (Babbie, 1992). The larger the difference, the larger the error. If there is a sampling error of plus or minus four points (±4), it means that if 50 percent of the sample say they did something, then the true percentage would be between

Table 2.5(1)

Table for Determining Sample Size for an Evaluation
(adapted from Krejcie and Morgan, 1970)

Population	Sample	Population	Sample	Population	Sample
10	10	220	140	1,200	291
15	14	230	144	1,300	297
20	19	240	148	1,400	302
25	24	250	152	1,500	306
30	28	260	155	1,600	310
35	32	270	159	1,700	313
40	36	280	162	1,800	317
45	40	290	165	1,900	320
50	44	300	169	2,000	322
55	48	320	175	2,200	327
60	52	340	181	2,400	331
65	56	360	186	2,600	335
70	59	380	191	2,800	338
75	63	400	196	3,000	341
80	66	420	201	3,500	346
85	70	440	205	4,000	351
90	73	460	210	4,500	354
95	76	480	214	5,000	357
100	80	500	217	6,000	361
110	86	550	226	7,000	364
120	92	600	234	8,000	367
130	97	650	242	9,000	368
140	103	700	248	10,000	370
150	108	750	254	15,000	375
160	113	800	260	20,000	377
170	118	850	265	30,000	379
180	123	900	269	40,000	380
190	127	950	274	50,000	381
200	132	1,000	278	75,000	382
210	136	1,100	285	100,000	384

46 percent and 54 percent. The smaller the error range, the more accurate the survey. Error can be allowed in evaluation projects, but care must be taken as to how much is allowed. If an evaluator wants to look at subgroups within a sample, a larger sample will have to be drawn. Good survey practice includes calculating

sampling errors, when possible, so that the percentage points above or below an item can be known. The calculation of the standard error, a measure of sampling error, is:

$$S_{error} = \pm \sqrt{\frac{P_1 \times P_2 \times \cdots \times P_x}{n}}$$

S_{error}: standard error
P_1: population parameter $_1$
P_2: population parameter $_2$
P_x: last population parameter
n: number of cases

The standard error(s) is the square root of the population parameters (in the example below, P_1, and P_2, although more than two population parameters can be used with this formula) multiplied together and divided by the number of cases (n). P_1 and P_2 are the population parameters or the percentage of agreement with a particular item. These population parameters are calculated by subtracting the percentage from 1. If we knew, for example, that 60 percent of the participants were satisfied with a program and 40 percent were not, and there were a total of 30 participants, the standard error would be 0.089 or rounded off to plus or minus 9 percent.

S_{error}: standard error
P_1: 60%, or (1.0 − 0.60) = 0.40
P_2: 40%, or (1.0 − 0.40) = 0.60
n: 30 participants

$$s = \pm \sqrt{\frac{(0.40)\,(0.60)}{30}}$$

$$s = \pm \sqrt{\frac{(0.24)}{30}}$$

$$s = \pm \sqrt{0.008}$$

$$s = \pm 0.089442719$$

$$s = \pm 0.089, \text{ or } \pm 9\%$$

Thus we could conclude that the true approval rate lies somewhere between 51 percent and 69 percent. It is important to remember that the standard error is a function of sample size. As the sample size increases, the standard error decreases.

In the sample above, if there were 60 participants, the standard error would be six percent so the actual approval rate would be somewhere between 54 percent and 66 percent.

Nonsampling errors have no simple and direct method of estimating. Nonsampling errors concern the biases that may exist due to who answered a questionnaire or participated in an evaluation project compared to those that did not. Errors also may be created by biases. These biases come from sampling operations, noninterviews, participants not understanding the ideas being measured, lack of knowledge of respondents, concealment of the truth, loaded questions, processing errors, and interviewer errors. For example, according to Rossman (1982), a nonsampling error might occur in giving out evaluations during the latter part of a program when drop-outs and absentees would not get included. The drop-outs are probably dissatisfied, but since that is not known reliability could be a significant problem. Therefore, to avoid nonsampling error, you need to sample all registered people, not just those in attendance. Only then can you be sure that high satisfaction was not the result of poor sampling because the dissatisfied people left an activity. The evaluator controls as much nonsampling error as possible by designing good evaluation projects and using appropriate methods and measures.

Probability sampling theory suggests that all units must have a known, nonzero chance of being included in the sample, and sample design must be explained in sufficient detail to permit calculation of sampling errors. When these guidelines are followed, inferences can be drawn from the sample to the appropriate population. The types of samples range from simple random samples to highly complex sample procedures. Quantitative data collection usually involves probability or nonprobability samples which will be discussed first. Table 2.5(2) gives a summary of the types of sampling that an evaluator might choose.

Table 2.5(2)

Sampling Types That May Be Used by an Evaluator

—Probability—	—Nonprobability—
• Simple random sampling	• Purposive sampling
• Stratified random sampling	• Convenience sampling
• Systematic sampling	• Quota sampling
• Cluster sampling	• Expert sampling
	• Snowball approach

—Theoretical—

Probability Sampling

Every unit or person who makes up a population has a chance of being selected in probability sampling. *Random sampling* is the most common type of probability sampling and is superior over nonprobability sampling. Mills, Um, McWilliams, and Hodgson (1987) examined the importance of random sampling when conducting visitor surveys. They used haphazard or convenience samples (nonprobability) and a random sample from the same visitor population. By comparing the data from probability and nonprobability samples they concluded that random sampling provides the most reliable data.

If a good job is done in selecting a random sample, the sample will resemble the population in demographics and background. The evaluator can select the sample using the table of random numbers or literally put all numbers or names from a population into a hat and draw out the number of individuals needed.

Selecting from a table of random numbers may be the most unbiased and useful tool to use in random sampling. The basis of the number configurations on the table is completely unbiased. Hudson (1988) has given a good example of how to select random numbers for use in an evaluation project. If an evaluator had a known population of 1,500 people and was going to select 306 people, she or he would first number each of the people from 1-1,500. Then determine the number of digits needed. Since 1,500 has four digits, four digits will be used. [Turn to the table of random numbers found in Appendix A (page 343). Notice several rows and columns of five-digit numbers. You can decide to select a five-digit number but use only the first four numbers. Deciding where to start is a matter of choice. Most people close their eyes and point a finger. This assures that no biases existed in choosing the number. From that starting point move either across or up and down, however you choose, but do it consistently. Ignore any number outside the range of 1,500 and go to the next. Keep on with the procedure until you have selected 306 different numbers out of the 1,500 with which you started.]

A *stratified random sample* is used when proportionate representation is sought. It might be based on age, sex, or activity involvement. For example, an evaluator might want the number of African-Americans surveyed in the evaluation project to represent the number of African-Americans in the population. Or, she or he might want to stratify a sample so that a proportionate number of boys and girls are observed. If the population consisted of 70 percent male and 30 percent female, we would randomly draw 70 percent of the sample from the list of boys and 30 percent from the list of girls. Stratified random sampling requires drawing samples from separate lists. Thus, it is possible to know the desired strata and the proportion of each stratum in the population.

Systematic sampling determines a rationalization for some kind of routine sample. It is somewhat easier to do than simple random sampling, and individuals have a somewhat similar probability of being chosen. All selections are determined by the first selection, and then every "n^{th}" one after that is chosen. If you knew there were 2,000 members of an organization and had enough money to sample 200, you might go through and pick every tenth name on the organizational list until 200 names are drawn. An important point is to choose a random starting point by taking a number from the table of random numbers or with closed eyes point to a random spot on the list. Systematic sampling is less cumbersome than some other sampling strategies, but not everyone has the same chance of being chosen after the first person is selected. The technique, however, is still considered a form of random sampling.

Cluster sampling subdivides a population into groups or units rather than individuals such as geographic areas, city blocks, or recreation centers. These subgroup units would be listed and the evaluator would then choose subgroup units randomly and collect data from the people within those groups. This method is a time saver, but care must be taken to assure that the units or groups are somewhat homogeneous.

Nonprobability Sampling

Using probability sampling is most desirable but not always possible in collecting quantitative data. Nonprobability sampling includes the procedures used when the sample is not drawn by chance from a general population. We do not know the probability of selecting a single individual so it has to be "assumed" that potential respondents have an equal and independent chance of being selected. Biases may occur, and caution is suggested in making generalizations to the broader population, although evaluators frequently do generalize. Several types of nonprobability sampling might be rationalized in an evaluation project.

Purposive sampling is arbitrarily selecting a sample because it is believed that evidence supports that the sample represents the total population. In using this sampling process, an evaluator will need to be able to justify clearly why you believe a particular sample is representative. Purposive sampling also may be used not only for deciding what people to observe and interview, but which activities to observe, what locations, and what time periods. For example, to sample university first year students' attitudes toward building a new recreation center, we select students from classes in English composition because we believe they represent all first year students.

Convenience sampling, or incidental sampling, refers to a sample that happens to be available for an evaluation project. This haphazard sampling technique has very weak generalizability and external validity. It generally does not serve a useful purpose, although there may be some justification for it if no other sampling techniques are possible or affordable. Convenience sampling is easy because the audience is captive and available, and may be representative but that fact isn't certain. You are taking a chance in drawing conclusions for a larger population. For example, to survey students on a college campus, a convenience sample might involve passing out questionnaires within the courses in which that the evaluator is enrolled, or to which she or he had easy access.

Quota sampling is based on dividing the population into subgroups and drawing a sample to fulfill a specific quota. For example, you may wish to survey an equal number of men and women even though that may not represent the population of an aerobics program. In quota sampling, you would simply choose an equal number of males and females until the number that you wanted was reached. The problem in quota sampling is that the evaluator does not know if the people chosen represent the population. Further, once the "quota" is reached, no one else has a chance of being selected. A bias may exist toward individuals who are willing to cooperate with such a sampling procedure. Quota sampling is not a bad strategy, but one can never be fully confident that error does not exist.

Expert sampling, or judgment sampling, is a process where people are chosen on the basis of an informed opinion that they are representative of the population. This "best guess" form of sampling is similar to purposive sampling but is based on a good deal of prior knowledge. Case studies are frequently selected on the basis of expert judgment as well as Delphi studies.

One might also get a sample by using the *snowball approach.* The evaluator gets people she or he knows to recommend others to be the sample for a project. The researcher may ask friends, go to an agency and ask for suggestions, or advertise for volunteers just to get the process started. The initial respondents are asked to recommend others. Obviously a bias exists in this form of sampling, but if one does not know the make-up of an entire population, a sample can be obtained in this way.

Theoretical Sampling

A third form of sampling that is frequently used in collecting qualitative data is different than either probability or nonprobability samples. Theoretical sampling does not focus on numbers of respondents, but the contribution each person makes to addressing the evaluation purposes. Theoretical sampling (Glaser and Strauss, 1967) includes the selection of informants through the stages of the interview or field observation process. The evaluator makes decisions on who and how many to sample as information begins to unfold and as it becomes apparent that certain views are or are not being represented.

Sampling, in the context of collecting qualitative data, means deciding what group of people is to be studied. Further, it involves realizing that you cannot observe everything, so you can only address certain aspects related to people, settings, events and social processes. In other words, the evaluator, by using interviews and/or qualitative observations, is not concerned about adequate numbers or random selection, but is trying to present a working picture of the broader social structure from which the data are to be drawn. Within qualitative approaches, the evaluator is interested in sampling so that the observations made or data collected are representative of the more general class of phenomena. The evaluator is also interested in whether the observations or interviews made are representative of all the possible observations or interviews that could have been conducted.

The exact number or type of informants is not specified ahead of time in theoretical sampling, although the evaluator may have some sense of what those numbers might be. In some cases, the evaluator may need to spend more time in the field or interview more people than was originally proposed to get data that are trustworthy. In other cases, the data may be grounded more easily and quickly than was initially planned. After the first few cases, you may select the sample purposely to get a number of perspectives. Toward the end of data collection, the researcher will focus more on interpretation and verification of data with the respondents. The more variability in responses or observations one uncovers, the more sampling the evaluator will need to do.

Samples used for qualitative evaluations are usually small and purposive. About 10 to 30 people is the usual number. Saturation is reached with simultaneous data gathering and analysis; it occurs when the evaluator realizes that the data collected is repetitive and no additional information is being uncovered. In any sampling done to collect qualitative data, you should consider how each respondent or situation contributes to an understanding of the evaluation criteria that have been established.

Other Aspects of Sampling

Several other strategies are frequently used in evaluation projects. One example is *random digit dialing* as a random phone sampling method. According to Dillman (1978), random digit dialing is based on identifying all working telephone exchanges for an area, generating the last four numbers from a table of random numbers, and calling. The nonworking numbers reached are discarded and the interview is administered to numbers reached. A lot of wasted effort results in this process because of missing phone numbers, but it is a way to get a representative sample from a population.

Another form of telephone sampling is via telephone directories. You might use random numbers to locate a starting page and then use another random number to locate a name on the page. It is convenient, and still allows randomness.

No matter how hard we try, it is unlikely that we will get a sample that perfectly represents the population. An evaluator can use an entire population, which is often done in smaller evaluation projects, and then won't have to worry about sampling. However, you have to be concerned about both sampling and nonsampling error.

From Ideas to Reality

Sampling is obviously an important aspect of evaluation projects. Sometimes it is not necessary to be overly concerned about sampling because an entire population is used, but other times it is important if projects are to be trustworthy. The possibilities for sampling described in this chapter should provide a basis for the sample decisions needed to undertake in your projects. If the suggestions are followed, you should be able to choose an appropriate sample and justify why it is appropriate given a particular situation.

2.06 SURVEYS: CHOOSING PERFECT VERSUS GOOD-ENOUGH SURVEY METHODS

Goals for Chapter 2.06:

—To describe why surveys are the most common method used in recreation, park, tourism, and leisure services;
—To explain the advantages and disadvantages of self-administered and interview surveys;
—To choose the appropriate survey technique based upon the criteria and resources that are available to you for a given evaluation project; and,
—To outline the procedures to follow given a particular survey project.

The most common type of descriptive design found in the evaluation of recreation and leisure services is the survey. Surveys refer to all types of self-administered questionnaires as well as phone, personal, and group interviews. All these methods are designed to get information from individuals. They may use open-ended or close-ended instruments and may collect qualitative or quantitative data. The choice of the specific method to use will depend upon the criteria to be measured, the sample selected, the expertise of the evaluator, the needs of the organization, and the availability of time and other resources. Choosing the best methods is essential for any evaluation project.

No survey method is perfect for every given situation, although idealistically we are always striving to find perfect methods for specific situations. Many times we have to settle for good-enough approaches to evaluation. It is essential, however, that we carefully consider the options for collecting data from surveys and then make the best possible choices. Sometimes we can collect data with more than one method, referred to as triangulation, but more often the researcher has to make choices.

Each of the survey methods has particular strengths and weaknesses. These strengths and weaknesses are presented in Table 2.6 (page 137) and will be discussed in this chapter. Self-administered questionnaires and interviews are the two major survey approaches used. Both require the development of questions for respondents to answer. Within these approaches, we may choose from among several techniques for gathering data: mailed questionnaires, drop off/pick up questionnaires, group administered questionnaires, call ahead/send questionnaires, telephone interviews, personal individual interviews, or group interviews.

The technique used will depend on the evidence needed to measure the evaluation criteria.

Self-Administered (Written or Paper/Pencil) Questionnaires

Self-administered questionnaires can be done by mail, in group administrations, by drop off/pick up, or call ahead/send methods. The advantage of these written questionnaires lies in the ease of presenting questions that may require visual aids. Questions that are long and may require more complex responses, such as staged questions (i.e., questions that require several items to get a response) can be done more easily with self-administered questionnaires. You can also ask a battery of similar questions without tiring the respondent. A high degree of anonymity is found in self-administered questionnaires assuming no identifying information is requested. The respondent also does not have to share directly in a face-to-face manner with the evaluator.

Disadvantages, however, exist with self-administered questionnaires. First of all, careful questionnaire wording and layout is needed because the evaluator has no chance to clarify the questions being asked. Second, long, open-ended questions usually do not work well in self-administered questionnaires because people do not like to write long responses. Finally, good reading skills of the questionnaire taker are required to do self-administered questionnaires.

Mailed Questionnaires

Advantages exist for self-administered questionnaires that are mailed. The cost is relatively low and an evaluation can be accomplished with minimal staff and facilities. A mailed survey can provide access to geographically dispersed samples as well as samples that might be difficult to reach in such as those who do participate in organized recreation activities. With self-administered questionnaires, the respondents typically have time to give thoughtful answers and/or look up information.

Written, mailed questionnaires are obviously easy to administer. Anonymity and confidentiality are clearly assured in this method even if code numbers are used to keep track of questionnaire returns. With mailed questionnaires, one has access to high and low income groups, although a certain level of education is usually necessary to be able to respond to the questions. Weather does not impact the response rate and one can get a great range of questions answered. The technique of mailed questionnaires is particularly good for larger samples (more than 100). One can be confident with the results, especially with a 50 percent return rate or better. The instructions should result in objective responses if the directions are clear and the questions are well-worded.

Table 2.6
Advantages and Disadvantages of Survey Techniques

Technique	Advantages	Disadvantages
Self-Administered — *Overview*	Ease of presenting questions Longer, staged questions can be used High degree of anonymity	Requires careful wording No chance to clarify misunderstandings Reading skills required Not good for open-ended questions
Mailed Questionnaire	Low cost Minimal staff/facilities required Widely dispersed samples Time for respondent to respond Easy to administer Anonymous and confidential Weather not a factor Good for vested interest groups	Low response rate possible Wrong person may fill it out No personal contact Nonresponse bias Can't pursue deep answers
Drop Off / Pick Up	Same as mailed questionnaire Can explain person-to-person High response rate	Costly for staff time and travel Access may be a problem Safety of staff
Group Administrations	High cooperation rates Low cost Personal contact	Logistics of getting people together
Call/Mail	Usually a higher response rate Personal contact Time/money not wasted on nonresponses	More costly with phone calls
Interviews — *Overview*	Ability to probe Establish and maintain rapport Questions can be clarified Low literacy rates can do well Unplanned information possible Interviewer can be adaptable	Time and personnel requirement Trained interviewers needed Simple questions asked Usually smaller sample size
Telephone	Lower costs than personal possible Random digit dialing sampling Broad geographic area covered Data can be collected quickly Control over data collection Possibility of call-backs Rapport, but not face-to-face	Sampling limitations for those without phone People can hang up Visual aids can't be used Sometimes superficial Timing is important
Personal	Elicit cooperation Probing and follow-up used Other observations to use Establish rapport Longer interviews High response rate Spontaneous reactions	Costly Requires highly trained interviewers Long data collection period Some populations not accessible Small geographic area Possible interviewer bias
Group Interviews	Fast to conduct Same as personal	Logistics of getting people together Leader must work to get all opinions

Disadvantages of mailed questionnaires lie in limited ways to check for reliability and validity. The possibility of a low response rate exists. It is possible to miss some homeless people if they do not have mailing addresses or some people who may not be able to read or understand English. Further, you cannot determine how an individual perceives the questions, and whether the person intended is filling out the questionnaire. With a mailed questionnaire, the evaluator has limited ability to pursue answers deeply. Questionnaires often require "accurate memory" which is not always possible. Mailed questionnaires are sometimes an ineffective way to get cooperation because there is no personal contact. In addition, the mailed questionnaire technique also takes time to collect data. Incorporating the steps of sending out a questionnaire, allowing several days for response, and collecting questionnaires that are eventually mailed back takes time.

You must be sure to have accurate mailing addresses and recognize that people without postal addresses will not be included in the survey. Mailed questionnaires are seldom used with the general public because names are not available and response rate is low. It is possible, however, to obtain or purchase mailing lists from local government tax rolls, utility companies, and telephone companies although these lists will also have limitations.

On the other hand, mailed questionnaires are usually highly useful for particular groups that have a vested interest in an activity. For example, if we wanted to know what Girl Scout leaders thought of the training they received, a short, mailed questionnaire might be a good way to receive feedback with the likelihood of a fairly high response or return rate.

In administering any kind of mailed questionnaire, an evaluator must be concerned about nonresponse bias. In other words, it is likely that those who do not respond to a survey may be different from those who respond. As discussed in the chapter on sampling and administering questionnaires, the evaluator must do as much as possible to assure that a high response rate is obtained and that nonrespondents are not different from those who respond.

Drop Off/Pick Up Questionnaires

Dropping off questionnaires one day and picking them up at a later date has some advantages beyond what has already been discussed relating to self-administered questionnaires. With a drop off/pick up technique, the evaluator can explain the study and answer questions when the questionnaire is dropped off. If someone is unable to do the questionnaire, then they can say so. Thus, the return rate is likely to be higher than with mailed questionnaires. Having time with the questionnaire also provides the individual with the opportunity to give thoughtful answers.

Some disadvantages exist in the drop off/pick up method. Frequently the costs are as high as personal interviews because field staff and travel money are required to do this legwork. Getting access to sites may also be a problem, as is making arrangements to have the questionnaires picked up.

Group Administrations

The group administration of paper/pencil tests has advantages in getting a high cooperation rate. This group administration process is similar to what a teacher does in the classroom when she or he gives a test. Each respondent is given a questionnaire (test) to do and can take as long as needed. The evaluator also has the chance to explain and answer questions about the survey. Frequently, the cost for this technique is low.

Disadvantages of group administrations include the possibility of only collecting a small number of surveys because of the logistics of getting people together in groups. If people already exist in a group, however, logistics and numbers generally are not a problem.

Call/Mail Method

A final method for self-administered questionnaires is to call people to enlist their cooperation and then to send them a questionnaire. Once people make a telephone commitment, they are more likely to complete the survey. This technique usually has a relatively high response rate, because the evaluator can answer any questions about the evaluation in the beginning. Additional expense of staff time is added in phone calls, but this cost may be offset with the assurance that questionnaires are not wasted on people who do not want to return them.

Interviews

Interviews may be divided into three categories: telephone interviews, individual personal interviews, and group interviews. The general advantages of interviews include the evaluator's ability to probe to a greater depth, the opportunity to establish and maintain rapport, and the possibility of clarifying questions. People with lower literacy levels can often do well with interviews. The evaluator may also get unplanned or serendipitous information and may gain insight into the true feelings of respondents. The evaluator can encourage respondents to answer questions and can be somewhat flexible and adaptable to the situation.

Weaknesses of interviews, in general, include the great amount of time and personnel that are usually needed. Trained interviewers are usually required, and interview biases are always a concern. Although interviews may be quantitative, the questions need to be simpler than self-administered questionnaires because respondents will have to listen rather than read. Open-ended questions provide rich information but may be more difficult to analyze than close-ended questions. In addition, interviews usually result in a smaller sample size.

Telephone Interviews

Telephone interviewing has a number of advantages. The costs are lower compared to personal interviews and moderate compared to mailed questionnaires. Sampling processes like random digit dialing can be used. The evaluator has access to certain populations in a broad geographic area. Further, the potential exists for a short data collection period. A smaller staff is needed compared to personal interviews, but more people are generally needed than for doing a mailed questionnaire. You have a little more control over the data collected in an interview because the interviewer can explain questions if needed. It is often easier to get sensitive data over the phone because individuals do not have to see the interviewer. A telephone conversation sometimes seems more anonymous. You are likely to get a better sample because of the personal contact and possibility of call backs. In some cases, letters are sent ahead of time to "warn" respondents that they will be receiving a call in the next week. In some telephone surveys, an initial call is made to ascertain cooperation and to set up an appointment for a more convenient time.

Disadvantages of telephone interviews include sampling limitations, particularly for those people without telephones or with unlisted numbers. Since phone interviews rely on verbal communication, response alternatives are limited with the impossibility of visual aids and visual observations. For example, it would not be possible to ask people to rank more than three or four items in a phone interview. Some superficiality may result because you cannot probe as deeply with phone interviews. Without prior contact, telephone interviews may be less appropriate for personal or sensitive questions. One must consider timing if the calls are to be successful. In addition, telephone marketing is so popular these days that people often are not excited about spending time with someone they do not know on the phone, and will hang up.

Personal Interviews

Personal interviews with individuals are a frequent form of survey data collection. The data collected may be quantitative or qualitative. These interviews may be brief encounters such as someone in a shopping mall stopping to ask people four or five close-ended questions, or personal interviewing can be done with in-depth oral histories/case studies that may last an hour or more.

Personal interviewing is an effective way to enlist cooperation. Accurate responses to complex issues are possible because the interviewer can probe and encourage responses. In addition to the words, you can also get additional data through observations and visual cues. Rapport and confidence building is easier in a face-to-face situation. In addition, longer interviews can often be undertaken. The success of interviews, however, often depends on the interviewer and her or his ability to get information. Personal interviews usually result in a high response rate and allow the evaluator to control the process to address the purposes of the evaluation project.

Disadvantages of personal interviewing include the cost and the need for trained interviewers who live near those to be interviewed. Unless there is a great deal of money, the sample size will likely be small. Further, data collection may take a longer period of time. Some populations may not be accessible for personal interviews, such as people in high crime areas or elite people. Logistics must be taken into account as it is difficult to interview over a large geographic area.

Group Interviews

Group interviews, commonly referred to today as "focus groups," have advantages because they are faster to do, even though logistics exist in getting people together. The interviewer in a group situation has to work hard to make sure that everyone has her or his say. Disadvantages include the ways that some people may take over an interview, leaving shy people unable to say as much as they would like.

From Ideas to Reality

The survey technique chosen will depend upon the purpose of the evaluation project and the use of the evaluation. Many survey possibilities exist. The use of the right technique coupled with a good questionnaire or interview schedule will contribute to the success of survey methods. If an evaluator follows these suggestions for making decisions, she or he should be able to conduct the best possible survey evaluation project.

2.07 SURVEYS: ADMINISTERING QUESTIONNAIRES AND TELEPHONE INTERVIEWS

Goals for Chapter 2.07:

—To conduct a pilot test for a survey evaluation study that you would like to undertake;
—To describe the steps in implementing a mailed questionnaire so that you will get the highest possible return rate;
—To write a cover letter; and,
—To determine the steps that need to be followed to complete successful telephone interviews.

When using a survey, one must consider the best way to actually administer the survey. The purpose of this chapter is to identify some of the procedures to be followed in administering questionnaires and conducting interviews. We assume that the criteria are well-established for an evaluation project and that you have selected or developed a reliable, valid, and usable instrument.

Pilot Testing

All evaluators should pilot test their instruments with a sample similar to the one that will be used in the actual evaluation. Usually the pilot test is done to see if any problems exist with the instrument or the sample. This recommendation was discussed to some extent in the chapter on choosing and developing instruments, but the importance of pilot testing cannot be emphasized enough. Changes may need to be made in the instrument after the pilot is completed. The data obtained in the pilot test also can be used to develop plans for sampling or for data analysis.

A pilot test usually consists of going to a small sample (five to ten people) who are similar to the individuals who will ultimately receive the survey. The evaluator will give the survey exactly as it will be administered and note the responses from the sample. In addition, people taking the pilot might be asked if all the items on the questionnaire were clear and understandable. Some problems may also be evident as the way that people responded to the questions is assessed. As indicated previously, you must pay attention to the information you obtain in the pilot as it can supply a great deal of information to consider before actually beginning to collect data.

Some people also use the pilot to test the reliability, validity, and usability of an instrument. The pilot test will determine if, in fact, an instrument can be successfully administered over the phone or whether another method would be better. If a standardized test is used, a pilot test may not be necessary, but doing one may help to assure that the instrument is valid for its intended use.

Implementing Mailed Questionnaires

In conducting mailed questionnaires, several aspects need to be considered including cover letters, mailing procedures, and follow-ups.

Cover Letters

A questionnaire should never be mailed that does not include some explanation of the evaluation project or research study. This description is usually done with a cover letter. The letter should contain a clear, brief, yet adequate statement of the purpose and value of the survey. If possible, the letter should be personally addressed to the respondent. With computer mail merge programs, we can easily address by name the individual to whom the questionnaire is being sent. The cover letter should engage the potential respondent in a constructive and appealing way and should provide good reasons why the respondent should take time to complete the questionnaire. The respondent's professional or public responsibility, intellectual curiosity, or personal worth are typical response appeals. The tone should be one that is inviting and not authoritarian.

The cover letter should indicate a reasonable, but firm return date. Usually people need two to three weeks to respond. Make sure a deadline is given or questionnaires will arrive months after the completion of the project. An offer to send the respondent a report of findings is an ethical responsibility. This offer should only be made, however, if you are committed to following through on this point. The use of letterhead, signature, and organizational endorsements lend prestige and official status to the cover letter.

The cover letter should guarantee anonymity and confidentiality or explain carefully how the data will be used. The letter should be signed personally by the evaluator, if at all possible. It is often best to avoid using words like "questionnaire" and "study" as these terms sometimes are not perceived as positively as are words like "project" and "survey." Table 2.7(1) shows a sample cover letter that might provide a prototype to follow when designing the letter.

Table 2.7(1)

Sample of a Cover Letter

Curriculum in Leisure Studies and Recreation Administration
CB #3185 Evergreen House
University of North Carolina at Chapel Hill
Chapel Hill, NC 27599-3185

December 1, 1995

Dear *(name)*:

Summer staff salaries are an issue each of us will address shortly. For some time, many camp directors have wondered how their summer camp staff salaries compared to other position in the same region and in comparable camp settings. Baseline data about summer camp staff salaries may be useful information for the camping movement in general, as well as for specific camps.

Your camp has been randomly selected for participation in this project. We are asking only a small percentage of accredited agency, religiously affiliated, and independent day and resident camps across the United States to complete and return this short questionnaire. Therefore, your participation is extremely *important*.

You may be assured of confidentiality. The questionnaire has an identification code number for mailing purposes only. This coding is done so that we may check your camp name off the mailing list when your questionnaire is returned.

The results of this survey will be made available to the American Camping Association and will be distributed at the next ACA Conference in San Diego. You may receive a copy of the results in mid-February if you send us a self-addressed, stamped envelope with your questionnaire.

To get the results tabulated by February, it is necessary to have the data as soon as possible. We are asking that you please return the questionnaire by December 18. Since ACA is doing this study on a small budget, you will contribute to the organization by putting your own stamp on the return addressed envelope enclosed.

We appreciate your assistance. We believe we are undertaking a valuable and useful project. If you have any questions, please call us at 919-962-1222. Thank you again.

Sincerely,

(names)
(titles)

Mailing

Depending on the number of questionnaires to be sent, and time constraints one may use bulk mail or first class. First class is faster, but more expensive. Bulk rate may take up to two weeks for delivery, but is less expensive. Usually 200 pieces of mail are needed to use bulk.

The higher your response rate, the more confidence the evaluator can have that the survey represents the views of the sample. Dillman (1978) talks about having a goal of getting a 100 percent response rate. He offers several suggestions to use to accomplish this goal. Always enclose a stamped, self-addressed envelope. A business envelope will also work. Business reply envelopes are usually more desirable financially, because you are only charged postage for the questionnaires returned. Response rates are generally higher if it is as easy as possible for someone to return a questionnaire. Some evaluations may use self-mailers in which the respondent simply folds the questionnaire, staples or tapes it, and puts it in a postal box. You will need to decide the best way, but keep the method of mail back as easy as possible for the respondent.

Although 100 percent is a possible goal, for most mailed surveys you should expect no less than a 50-70 percent response rate. The shorter the questionnaire, the better the response rate. If the response is lower than 50 percent, there may be nonrespondent bias resulting in problems with validity. Response rate is calculated by dividing the actual number of responses returned by the number in the sample size, minus any who were not reachable (such as questionnaires returned due to incorrect addresses or no forwarding address), and then multiplying by 100. The fraction should be as close to 100 percent as possible. For example, if there are 80 names on a list that received questionnaires, and 48 of them returned the questionnaire and three letters were undeliverable, we would have a response rate of $48/(80-3) \times 100 = 62$ percent.

A low response rate does more damage than a small sample size since no valid way exists of scientifically inferring the characteristics of the population represented by nonrespondents. People likely not to respond often have little or no interest in the topic, are low income and blue collar workers who tend to express themselves less frequently in written form, and citizens with little formal education (Michigan State University, 1976).

Sometimes incentives such as a small amount of money, pencils, newspaper clippings, gifts (a small memento), or a promise of a copy of the results to encourage people to respond can be provided. Providing incentives adds additional expense to the survey, but may be possible in some situations, such as a health club that offered two free guest passes to any member who returned a completed evaluation questionnaire. The best thing to do, however, to assure a high response rate is to convince people of the value of their input regarding the mailed questionnaire.

Many evaluators use a code number system to keep track of who and how many people return questionnaires. This code is accomplished by giving each respondent a number associated with her or his name and address. This number is then written somewhere on the questionnaire. The cover letter should explain what the number means. When the questionnaire is returned, the name can be crossed off the list so that no additional money is wasted on follow-up reminders, sparing the individual what would essentially be "junk" mail. Destroying the list of names and numbers after the data are coded and tabulated also assures the respondent of anonymity.

Follow-up contacts should also be conducted to obtain a higher response rate. Dillman (1978) suggested that a reminder postcard be sent to individuals who have not returned questionnaires after the first ten days or so. It is just a friendly reminder. A second follow-up letter should be sent several days after the initial due date. It should include a second cover letter with much of the same information as in the first, including a plea to complete the questionnaire by a new due date. This follow-up letter might suggest that the evaluator hopes the questionnaire is in the mail, while also reaffirming the value of the evaluation project. Another questionnaire and a self-addressed, stamped envelope should be included with the second follow-up letter. A final contact in the form of another postcard should be mailed about ten days after the second letter is sent to anyone who has not returned the questionnaire. If a good response rate has not been received, a telephone call to nonrespondents might be initiated to either ask them to return the questionnaire or, if possible, complete the questionnaire over the phone.

For some evaluation studies, you may want to determine nonresponse bias. In other words, are those people who did not respond different than those who did? Calls can be made to get demographic data or check if late respondents are different demographically from early respondents to the survey. If a high response rate is obtained (high is usually 60-70 percent), determining nonresponse bias is probably not necessary.

Administration to Groups

Administration of surveys to groups mainly requires getting people together to give them an evaluation instrument. You may need to provide them with a writing utensil and a place that is conducive to filling out the instrument. Clear directions should be given about the purpose of the survey and what to do once it is completed. The response rate is much higher when people are required to complete a questionnaire on the spot; however, sometimes it may be necessary to allow people to take the questionnaire with them. In that case, it may be desirable to use a code procedure similar to what was done with the mailed questionnaire so that postcards can be sent or phone calls made as reminders to those who do not return their questionnaire. If people are asked to return a questionnaire, they must be told where and when. In some situations, mailing may be easier than a drop off. Provide the address and a stamped envelope along with the questionnaire when it's distributed.

Telephone Interviews

Telephone interviews may be conducted by sending a preliminary letter or by simply calling the interviewee on the spot. Forewarning is usually helpful if the individual needs time to consider the topic and it alleviates the suspicion that a call may not be legitimate. The advance letter, similar to the cover letter, is written with the details about the project and when the phone call is going to occur.

Timing is often critical for telephone interviewing. The best time to catch people at home is between 6:00 and 9:00 p.m. However, this time slot is not always the most convenient time to interview people. Most telephone interviews are not completed during the first contact, and several calls are often required to complete the interview if it initially requires more than a couple minutes on the phone.

You may call from a predetermined list, use a random sample from a directory, or do random digit dialing. When making the call, the first thing to do is to confirm that the phone number is correct or that the appropriate residence has been reached. If a particular person is wanted in the household, this person should be requested. The interviewer should then state to the desired respondent who she or he is and why a phone survey is being done. A brief description of the evaluation project should be given (two or three sentences). You might also want to explain how the phone number was obtained and/or remind her or him that a letter was sent previously. The individual should be told how long the interview will take and ask if now is a convenient time. If it is not, another time that would be more convenient should be scheduled if possible. Remember that getting a high response rate is the goal, so all should be done to get the interview completed. If someone hangs up, they are considered a nonrespondent or no return. As discussed previously, we want the return rate to be as close to 100 percent as possible.

Proceed through the survey on the phone as quickly as possible, but make sure the individual is allowed time to respond. If you are tape-recording the conversation, it is necessary to inform the individual of the recording. If not, mark her or his responses to the questionnaire accurately or enter them into the computer appropriately. Many telephone interviewers now use computers that immediately enter the data and, depending upon the response, will move the interviewer to the next appropriate question. Table 2.7(2), on pages 150-151, shows an example of a telephone interview schedule. Note that 7. dk (don't know) and 9. NA (not applicable) is used consistently throughout the interview.

Interviewers doing telephone interviews will need to be thoroughly trained. Sometimes volunteers will do phone interviews, but often you will need to hire people. Regardless of whether paid or volunteer, the interviewers must know how to conduct the interview. For example, interviewers must learn to read the questions exactly as they appear. They must understand the telephone system and must know how to respond to questions. It is usually best if all interviewers operate from a central location for ease of supervision. One of the best ways to train interviewers is during the pilot test so they can practice their responses before the real data is collected.

The big difference between telephone interviews and mailed questionnaires is the need to have a third person between the evaluator and the respondent. Thus, much effort goes toward making sure the interviewer is adequately prepared.

Table 2.7(2)

Sample Telephone Interview for Recreation Trails Survey

1. As we have said, this survey is about the use of any designated recreational trails in Wisconsin. By this we mean any trail in Wisconsin that is marked and maintained specifically for recreational activities. Did you use any of these trails at all in 1984?

      1. yes (Go to Q2)   2. no (Go to 1a)   7. don't know (dk)   9. NA.
                                                                            (skip to Q 46)

   1a. Is it very likely, likely, unlikely, or very unlikely that you will be a user of Wisconsin trails five years from now?
      1. very likely   2. likely   3. unlikely
      4. very unlikely   7. dk   9. NA

   1b. Have you heard of these trails, or didn't you ever know they exist?
      1. heard (Go to 1c)   2. didn't know they exist (skip to Q46)
      7. dk (skip to Q46)   9. NA (skip to Q46)

   1c. Was there anything that kept you from using these trails in 1984 if you had wanted?
      1. yes (skip to Q33)   2. no (skip to Q46)
      7. dk (skip to Q46)   9. NA (skip to Q46)

2. During 1984, about how many times did you use a designated recreational trail in Wisconsin for any of the activities I'll name?

   First: for backpacking? (ENTER "O" IF NONE)   #:____

3. ...hiking without backpacks? #:____

4. ...biking? #:____

5. ...horseback riding? #:____

6. ...cross-country skiing? #:____

7. ...snowmobiling? #:____

8. ...driving or riding motorcycles or off-road vehicles? #:____

9. ...canoe trails? #:____

10. What other activities, if any, did you use the trails for in 1984, and about how many times did you do each one?
      0. none.
      a. _____ #:____
      b. _____ #:____

Interviewer: If "0" to Qs 2-10, return to question 1.

Table 2.7(2) continued

Sample Telephone Interview for Recreation Trails Survey

11. In 1984, did you tend to use these trails more on weekdays or on weekends?
    1. weekdays   2. weekends   3. no difference
    7. dk   9. NA.

12. How many different designated recreational trails in Wisconsin did you use last year?

    #:____

13. In 1984, did you use any nationally-operated trails in Wisconsin?
    1. yes   2. no   7. dk   9. NA.

14. Any state-operated trails?   1. yes   2. no   7. dk   9. NA.

15. ...county-operated trails?   1. yes   2. no   7. dk   9. NA.

16. ...city-operated trails?   1. yes   2. no   7. dk   9. NA.

17. ...privately-operated trails?   1. yes   2. no   7. dk   9. NA.

18. Do you usually use these trails with a friend, or with a relative, or do you usually go alone?
    1. friend   2. relative   3. alone
    4. both   7. dk   9. NA.

19. When you used any of these trails, was it usually on outings sponsored by a club or organization?   1. yes   2. no   7. dk   9. NA.

20. Do any members of your household use designated recreational trails in Wisconsin that you do not use?
    1. yes   2. no   3. single person household
    7. dk   9. NA.

From Ideas to Reality

Survey administration is a necessary step in data collection. This aspect of the evaluation project is not difficult to do but the tips provided should help to make sure that the process goes smoothly. Evaluations are challenging enough as they are and you will want to do everything possible to expedite the efficient and effective collection of data.

2.08 Surveys: Personal Interviewing

Goals for Chapter 2.08:

—To identify the four approaches that can be used to organize interviews;
—To develop an interview schedule using one of the four approaches including the determination of question content, sequencing, and possible follow-ups and probes;
—To train interviewers about the skills that they will need to be effective as interviewers;
—To design an evaluation project that would make use of group interviews or focus groups;
—To identify possible problems that might occur when using interviewing methods; and,
—To implement a procedure for collecting interview data.

The purpose of interviewing is to find out what is in and on someone's mind. It allows evaluators to enter into another person's perspective. We assume that the perspective is meaningful, knowable, and able to be expressed. Interviewing may be done over the telephone or in person. The questions asked may collect quantitative or qualitative data, although personal interviews often have been used to collect qualitative data.

The value of interviewing is in finding out those perspectives of an individual that we cannot directly observe. For example, feelings, thoughts, and intentions cannot be observed, nor can we observe behavior that took place at some previous time. We cannot see how people have organized the world and the meanings they attach to what goes on in the world. People must be asked about these things.

Interviewers sometimes feel they are imposing on people. Handled appropriately, however, what could be more flattering to an individual than to be asked to talk about her or his views about various issues? Most people like to talk about themselves and the interviewer can encourage them to talk. Nevertheless, as in all survey situations, the interviewee is giving a gift of time and emotion so she or he should be respected for that contribution as well.

Approaches to Interviewing

Four approaches, according to Patton (1980b), may be used in conducting personal interviews, whether they be done one-on-one or in a group situation. The first, *closed-quantitative*, has already been discussed in Chapter 2.04 on developing instruments. In this first approach, an interview schedule is developed ahead of time, and the interviewer simply asks the quantitative questions as they appear on the preestablished questionnaire. As indicated previously, telephone interviews typically use this approach where the respondent is provided with a series of close-ended responses from which to choose.

The remaining three basic approaches are open-ended and are used to collect qualitative data. The three approaches require different types of preparation, conceptualization, and instrumentation:

1. the standardized open-ended interview (structured);
2. the interview guide approach (semi-structured); and,
3. the conversational interview (unstructured).

In the structured approach, the interviewer must follow verbatim what the questions are. The *standardized open-ended* interview consists of a set of questions carefully worded and arranged with the intention of taking each respondent through the same sequence and asking each respondent the same questions in the same way. Flexibility in probing is limited. Sometimes you can only interview each participant once for a limited period of time. The questions are written in advance *exactly* how they are to be asked. Each question is carefully worded with the probing written into the questions.

The standardized open-ended technique minimizes interviewer effects by asking the same questions. Interviewer judgment does not enter into the interview, and data organization is relatively easy to do. Three good reasons to use this approach are: (a) the exact instrument used is available for inspection, (b) variation among interviewers can be minimized, and (c) the interview is highly focused so interviewee time can be carefully used. In general, this approach minimizes issues of legitimacy and credibility. The weaknesses are that the interviewer is not permitted to pursue topics or issues that were not anticipated when the interview schedule was written. Further, individual differences and circumstances might be reduced using this structured interview.

The semi-structured or *interview guide* approach allows freedom to probe and to ask questions in whatever order seems appropriate. In the general interview guide a set of issues is outlined and explored with each respondent. The questions are prepared to make sure the same information is obtained from a number of people by covering the same material. The issues are not necessarily covered in a particular order, and the actual wording of each question is not determined ahead of time. The interview guide serves as a basic checklist during the interview. The interviewer must adopt the wording and sequence of questions in the context of the interview.

The interview guide provides topics or subject areas so the interviewer is free to explore, probe, and ask questions that will elucidate and illuminate that particular subject. The interviewer can remain free to build a conversation within a particular subject area and to establish a conversational style. The guide allows the interviewer to take as much time as needed to cover all the aspects of the guide. Those interviewed can provide more or less detail depending on their interests and the follow-up probes done by the interviewer. Other topics may emerge during the course of the conversation, and the interviewer must decide whether or not to pursue those additional ideas. Interview guides are especially useful for group interviews.

Unstructured approaches are also referred to as *informal conversational* interviews. They have no preestablished questions, but result from a conversation. In this informal approach, spontaneous generation in the natural flow of interaction results so the respondent may not realize she or he is being interviewed.

The strength of unstructured interviews is that they allow the interviewer to be highly responsive to individual differences and situational changes. The technique, however, requires a greater amount of time and conversational skill to collect systematic information. The interviewer must be able to interact easily with people in a variety of settings, generate rapid insights, formulate questions quickly and smoothly, and guard against asking questions that impose interpretations on the situation by the structure of the questions. In the unstructured approach, the evaluator gets great quantities of data that will result in much time devoted to data organization and data analysis. Table 2.8 (page 156) provides a summary of the strengths of these four interview approaches.

Content of Interviews

Similar to any type of instrument development, one must determine and develop the content of interview questions. You must decide what questions to ask, how to sequence questions, how much detail to solicit, how long to make the interview, and how to word the actual questions. In developing questions for any survey, the evaluator may address the past, present, or future and may ask about behaviors, attitudes, knowledge, feelings, and/or background.

In conducting personal in-depth interviews, the sequencing of questions is important although no fixed rules exist. An evaluator usually starts with fairly noncontroversial questions to get the person talking. Asking questions about behaviors, activities, and experiences is usually a good place to begin. Then you can ask about interpretations, opinions, and feelings. Questions about the present are usually easier to answer than questions about the past or the future.

Asking open-ended questions is an art, just like asking close-ended questions. The questions should be neutral, singular, and clear. Try to avoid "why" questions because they presume a cause and effect. Many possibilities are evident in "why" questions; use words other than "why" to get at specific philosophical, economic,

Table 2.8

Variations in Evaluation Research Interview Approaches
(adapted from Patton, 1980b)

Type of Interview	Characteristics	Strengths	Weaknesses
Informal Conversational	Questions emerge from the immediate context and are asked in the natural course; no predetermination of question topics or wording.	Increases the salience and relevance of questions; interviews built on and emerge from observations; interview matched to individuals and circumstances.	Different information collected from different people with different questions. Less systematic. Data organization difficult.
Interview Guide	Topics and issues to be covered are specified in advance. Outline form. Interviewer decides the sequence and wording of questions in interview. Interview is conversational and situational.	The outline increases the comprehensiveness of the data; systematic data for each respondent. Logical gaps in data can be closed.	Important and salient topics may be omitted. Comparability of responses is reduced.
Standardized Open-Ended	The exact wording and sequence of questions are determined in advance. Same basic questions in same order.	Respondents answer the same questions; increased comparability of results. Reduced interviewer effects and bias when several individuals and interviewers are used. Permits decision makers to see and review the instrumentation used in the evaluation. Facilitates organization and analysis of the data.	Little flexibility in relating the interview to particular circumstances. Wording may constrain and limit naturalness and relevance of questions and answers.
Closed Quantitative	Questions and response categories are determined in advance. Responses are fixed; respondent chooses from among these fixed responses.	Data analysis is simple; responses can be directly compared and easily aggregated; many questions in a short time.	Respondents must fit their experiences and feelings into researcher's categories; may be perceived as impersonal, irrelevant, and mechanistic. Limited response choices.

outcome, or personality factors you wish to explore. Instead of "Why did you join?" you might ask, "What is it about the program that attracted you to it?" or "What is it about you that attracts you to this activity?" "Why" questions are often difficult to analyze with any comparability unless they are made specific.

Collecting qualitative data through personal interviews requires that the interviewer use probes and follow-ups to deepen responses. An interviewer may want to think about probes such as "who, what, where, how, and when" while listening to someone describe their experiences. These follow-up questions can prompt the interviewee to elaborate and give more detail. Such nonverbal signs as head nodding may also elicit more information. Probes and listening responses are seldom written into an interview schedule, but a successful interviewer knows how to use them appropriately.

The general conduct of any interview will require that both the interviewer and interviewee see themselves engaged in two-way conversation. The interviewee must be willing to talk. The interviewer must ask for the information desired, explain why it is important, and let the interviewee know how the interview is progressing. Further, the interviewer must maintain control of the interview. Encouragement should be given, but you may also want to stop an interviewee if she or he takes an irrelevant tangent. It is wrong to let someone go on about something that isn't appropriate for the particular evaluation project or research study. It wastes everybody's time. In qualitative data collection through interviewing, however, an interviewer sometimes does not know how relevant someone's tangent might be to better understanding a phenomenon.

Setting up the Interview

Contact should be made with interviewees by mail or phone. The time, place, and other logistics of the interview should also be described and discussed. Usually an in-depth interview will take one half to two hours; a place should be scheduled where privacy is possible. Enough time and the proper place can greatly affect the nature of the interview. Let the interviewee know whether or not the conversation will be taped when you first contact her or him. The evaluator must be clear about the evaluation intentions and assure the anonymity of the respondents. You will probably want to explain the general topics that will be covered in the interview and offer the interviewee an opportunity to receive a copy of the evaluation report.

Recording the Data

Recording the data will depend upon the interview approach used. In a closed-quantitative interview, the interviewer can mark a response sheet much as would be done if a questionnaire was self-administered. For any of the other three approaches, the primary raw data are quotations so the interviewer must try to capture the actual words said. Data interpretation and analysis involve making sense of what people have said, looking for patterns, putting together what is said in one place with what is said in another place, and comparing differences. Since this process is necessary for analysis, what is said must be recorded as fully and fairly as possible during the personal interview.

A tape recorder is indispensable for in-depth interviewing. The use of tape recordings frees the interviewer to concentrate on interviewing, improves the fullness and quality of responses, avoids an interviewer's selective listening, and allows the evaluator to check up on interviewer technique. Most research suggests that tape recording does not increase resistance, decrease rapport, or alter people's responses (Weiss, 1975). If a tape recorder cannot be used to get verbatim responses, then the interviewer must take thorough notes. Taking verbatim notes is extremely difficult. Not only does the tape recorder increase accuracy, however, it also allows the interviewer to give the interviewee full attention during the interview.

When using a tape recorder, the interviewee must know why it is being used and how the tapes will be handled. Further, using a tape recorder does not mean that some notes shouldn't be taken. In addition to using a tape, the interviewer ought to jot notes in case of a mechanical problem; these jottings will also help to supplement the transcription. Notes help formulate new questions and help organize information on the tape. In tape recording, use high quality tapes, lapel mikes (if possible), and always carry a back-up tape recorder. A back-up tape may be made if there's a chance that a tape cannot be transcribed immediately. The tapes should be labeled and protected so that they do not become damaged. Remember, when using qualitative data, the words are the data; don't lose the tapes.

Making a full transcription of all tape recorded interviews as soon as possible after an interview is highly desirable. Transcribing tapes, however, is time-consuming. The ratio of transcribing to tape time is 4 : 1. It takes at least four hours to transcribe one hour of tape. Transcribing can be costly as well, but an evaluator must consider its usefulness and how the benefits may outweigh the costs. If resources are not available for transcribing, you can work back and forth between tape and notes, although in the long run this method may be more time-consuming than simply doing the transcribing.

Notes on Notes

As soon as an interview is complete, it is important to make notes about the interview. You should list proper names and any unfamiliar terminology that may have been encountered; make notes about anything observed that had relevance to the interview like where the interview occurred, who was present, how the interviewee reacted, observations about the interviewer's role, and any additional information that might be important. You should also make "notes on notes" about how you felt the interview went. To do a good job of personal interviewing, you should spend time after the interview reviewing and reflecting on what occurred.

Depending upon the nature of the interview, particularly if it is qualitative, it may be desirable to follow-up for a second interview with an individual. Therefore, the interviewer will want to keep in touch with the people initially interviewed through a thank-you note or some other formal communication. When doing the initial interview, you may want to see if that person would be willing to do a second interview if needed.

Training and Supervising Interviewers

The comments in the first part of this chapter have assumed that the evaluator will be conducting the interview. The evaluator will need to decide whether interviews can be done better by existing program staff or whether they ought to be done by outside (volunteer or paid) people. Sometimes organization staff are too busy to do data collection. On the other hand, they know the participants well, and sometimes there is no choice but to use them due to financial constraints. Hiring interviewers is costly and time-consuming, but may be a viable option if staff is not available.

Regardless of who does the interviews, training is essential. Hiring or using interviewers who have experience is best, but experienced interviewers may not be easy to find. If experienced interviewers cannot be hired, extensive training must be conducted. In hiring or choosing interviewers, sometimes peoples' attitudes may make a greater difference than their actual skills. Middle-age women are often the least threatening to interviewees and it is often useful to try to match race if possible. The research on race matching as well as sex and age, however, has been inconsistent. Indigenous interviewers may be good in establishing rapport, but may not always have the best interview skills.

The purpose of training is two-fold: to explain the details and objectives of the study and to familiarize individuals with the interview schedule and allow them to practice. Several key ideas might be emphasized in interviewer training. First the interviewer must learn to recognize and control any subtle or pervasive bias and become as neutral as possible. The interviewer should be told to always carry identification concerning the project so that any safety concerns on the part of interviewees can be allayed. The interviewer should not dress to any extreme (rich or poor) but should look neat, conservative, and casual. The interviewer should show interest and concern without seeming to spy on respondents. In general, however, the interviewer is only as good as the training she or he gets (Michigan State University, 1976).

Problems Associated with Interviewing

In conducting interviews, certain problems may be encountered. One problem relates to the influence of social desirability on validity. For example, people will often over-report participation because they think they should. Income is the exception to desirability; people often underreport it. To avoid issues of social desirability, the interviewer should show complete acceptance of answers and reassure the interviewee that answers are confidential. Providing opportunities to explain rather than just answer yes/no may also encourage a respondent to answer honestly. An individual is more likely to give an honest answer if she or he understands the questions being asked.

The language used in any personal interview must also be considered. A respondent has the opportunity to ask for clarification if she or he doesn't understand a question, but using the wrong language or unknown jargon may result in problems in communication. People are sometimes reluctant to admit they don't understand. While interviewing, we must also be concerned with different cultural perspectives. Interviewers must recognize that language and speech patterns may result in data different than initially expected. Being able to understand leisure interests and behavior through different cultural experiences may be of considerable value when using in-depth interviews in evaluation.

Some controversy surrounds the paying of respondents. On the positive side, some evaluators say the answers are better, the interview is put in a commercial light, and the payment reflects the value of the time and energy spent giving information. Those who are against paying respondents say that it increases the cost of a project. Further, respondents may come to expect to be paid, and a bad precedent may be set for other evaluators or researchers. Other opponents feel paying respondents may affect validity of the interview because people will respond in more socially desirable ways. Many times evaluators do not have money available for paid interviewees, so payment is not an issue. Other times it may be a possibility to consider.

Interviewing is not always done with individuals who are educated, middle-class, and articulate. To get information about a diversity of people who are potential users of recreation services, a variety of people ought to be interviewed. Malik, Ashton-Shaeffer, and Kleiber (1991) have described some of the aspects to consider in interviewing people with mental retardation, for example. They believe interviewing can be successful and helpful because it deobjectifies a person and allows the evaluator to get more information that couldn't otherwise be obtained. Designing questions so that the individuals with mental retardation have the ability to understand and can accurately convey facts and opinions is important. They suggest that an interview session can be enhanced by considering the time, place, length of interview, and interviewer rapport. An interview should be conducted where the fewest distractions exist; usually thirty minutes is an appropriate length of time. For many people with mental retardation, yes/no and either/or questions are easiest to answer.

Every evaluator should seek to minimize the degree of interview error in the evaluation project. Because of authority relationships, direction of desirability of response, and the nature of the subject matter, response accuracy is always suspect. Interview error may occur due to the predisposition of respondents such as whether they are suspicious, hostile, indifferent, unmotivated, lacking information, lacking insight, or have limited language. Error may also be due to the predispositions of the interviewer who may be uncomfortable with the people interviewed, shy, ill at ease, unable to establish rapport, lacking in an understanding of the language, or who may have stereotyped expectations. The procedures of the project are, however, under the evaluator's control and the evaluator must try to reduce as much error as possible.

Specific Examples

Not only do leisure service professionals use interviews of the general public or participants such as through community needs assessments or formative evaluations, but there also may be some special clinical applications of interviews. Ferguson (1983), for example, has described the components of a therapeutic recreation assessment interview technique. The purpose of the assessment interview is to gather information for inferring the leisure needs of the client. An interview usually involves assessing client readiness for treatment, assessing client rationality and appropriateness, identifying leisure behavior patterns, gaining insight into personal leisure values, determining relationships between client and family, ascertaining personal strengths and assets of the client, determining needed lifestyle adjustments, analyzing available leisure systems, and examining economic factors.

Clinical interviewing techniques are not the focus of this book, but they relate to evaluation interviewing in general. Clinical techniques apply to any interview session, but they are particularly useful for purposes of the assessment interview. Ferguson (1983) suggested it is best to use open-ended and not yes/no questions, make questions short and specific, don't use "why" (i.e., use "how" instead because it is less threatening), ask one question at a time, give the client time to think, ask questions that address the purpose of assessment, show empathy, use client's first name, and clarify mixed messages. This advise is good as a summary for *any* interview situation.

Staff performance appraisals are another example of regular interviews conducted each year. A supervisor can apply the principles of interviewing as she or he interacts with an employee by establishing rapport and communicating in a two-way conversation.

Group Interviews

Leisure service professionals may want to consider the use of meetings or group gatherings to collect data from individuals. Ewert (1990) suggested the possibilities of decision making through public participation by using open public meetings, meetings for specific users, advisory committees, and focus groups. According to Krueger (1988), a focus group includes people who possess certain characteristics and who provide qualitative data through a focused discussion. These group focus interviews are beginning to be used more frequently and offer possibilities for evaluators to consider. The value of group interviews lies in their ability to stimulate new ideas among participants by allowing spontaneity and candor.

Group interviews with two to six respondents can often save time and money. In a group interview, interviewees can direct thoughts to each other and not just the interviewer. The evaluator can also directly observe group process. The group interview can serve as a useful scouting device for other situations and is especially good for groups who have some common denominator, such as people who live in the same geographic location or who share the same activity interest. Another use of the interview is to test an evaluator's interpretation of evaluation findings from a survey or to establish the questions to be asked for a more quantitatively oriented questionnaire.

Krueger (1988) summarized the advantages of the focus group by stating it is a socially oriented evaluation procedure that allows the interviewer to probe, is relatively low cost, can provide speedy results, and can use fairly large samples if several small groups are combined in data analysis. The limitations of focus groups are that there is less control in a group interview, data are sometimes difficult to analyze, the interviewer must be carefully trained, groups may vary considerably, groups may be difficult to assemble, and the discussion must be in an environment conducive to conversation.

In conducting a group interview, the evaluator will first need to arrange to get people to attend a gathering. Sometimes a group already exists; at other times it may be necessary to form and assemble a group. Focus groups run by commercial organizations sometimes provide a complimentary meal and may offer a stipend for being involved, but a monetary incentive is not always the case. Individuals need to know in advance the purpose of the group interview and the parameters including time commitment, remuneration, or whatever compensation will be given. The evaluation planner will need to make a list of the administrative and logistic aspects necessary to conduct the group interviews or focus group.

In preparing for group interviews, the purpose of the forum/meeting (also known as the criteria), should be clearly established. Based on the purpose, an agenda will be developed. Questions should be prepared just as you would for any standardized interview schedule or interview guide. These questions are similar to a structured, open-ended interview in that the questions should be carefully prepared, presented within a context, and logically focused. You also will need to have the session videotaped or audiotaped and will need to make plans for transcribing and analyzing the data.

Another variation of a group interview used in leisure services is community forums. Citizen advisory groups can reflect the interests of the community for needs assessments and evaluation. Public meetings and workshops can be used to solicit citizen input, facilitate a two-way dialogue, and share ideas and emotions. Workshops can get people into small groups to identify needs. In these situations, people come together to address particular issues that may reflect assessment, formative, or summative evaluation. The participants in community forums are often self-selected rather than chosen, which could indicate some sampling biases. The disadvantage to community forums is that these meetings may not represent the entire community. An evaluator must be careful in drawing broad conclusions from only specific individuals. The advantages of community forums are the open access, low cost, and good ideas that may be generated.

From Ideas to Reality

Many options exist for doing personal interviewing. Individual and group interviews are useful as a way to get into "people's heads." To use interviews effectively, an evaluator must appreciate their value and train people adequately in how they can best be used. Interviewing is an interesting and useful way to conduct evaluation and research projects. Interviewing should be tried if it seems appropriate for the evaluation project to be undertaken.

2.09 Observations:
"On a Clear Day You Can See Forever"

Goals for Chapter 2.09:

—To describe the differences between qualitative and quantitative observations;

—To choose the appropriate roles that an observer will take given a particular evaluation project;

—To develop a quantitative checklist using two or more of the strategies described;

—To explain to an administrator the value of using professional judgments as a means for evaluation within an organization;

—To take descriptive notes within a field observation setting; and,

—To critique whether a field observation project has been undertaken appropriately.

Observation methods are available to leisure service professionals for evaluation projects. Evaluation by judgment through accreditation and standards programs, and various kinds of checklists such as maintenance checklists are common examples of observations. This chapter will examine observations by addressing checklists, professional judgments, and field work or participant observation. All methods share a commonality in using observational techniques, although they may be applied differently.

Becoming a good observer requires practice. Many people take observation for granted or do not realize the extent to which they have learned to be selective in what we observe. To be a good evaluator, one has to watch, listen, concentrate, and interpret data apart from gathering it. Just as most people were not blessed inherently with the ability to do math without being taught and given chances to practice our mathematical and analytical abilities, evaluators have to learn observational techniques and practice them to become good.

Roles of Observers

The most common roles of observation include a range from outside observer to full participant and unknown to known. Figure 2.9 (page 166) illustrates these continua. Depending on the placement on each continuum, the evaluation outcomes may be influenced.

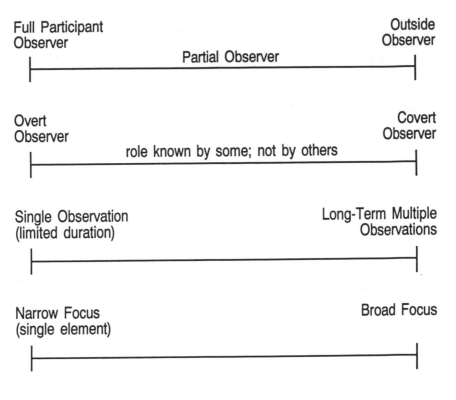

Figure 2.9 Dimensions of Approaches to Observation
(adapted from Patton, 1980, p. 138)

A nonreactive or outside observer might remove herself or himself completely from involvement with the group observed. An example of nonreactive observation might be someone analyzing the way the leisure behavior of women is portrayed on television by watching the shows or viewing videotapes of television programs. Outside observers, similarly, usually try to be as invisible as possible and seek to elicit very little reaction to themselves from the individuals being observed. The full participant or participant observer, on the other hand, is completely involved, and observing is not her or his only role. A danger with the participant observer role is the possibility of becoming highly involved as a participant and losing objectivity or losing concentration on the events occurring. As indicated, it is also possible to be a partial observer which would combine aspects of full participant and outside observer roles.

An unknown observer (covert) is not known by the participants whereas the known (overt) observer has identified her or his role. The covert observer becomes a group member and, in essence, is posing as an "undercover agent." The overt observer is an outsider who makes her or his intentions clear. The known evaluator does not try to pass as anything but known. Being in a situation where some participants know they are being observed and others do not is also possible within this continuum.

Similarly, the role of the observer may range from single observations to long-term, multiple observations and from a narrow focus to broad foci (Patton, 1980b). If a goal-attainment model is being used for evaluation, and the data being collected are quantitative, a single selected observation using a narrow focus may be appropriate. On the other hand, if the goal-free model is being used, and the evaluator is not sure what may result from an observation, long-term multiple observations may be used with an initial broad focus. These observations may become narrower as time progresses. As on any continuum, variations of these ranges may exist depending upon the particular evaluation criteria being measured.

No one observation role is best. Each role has value in certain situations. The evaluator may want to keep in mind the possible ethical problems discussed in Chapter 1.10 that addressed covert observation including invasion of privacy and what may happen to the evaluation project if one is "found out." Therefore, different situations with specific evaluation criteria will require both ethical and methodological considerations.

Regardless of the roles played by observers, the basic procedure followed in any observation is the following:

- choose a behavior or situation to observe;
- decide on mode for recording observations and collecting data (quantitative vs. qualitative);
- determine sampling strategies;
- train observers or practice in the situation;
- analyze data; and,
- evaluate observation instrument.

Quantitative Observations

Stumbo (1983) believes that in areas such as therapeutic recreation, systematic observation instruments are needed to reliably assess behaviors. The systematic observations usually include a checklist or a standardized form with units of analysis identified. The more structured an observation, the more likely analysis will involve scoring and statistical analysis (Denzin, 1978).

The most common quantitative observations use checklists and similar recording scales. These checklists are measurement instruments that the evaluator completes, not the person(s) being evaluated. Evaluators using checklists assume that *a priori* (i.e., before the observation) factors can be identified. The design of these instruments, thus, must follow the same design principles as addressed previously when developing questionnaire instruments was discussed. The criteria measured must be determined, followed by the development of measurement scales.

Checklists are a technique for recording whether a characteristic is present or absent and/or whether an action is taken or not. Often a yes/no response is used, but several checklist formats might be considered. Rating scales are used to indicate the degree of a characteristic or action. Other similar methods include frequency counts and duration recordings. These techniques may be useful, for example, in observing activities done during instruction, in therapeutic recreation settings, or for the recording of specific behaviors in the outdoors.

Just as one may ask questions about a number of aspects of people's lives, you can also observe many aspects of their lives. Several possibilities might be considered for quantitative observations. It is possible to measure the affective or emotional component of what people do. How many times did they smile or act out? The cognitive observations examine intellectual components and thought processes. How does an individual work through a situation? Procedures and routines might be observed. For example, you might observe in what ways a lifeguard describes and enforces the safety rules at a pool. Often in recreation settings physical environments such as space and equipment can be observed. Psychomotor aspects such as posture, position in relation to others, types of movement, and facial expressions might be observed as well. Sociological structure relates to who is talking to whom, the roles that people take on in a group, and the numbers and types of people interacting. Finally, we might observe the activities in which people are engaged.

Different coding units are also used in observation. Sometimes you will simply be counting and will use frequencies or percentages. Other times rating systems that are predetermined and defined will be used. These systems might be scales that determine amounts or judgments of quality such as poor, fair, good or hierarchical ratings such as not at all, seldom, occasionally, constantly. No matter what unit, the observer must clearly define what each of these words mean if they are used in a checklist system.

Strategies to Obtain Observation Information

Several strategies may be used to obtain quantitative observational material. The first is *interval sampling* whereby a series of brief intervals are observed and the evaluator notes what was observed. The interval sampling may be systematic (e.g., doing a recorded safety check of a swimming pool every day) or may be used as a running account of what happened sequentially during a prescribed period of time. The running account might be a rough estimate of frequency and duration.

In interval sampling, the evaluator records for a brief period of time (e.g., ten-second blocks) some particular task—like a child playing with a particular toy. Both the relative frequency and the duration of behavior are reported. The rate of behavior needs to be low enough to count, and you need to be able to determine the size of intervals and mark whether a behavior occurs.

A second strategy uses *frequency counts, event recordings,* or *tally methods.* The frequencies are converted to percentages. In this strategy, one counts the number of discrete events of a certain class of behavior as they transpire during a given time (e.g., minute, hour, day, week). The behavior needs to be clearly defined. This strategy is useful when determining behaviors or seeing what more than one individual is doing. One example is counting the number of complete and incomplete tasks performed by a client in a therapeutic recreation program. You also might record the number of times a behavior is done appropriately or inappropriately. Frequency counts are relatively easy to do. In some situations, the observer could use a wrist-golf stroke counter or grocery store counter or put tally marks on a paper to keep track of how many times a particular behavior is occurring.

Observing *duration* is another quantitative observation strategy. Duration refers to the length of time spent in a particular behavior or how long a behavior occurs. As in other situations, the behavior must be readily observable. The duration is then converted into percentages. For example, one might determine the popularity of a piece of playground equipment by how long children use it. A stopwatch or other timing device would need to be used in this observation. This strategy is time consuming, and one needs to pay constant attention.

A related strategy is *latency recording* where the time elapsed between a cue and the response is measured. For example, one might measure the time between telling a child to put away toys and when she or he actually begins the process. A stopwatch is used in measuring latency time.

Time sampling or *spot checking* involves recording behavior at a particular point in time. In this strategy, the observation occurs periodically at predetermined time intervals. The evaluator specifies in advance the timing, number of observations, and type of observation within a particular context. These observations are usually done in equal intervals with a recording of the number of times something occurs. This spot checking may include ascertaining the total number of participants using a picnic area at different times of the week, for example. It is not possible to observe picnicking all the time, but a systematic time sampling could give you valuable information.

Quantitative Observation Tips

For sophisticated quantitative observation systems, rigorous training periods for observers are needed. Observation systems with few categories require less training, are easy to learn, and result in greater inter-rater reliability. Most quantitative observation systems used in leisure services fall between these two extremes.

The evaluator needs to be concerned about several aspects of doing observations or in supervising others who may be doing quantitative observations. First, behaviors to be observed must be defined carefully. Since few standardized procedures exist for observations, the evaluator will often need to develop the measurement instruments carefully and pilot test them in the situation where they will be used. Second, the interaction between the observer and the participants must be noted. Are there any reactive effects? How did behavior change because of the observer? Did the observer impose consciously or unconsciously any of his or her biases on the events so the meaning became different? Were any self-fulfilling prophesies evolving? Did the observer overidentify with the participants or a faction of them? Third, reliable measures are needed. Thus, the observer will need to be sufficiently trained, use an instrument with clearly defined and nonoverlapping categories, and use a small manageable number of categories that can be sufficiently observed.

Inter-rater reliability is also a concern. Do all observers see the same things? The formula for reliability is number of agreements divided by number of observations (including agreements and disagreements) multiplied times 100 which equals the percentage of agreement:

$$\frac{\text{Agreements}}{\text{Observations}} \times 100 = \text{percent of agreements (i.e., inter-rater reliability)}$$

For example, if two observers agreed on twenty-four items and disagreed on five, we would divide twenty-four by twenty-nine and then multiply this quotient by 100 resulting in 83 percent inter-rater reliability. This result should be as close to 100 percent as possible. Observers should be trained until they can reach a high agreement which could be defined as anything over 90 percent.

Professional Judgments

Professional judgment is the direct observation and evaluation by an expert or someone familiar with a particular program. Professional judgments are based on intuitively evaluating the quality of something based on formal and/or informal criteria.

Some evaluation procedures use professional judgment in conjunction with preestablished criteria. In other cases, experts may be invited into a situation to observe and to use their expertise as the criteria. The advantages of using professional judgment observations are the ease of implementation and immediacy of judgment. Precautions are urged, however, in having outsiders rather than staff evaluate a program, as discussed regarding internal and external evaluators in Chapter 1.09. A value exists in having several judges, making sure the professionals clearly understand the criteria, and providing some training about the factors to consider and their relative importance for a particular situation (Weiss, 1972).

The accreditation processes used in various areas of recreation are examples of professional judgment observation. In cases of accreditation, certain standards are established ahead of time and are then observed. The experts answer questions or write a report concerning their responses.

In therapeutic recreation, a peer program review process has been used successfully in some organizations (Coyne and Turpel, 1984). The peer program review is a method of program evaluation that utilizes established professional standards. The process facilitates making these standards a pattern of practice. Two techniques encouraged within this system are program observation and case review. The process is initiated by therapeutic recreation practitioners who ask peers to observe and evaluate what they are doing. In addition, within other therapeutic recreation agencies, professional judgments are made in the form of internal service audits that give therapeutic recreation specialists information about how their record keeping is done.

Staff/personnel reviews are further examples of professional judgment. In performance appraisals or staff reviews, the supervisor is the professional judge. Other data besides the supervisor's expertise may be collected, but frequently it is up to the supervisor to take all input and use her or his professional judgment to make an evaluation. This process of staff evaluation works best when clear performance criteria have been set through the job description, the supervisor knows the organization well, and when the supervisor's personal biases do not enter into the evaluation.

Qualitative Observations

Advantages exist in using qualitative observations, also referred to as field observations. These techniques may be used to collect anecdotal material and critical incidents that may not be recorded elsewhere. They are in-depth, and the evaluator is able to examine the background and meanings of what may be happening in a program or organization. Flexibility exists regarding what to observe and what data to collect. Qualitative observations are only unscientific when improper techniques are used. Otherwise, the techniques are a highly valid and reliable form of data collection. To qualitative observations, however, requires a highly trained individual or group of individuals that will expend much time and energy.

Doing qualitative observations is often time-consuming. Another disadvantage of these techniques is the possible introduction of bias. This bias, however, can be reduced by including quantitative observations as well as using multiple observers. A further disadvantage may be that single conclusions should not be drawn, but multiple explanations, conclusions, and descriptions for a phenomena are usually the result of qualitative observations.

Qualitative observations may be done in two major ways. One method is to keep an account of anecdotal records and critical incidents. Anecdotal records are factual descriptions of meaningful incidents and events and/or detailed accounts or running logs, often referred to as progress notes. To use these for evaluation, the interpretation is kept separate from factual description. Critical incidents refer to unusual situations that occur that are recorded and described in detail. In analyzing critical incidents, one also attempts to describe the antecedents, behaviors, and consequences.

A second major method of qualitative observations is field observations where the evaluator goes into a "natural" or "normal" situation, such as a playground or a staff meeting, to observe what is happening. Conclusions are then drawn about what is occurring based on volumes of descriptive notes that are taken. The process of field observation involves defining the purpose, populations, samples, and units of analysis to be included, just as is true with any other method of evaluation. The data are analyzed to draw conclusions. The field observation techniques often are combined with other techniques such as interviews, case studies, or document analyses.

Prior to beginning a field observation project, the evaluator would need to become acquainted with the site or program if she or he isn't already, assume a role as known or unknown, and prepare an initial broad focus checklist of things to observe. The process is one of scheduling and becoming involved with the organization. As you begin to collect data through taking extensive notes, themes will develop. In the interpretation process, these themes will be tested, refined, reinterpreted, expanded, discarded, and new data will be observed until final conclusions have been reached.

Taking Notes

Data are collected in field observations by recording information through note-taking by the evaluator(s). The evaluator is, thus, the data collection instrument. Since the notes are the data, they are central to qualitative observations. Notes are taken prolifically. Even in a complete participant role, the evaluator must write down notes as often and as completely as possible. The less time between an observation and recording it through notes, the more accurate the data will be. The notes are taken within the context of what is observed and will depend upon the criteria being evaluated. Often information like weather, people present, the observer's mental state, start and finish, location, changes in environment, and formal roles observed are important to note.

The field observer should be careful to separate facts from interpretation when taking notes. The observer should be particularly careful to identify whether the idea recorded is a fact, quote, or interpretation. The evaluator as observer must indicate what she or he knew happened, as well as what she or he thought happened. Just as you cannot observe everything, you cannot record everything, so the evaluator must practice recording the most important observations. Table 2.9 (page 174) shows an example of note taking. In addition, Henderson (1991) offers several considerations in note taking:

- Record any notes as soon as possible after making the observation.
- Write, type, or word process the notes in detail. The notes should include a running description of events, people, things heard and overheard, conversations among people, conversations with people, and incidents that occur.
- Make copies of the notes as soon as possible. If something happens to the notes, the data has been lost.
- Indicate on the notes whose language was used. Who exactly said what? Did you? Did someone else? Include verbatim quotes, if appropriate, and always use concrete description with specific detail.
- Leave wide margins on the note sheet so that ideas can be written in or note additional interpretations as they occur to you. Start new paragraphs often so the note sheets can be easily read.
- The length of field notes will differ considerably. A rule of thumb might be several single-spaced pages for each hour of observation.
- It is possible to dictate your field notes into a tape recorder and then have someone else transcribe them. If this seems appropriate, the evaluator will need to review the transcriptions as soon as possible.
- Do not be afraid to record notes about what is not understood. Something may not make sense at one time, but it will possibly become clearer later. Record notes at will and do not be afraid of making mistakes.
- Continually monitor yourself as a data gatherer. Tiredness, emotional reactions, relationship with others, energy level, use of discrete observations, and technical problems may all affect the data collection and these manifestations should be noted.
- The length of time spent in note taking will depend on the evaluation questions being asked.
- And finally, remember "If it is not written down, it never happened" (Taylor & Bogdan, 1984, p. 52).

Table 2.9

Sample Notes from Observations of Leisure Education Class

Facts	Interpretations
March 25, 1991	
The C.T.R.S. meets with Richard in the seventh class meeting: C.T.R.S. is slouched in the chair at the table with her arms folded across her chest waiting. Richard walks up, smiles and fumbles as he pulls the chair out to sit down. He sits forward in the seat with his hands holding up his head. C.T.R.S. continues to look at him as he wiggles in the chair. She begins with, "How are you?" He mumbles, "Fine." She says, "You look a little tired."	*Instructor looks tired*
He shrugs his shoulders. She waits a moment and then begins. She is still sitting with her arms crossed. "What did you do this weekend?" "Nothing," Richard replies. Silence for about five seconds. "Were you bored?" she asks. He shrugs his shoulders again. The C.T.R.S. pauses and then points to the decision-making board that has four words written on it—GOAL, OPTIONS, IF/THEN, DECISION. She says, "We are going to talk more about these today. Let's try to talk about leisure. What is your goal for leisure?"	*Both look tired*
	I wonder if people know when they are bored
	I'm not sure what she is asking

Tips on Qualitative Observation

In observation, the evaluator must be a reliable and valid measurer. As an effective observer, you must be trained to notice events and actions that are relevant to your perceptions as well as those that contradict your perceptions. Field observations take enormous amounts of energy to look beyond ordinary day-to-day observations to apply the rigor of scientific evaluation and interpretation.

Part of good observation is learning what to observe. Everything cannot be observed, and even if it could, total sensory overload would occur. Therefore, observation becomes more focused as the evaluator continues with her or his work on a particular evaluation or research project. Ultimately, the observations should result in a written report that will allow the reader to actually enter the situation and understand what was happening based on detailed descriptions of the observer.

At the observation site, it will be necessary to establish a role. You may choose to be a full participant, an outside observer, or something in between, such as a staff member or a volunteer. The role may affect your ability to gain acceptance within a group, so the role should be carefully chosen. In some cases, a staff member wants to use field observations to collect evaluation data. It is possible for her or him to adopt this observer role, but there must be an awareness of the possible biases that might be brought to the situation. No matter what role is used, as an observer one must be explicitly aware of the situation being observed, use a wide-angle lens, take the insider/outsider perspective, be introspective yourself, and keep good notes on both your objective and subjective feelings.

Establishing rapport in the field site will be an important early aspect of the field research. Taylor and Bogdan (1984) offered several tips for establishing social interaction including: remaining passive in the first few days; putting people at ease in whatever ways possible such as doing favors or helping out, collecting data as secondary to getting to know people, acting naive, paying attention to people's routines, introducing yourself, explaining what will be done with the data, trying to figure out what being at the right place at the right time means, beginning with small amounts of time and then increasing the time at the site, and keeping overt note taking to a minimum initially, and adjusting to more visible note taking as participants feel comfortable later. Above all, the field observer doing an evaluation should act interested, and the people being observed will see that she or he is serious about them and the project being undertaken.

Qualitative observation is an ongoing process of data collection and analysis. An evaluator may begin a project with some general criteria in mind, but these criteria may change and become redefined as she or he observes and interacts with people. In other words, an evaluator will develop new insights and new ways of obtaining information as new data is discovered. The qualitative observation process is one that will evolve over time. In addition, one's skills as an observer will improve over a period of time.

Field evaluation requires a high level of concentration to pay attention to what is happening. If the evaluator cannot take notes immediately, concentration is required to imprint the notes in mental photography. The observer must look for key words in people's remarks, concentrate on the first and last remarks of each conversation because those are generally the most important, and be able to play back the observation or conversation easily in the mind.

A final, but not unimportant, aspect of field evaluation research is the utilization of key informants. Respondents are people who are observed or who answer questions with no particular rapport having been established. Key informants, on the other hand, are people who provide more in-depth information about what is occurring because the evaluator has established trust with them. Information is usually obtained from key informants by either formal or informal interviews. One way to regard these informants is as "evaluation collaborators." The value of key informants is to help the evaluator ascertain if people "say what they mean and mean what they say." Some informants may have general information about the past and their perceptions of the present, others may be representative of a group of people, and still others may serve as observers when an evaluator is not there to observe in person. Relationships with key informants will help the evaluator develop a deeper understanding of the setting being evaluated.

Sometimes the evaluator will run into hostile respondents. The evaluator needs to be friendly, but not pushy. She or he may want to employ some additional investigative skills to determine why the lack of cooperation is occurring. The field evaluator will often have to talk to people that she or he dislikes or distrusts. For an effective evaluation to be conducted, an evaluator must observe and talk to all types of people within the setting, and not just to the people who are likable and friendly.

From Ideas to Reality

In all cases, an evaluator is looking for accurate, reliable, valid data. A reliable observation is one that is not biased by idiosyncrasies of either the observer, the subject, or by the constraints of time and place. Observations are not always the easiest methods to use but they can provide information that will be helpful in determining what is actually happening in a particular situation.

2.10 UNOBTRUSIVE EVALUATION METHODS

Goals for Chapter 2.10:

—To identify when unobtrusive methods might be used in an evaluation project;
—To describe the differences between physical evidence, archives, and unobtrusive observations; and,
—To give examples of the uses of physical evidence, archival data, and unobtrusive observations.

Webb and his colleagues (1966) suggested that maybe too much emphasis has been placed on survey methods such as interviews and questionnaires. Perhaps evaluators ought to consider methods that may not be as obtrusive or that may not infringe on people's time and privacy. Unobtrusive methods may complement methodological weaknesses in surveys such as people's socially desirable responses and the tendency to survey people who are accessible, cooperative, literate, and verbose.

Unobtrusive, sometimes called nonreactive, methods refer to observing, recording, and analyzing human behavior in a situation where interaction with people generally does not occur and when people are unaware that their behavior is being observed. Some aspects of observations and unobtrusive methods may overlap, but they are different methods. Unobtrusive methods do not require the cooperation of individuals. These measures are often used to provide supplementary data for evaluation projects, or they may be used on their own. As in other methods, either quantitative or qualitative data may be collected.

These unobtrusive methods are sometimes called "odd ball" because they are unlike what is done in traditional evaluation projects. Their value lies in that they address some criteria that one could not easily measure by asking or observing people directly. These methods counter the notion of dependence on language for obtaining information.

In unobtrusive methods, the anonymity of people is almost certain. Usually some activity such as watching the behavior of individuals in a public park or tracing activity such as by counting the types of vandalism that occur in a park is observed. The data generally consist of physical evidence, archives, or unobtrusive and covert observations. The unobtrusive measures may be systematically identified and analyzed in an evaluation project, or they may be found accidentally when other survey or observation data are being collected. Examples of unobtrusive measures that may be used to obtain data about people's behavior include: observations of body language and other nonverbal behavior, short cuts or worn grass in a park indicating where people walk most frequently, types of graffiti and where it is likely to be found, noting the stations that car radios are tuned to in a parking lot to ascertain station popularity, the number of beer and soda cans in household garbage, litter frequency and type along a highway, and rental records for a business.

Sometimes these unobtrusive methods require detective-like tactics. Similarly, they offer clues to what people are doing. Some of the strengths of unobtrusive methods are the face validity, the simplicity and directness, the inconspicuous and noninterventional nature, their nonreactivity, their easy combination with other methods, the stability over time, and the independence from language (Guba and Lincoln, 1981). In evaluations of policies and administrative procedures, for example, evaluators may rely solely on records and archives.

Problems exist in using unobtrusive methods, however, because they are heavily inferential, information often comes in bits and pieces, and the situations cannot easily be controlled. Unobtrusive methods alone do not tell how people see and experience their activities. Additionally, if subjects are aware in some way that they are being observed, their actions may be distorted and unnatural. Hardware such as hidden cameras, gauges, and one-way mirrors may be used for data collection although some ethical problems exist in using these devices if people can be identified and their privacy is invaded. Further, unobtrusive studies also may have associated biases unless appropriate random sampling procedures are used.

The three ways that data are unobtrusively collected include physical evidence, archives, and unobtrusive and covert observation. Each will be discussed and applied to evaluation.

Physical Evidence

Physical evidence or traces from past behavior is one way to do unobtrusive evaluations. Physical evidence might include the wear on vinyl tiles in a museum as a measure of the popularity of certain exhibits. Another example would be to measure and categorize the food that is thrown away at camp to determine popularity of certain food items. Although the number and types of books checked out of a library would be an example of archival document data, the wear and tear on the books to show what was actually read would be an example of physical evidence. One could put a "Cal-trac device" on an individual to measure activity level and calorie expenditure as another example of physical evidence data.

The advantage of physical evidence data is the lack of conspicuousness. A major drawback to the method, however, is that one gets little information about the nature of the population that is doing whatever is being measured. For this reason, physical evidence *alone* is not necessarily the best method to use for evaluation.

Archives

Archives include any records or documents that exist. Archives include written materials that can provide a past or present historical perspective for the review of patterns. Documents and records are often used to supply data for content analysis. Records are used to keep track of events and serve as official chronicles. They are generally used for trend analysis and integration. Examples of records might be sales records or minutes of a meeting. Documents may be either personal, institutional or public, and they often provide a historical context for an evaluation project. These documents may be letters and diaries, brochures, or newspaper articles. They may be running records or may be episodic.

Archives are generally inexpensive to access, easy to sample, and provide specific population restrictions. A great advantage in using archives is cost savings because data collection is not needed. Sometimes it is difficult, however, for external evaluators to get access to some types of records. In addition, records are sometimes incomplete, out-of-date, and/or inaccurate. Another problem is records often were not collected for the same reason that the evaluator intended. Further, limitations may lie in the selective deposit of certain documents or archives and how well they survive over time.

Despite possible limitations in using archives, previously collected data are often helpful to an evaluator. Records that tell information such as density of population, population distribution, age distribution, sex distribution, racial composition, education level, occupation type, per capita income, family income, housing type, housing age, employment rate, birth rate, expenditure patterns, and crime rate and type are examples of archival records. Also of use are:

- city maps and photos,
- church records,
- building permits,
- state or federal organization records,
- public utility records,
- health and welfare records,
- large scale social studies,
- weather and traffic reports,
- sales records,
- business and professional groups,
- personal documents (e.g., collections, newspaper records, tax assessments),
- school records,
- real estate records,
- libraries,
- radio and TV stations,
- chamber of commerce data,
- actuarial records,
- voting records,
- public records (e.g., gas, water use),
- institutional records,
- financial institutions,
- information from scouting groups (and other youth serving agencies),
- planning agencies, and

- data from state organizations and National Recreation and Park Association (i.e., operating and capital expenditures, amount of recreation acreage, number of full-time and part-time staff, and populations served).

Good sources of archives are city planning departments, Visitor and Convention Bureaus, and Councils of Social Agencies.

Within leisure service organizations, several sources of archives might be interesting. These include budget/financial reports, attendance rosters, trip reports, annual reports made to the recreation commission or board, and old evaluation reports. Evaluators frequently use previous records to do various evaluation procedures such as cost-benefit and cost-effectiveness analysis. Program records and agency files are useful if good data have been kept. Inappropriate data for evaluation purposes, incomplete data, or changes in procedures may be problems in using leisure service agency archives. With the widespread use of computer systems, evaluation from agency records ought to become easier in the future. One secondary outcome in working with archives is that the evaluator learns to develop better record keeping procedures to help an agency with evaluations in the future.

Unobtrusive and Covert Observations

Observations that are unobtrusive and/or covert may occur in a variety of ways. One must be careful in using this technique of data collection because it can border on infringement of people's privacy. Contrived observation such as what is done with hidden cameras and listening devices should be avoided, but once in a while these observation techniques can be justified. Unobtrusive observation involves the evaluator being unknown and passive. These observations are often used to measure physical behavior through audiovisual analysis.

Physical signs may be used in a group to examine such simple aspects as expressive movement including facial expressions, finger and hand movements, rituals of athletes, physical location like proximity to the leader, seating, personal space, clothing, how people sit, and how people stand. These observations might also be used to analyze language behavior like the subject of conversations and with whom they occur. The values of unobtrusive observations are that no role-taking is associated, measuring these activities doesn't cause change in behavior, interviewer effects are not an issue, and data are collected first hand.

Observation in public places is one type of unobtrusive method used in studying recreation, parks, tourism, and leisure settings. In this unobtrusive method, an evaluator uses observation and personal introspection with the assistance of casual conversation. Observation in public places is sometimes hard to do, but an evaluator can get a sense of such aspects as exterior physical signs (e.g., clothes, bumper stickers, license plates), expressive movement, physical location of types of activity, conversational sampling, and time duration of particular activities. The data could be recorded and analyzed like other forms of qualitative observations or quantitative checklists.

Observations can also be recorded using tapes, films, and photos. Audiovisual aids allow the evaluator to examine a phenomenon a number of times. Audiovisual analysis can be divided into several categories. One category may refer to an analysis of media. This technique is essentially a content analysis of pictures, graphics, or words. A second category includes audiovisual analyses that may refer to using photos and media to collect data which can be replayed for analysis. For example, time-lapse photography may give information about patterns of movement in a park. After the photography is done, evaluators can use the data for analysis. A third variation of this category is to make a tape or film and then show it to people to get their reactions. This strategy has been used in park planning where pictures of outdoor areas are taken and shown to people. They are asked to describe their reactions to what is pleasing and not pleasing about particular places.

The method of using audiovisual devices to collect and analyze data has pros and cons. Sometimes the use of audio or visual recordings presents a way to get better samples if an evaluator cannot observe everything at one time. On the other hand, there is a problem with not being able to observe everything even when cameras or recording devices are being used. Most evaluators have found that initially people may be bothered by a video camera or tape recorder, but they forget the presence of these devices after a few minutes. It appears, in general, that the use of audiovisual equipment does not affect the data that may be collected. As in the other techniques, data collection and analysis using audiovisual devices may be quantitative or qualitative depending on how the evaluation project is designed.

From Ideas to Reality

Unobtrusive evaluation methods are not commonly used in leisure services projects but there is no reason why they cannot be. Less is known about the potential for these methods than for other more commonly used methods, but they are no less reliable, valid, or useful. They offer some possibilities to consider as one undertakes particular evaluation projects.

2.11 True Experimental and Quasi-Experimental Designs

> ## Goals for Chapter 2.11:
>
> —To explain the differences between true experiments, quasi-experiments, and preexperiment methods;
> —To describe why randomization and control groups are important in evaluation projects;
> —To analyze the advantages and disadvantages that are associated with using experimental designs; and,
> —To conduct a simple experiment using one of the methods described in the chapter.

The two major classifications of evaluation designs are experimental and descriptive, as introduced in Chapter 2.02. Quasi-experimental designs, as you will see in this chapter, might be classified as descriptive more than true experimental. True experimental and quasi-experimental designs, however, share some characteristics from a methodological perspective.

When attempting to show that a summative evaluation is really the result of an intervention, experimental methods are often used. For example, if an evaluator wanted to know if participation in a summer camp program resulted in increased self-esteem among young people, she or he would measure self-esteem scores before and after the camp session and compare those scores to before and after scores from young people who did not go to camp during that same period of time. Many types of experiments exist, but the true experiments are those where a randomized sample with a control group are used. Quasi-experimental evaluation methods, a "cousin" of experimental designs but more characteristic of descriptive procedures, do not necessarily control for randomized sample, control group, or use pretests. True experimental procedures are more valid if participants are "blind" about the group in which they are participating. That is, they know they are a part of an experiment, but they do not know to which group they have been assigned. In leisure service situations, however, individuals seldom are blind to the experiment.

Thus, the purpose of the experimental design in its purest form is to control as many of the factors as possible to minimize any outside effect that might account for change due to some intervention. In this way, the evaluator, as well as anyone using the results, can be assured that the results of the experiment represent what really happened. Experimental designs provide a way to measure the outcomes or impact of a program and/or what happened to individuals as a result of a particular intervention.

The Characteristics of Experimental Designs

According to evaluation textbooks, experimental designs range from "true" methods such as the pretest-posttest control group just described to single group methods that are essentially equivalent to one-group surveys or tests. For purposes of this discussion of experimental and quasi-experimental methods will be focused only on examples that use some type of comparison and/or pretest. To begin, however, we will discuss why randomization, control groups, and pretesting are important.

When no control group is used, several threats to the results concerning internal validity (i.e., whether the procedure really measured what it said it measured) occur. The first threat is maturation or whether a change might be due simply to a group maturing. For example, given a particular age group, basketball skills might improve naturally with practice regardless of what kind of instruction is given. To reiterate history or time passing may change people's abilities or knowledge. The effects of taking a test upon the scores of a second test may be a validity threat if a participant remembers how she or he answered the first time. Changes in the measuring instruments or changes in the observers or scoring can also pose a validity problem in conducting evaluations. The Hawthorne effect, or result of people improving just because they get attention, is also a possibility that can be addressed by using a control group. Sometimes no changes are seen in a group because of what is known as statistical regression. This phenomenon occurs when groups have extreme scores also known as the ceiling effect, and on a second testing, the scores tend to move back toward the mean because they were so high initially.

To randomize means to assign people to groups by chance. Randomization is important because selecting or choosing experimental and control units with different characteristics may affect the results. The mortality or differential loss of respondents must also be considered. Addressing the selection-maturation interaction, which is the different maturation of members of experimental and control groups, is a further value of using randomization in experimental designs. According to experts Campbell and Stanley (1963), randomization controls against many threats to the validity of the findings. Random assignment is highly desirable, although sometimes difficult, and often uncommon in many parks and recreation evaluation projects and research studies.

The major problem with using experimental designs is that controlled experiments are often impossible in real settings. Extra people may not exist who can serve as controls. Your professional obligations require that no one is denied services. Further, control group members may get angry if they don't get their choice about recreation services. These true experimental designs are difficult because the program must be held constant and formative evaluation isn't desirable in experimental designs. In using experiments in real life and not just in laboratories, a concern exists that evaluators often try to control too much and the recreation activity may become stale. Despite all these problems, experimental designs may still be a possible way to conduct useful evaluation projects.

Using Experimental Designs

Traditionally in research and evaluation books, certain symbols are used to indicate the procedure used:

E = group receiving the experimental treatment;
C = control group receiving no treatment;
R = randomized;
O = observation or testing done usually followed by a number; and
X = treatment.

The most common true experiment is the pretest-posttest control group with a random sample. For example, if you wanted to know if the skill level and knowledge of a group of children improved as a result of Saturday morning basketball instruction, you could set up an experiment whereby the children were assigned to two groups—one for instruction and one for free play. A pretest on skills could be given and then randomly divide the group in two with a similar skill level in each group. One group could be given instruction for six weeks while the other group engaged in free play. At the end of the period, the skill levels of both groups could again be tested and comparisons made of the differences between the pretest and posttest for each group. This experimental method would look like this:

| R | E | O1 | X | O2 |
| R | C | O1 | | O2 |

As is true in many cases in recreation, the evaluator may want to make sure that the control group does not miss an opportunity, so the group that did not receive instruction might be allowed to get six weeks of instruction after the experiment is completed. This procedure will assure that no ethical issues are being violated in doing harm to a group because the members of one group did not receive a program or treatment. In this case the design would look like:

| R | E | O1 | X | O2 | |
| R | C | O1 | | O2 | X |

The only possible problem with this pretest-posttest control group method is that the initial testing might have some effect on the results, but it is virtually impossible to control those effects unless you eliminate the pretest.

Other True Experiments

The Solomon Four-Group Design

The Solomon Four-Group Design is another example of a true experimental method. The configuration looks like this:

```
R    E    O1    X    O2
R    C    O1         O2
R    E          X    O
R    C               O
```

In the Solomon Four-Group design, four random groups are used. Two of those groups receive an observation or pretest at the beginning. One of those two groups then receives a treatment along with one of the other groups that was not pretested. At the conclusion of the treatment or the program, all four groups receive a posttest. This true experimental method assures that the pretest does not influence the results of the treatment of the posttest.

Posttest-Only Control Group

The Posttest-Only Control Group method does not have the problem of a possible interaction of having had a pretest. It resembles this configuration:

```
R    E    X    O
R    C         O
```

Two groups are randomly selected, and one receives a treatment. Both groups are then given a posttest to see if the treatment made any difference between the groups. The only problem with this method is that you are not always sure that you started out with similar groups, although the randomization ought to ensure that a similar baseline occurred.

Quasi-Experimental Methods

Quasi-experimental methods do not satisfy the strict requirements of the experiment. Campbell and Stanley (1963) have legitimized quasi-experimental methods as possibilities to be used in any number of settings. The best methods control relevant outside effects and lead to valid inferences about the effects of the program or treatment. Quasi-experimental methods, unfortunately, leave one or several threats to validity uncontrolled. These methods include the following examples:

Time-Series

In the time-series method, observations are taken several times before a treatment is applied and then, additional observations are used. The configuration looks like this:

E   O   O   O   O   X   O   O   O   O

One of the problems of the method is the inability to control the effects of history between measurements. Because a control group is not used, you would have to use this format in different situations to generalize the results more broadly. An example of a control group time-series is new playground equipment at a park. To conduct this time-series quasi-experiment, an evaluator would take several visitor counts at a park. New equipment would be installed and taking the counts at the park would continue (Ellis and Witt, 1982). You would see if participation increased in the park compared to what it was before the new equipment was installed.

Equivalent Time Samples

The equivalent time samples is an extension of the time-series method by alternating treatment and measurement. It looks like this:

E   XO   XO   XO   XO

The procedure is useful when the effects of the treatment are anticipated to be short-term. An example of its use might be in measuring how reality therapy could be used for patients with Alzheimer's disease in a therapeutic recreation program. You would do the therapy and make an observation and then do the therapy again and observe to see if repetition resulted in behavior changes. The disadvantage of this method is the inability to generalize the findings to other subjects in other settings.

Nonequivalent Control Group

This nonequivalent control group method has the same structure as the standard pretest-posttest control group with the exception that no random assignment of subjects to groups is made. This method assumes a random assignment. Often prearranged groups are used. For example, if an evaluator wanted to compare the gains in aerobic capacity made between people in a class taking step aerobics and a regular aerobics class, she or he could use the two groups that exist rather than randomly assigning them. The configuration looks like this:

E   O   X   O
C   O   O

Preexperimental Methods

Preexperimental methods are more descriptive than experimental methods, but they share some characteristics with true and quasi-experimental designs. The evaluator has to be careful, however, in referring to them as experimental methods because they result in descriptive (rather than predictive or cause-and-effect) outcomes.

One-Group Pretest Posttest

We will discuss the possibility of a one-group pretest posttest design briefly because it does have possibilities in evaluation even though it is more of a preexperimental or survey-oriented method than a quasi-experimental procedure. It looks like this:

$$E \qquad O \qquad X \qquad O$$

The advantage is the comparison between pre and post performances by the same subjects. The subjects would be tested for knowledge, attitude, or skill level before a treatment or program begins and then again after it is over. The disadvantage is the inability to accurately determine whether the differences from beginning to end are due to the treatment or some other variables.

Static-Group Comparison

The static-group comparison is also not technically experimental, but it has the comparison aspects of experiments in that a treatment is applied to one group of subjects. Testing or observation is then done on two groups, the one receiving treatment and another that had nothing. The method looks like this:

$$E \qquad X \qquad O$$
$$C \qquad\qquad O$$

The value of this preexperiment is that it can provide comparisons to evaluate a group after it is completed. The problem is the equivalence of the groups are unknown from the beginning.

One-Shot Case Study

A third common type of preexperimental method is referred to as the one-shot case study where a treatment is given and an observation is made. The basic configuration is this:

$$(R) \qquad E \qquad X \qquad O$$

This framework is used often in survey designs and will be discussed with surveys in the next two chapters. In the one-shot case study, the sample may or may not be randomized.

Making Experimental Design Decisions

As indicated above, a number of objections exist to experimental designs. Some people feel funny about being "guinea pigs" and some professionals do not wish to perpetuate that idea by using experimental designs for evaluation. In addition, the time and effort involved in planning experimental projects is obviously great. The values of using experimental and quasi-experimental procedures, however, cannot be discounted in doing summative evaluations and in assessing goal attainment. They are particularly good in assessing participant changes in behavior, skills, knowledge, or attitudes.

Experiments might be considered when a new program is introduced, when stakes are high, when there is controversy about program effectiveness, and when change or the value of something needs to be shown. Ultimately, experiments are best used to determine whether or not a program caused any personal or social change.

Regardless of how an experiment is used, several criteria must be considered. Adequate control must be guaranteed so the evaluator can be assured that the results were due to a treatment and not to something else. In the field of leisure studies, the results must apply to the real world. Comparisons are an essential component. Further, the measurement instruments must be sound. Thus, when you do experiments you will either have to choose existing instruments or develop instruments for measuring the pretest and posttest information. This information has been discussed in some detail in previous chapters. Finally, the experimental methods employed in leisure services evaluations need to be kept simple. Most evaluators lack the expertise to get into sophisticated evaluation projects using experimental designs. Figure 2.11 (page 192) shows a flow chart that may be useful in deciding whether to use experimental designs.

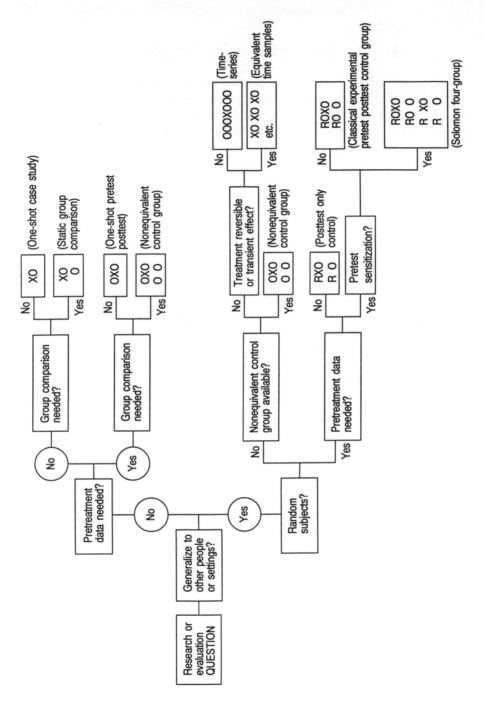

Figure 2.11 Decision Matrix for Experimental Designs
(adapted from Okey et al., 1977)

From Ideas to Reality

Experiments are commonly discussed in the scientific literature and have been a respected way that research and evaluation have been undertaken. These methods, however, are not always as easy to administer as are descriptive methods such as surveys and observations. Nevertheless, experiments have much to offer leisure service evaluators. They may be the most appropriate methods to use if we want to determine whether changes actually occur as a result of the programs and interventions that we conduct. Experimental designs are worth considering as options for particular kinds of evaluation situations.

2.12 SPECIFIC APPLICATIONS OF MEASUREMENT TECHNIQUES

Goals for Chapter 2.12:

—To describe how the evaluation methods might be applied to one or two specific situations; and,
—To analyze the possible strengths and weaknesses of any technique that might be applied to collecting data for evaluation.

This text has discussed descriptive and experimental designs and the broad method categories of surveys, observations, and unobtrusive measure. We will now examine some common applications of techniques used in evaluating leisure service organizations. Each of these techniques can be used to measure aspects of the five Ps (i.e., participants, personnel, places, policies, program) and can be applied to assessment, formative, and summative evaluations. The steps of determining criteria, selecting methods and samples for data collection and analysis, and using the information to make judgments applies to all of these techniques. We will address importance-performance, econometrics, case studies, single-subject designs, consensus techniques, sociometrics, and several other evaluation techniques.

Importance-Performance

A technique that has been popular in recent years is the use of importance-performance (I-P) questionnaires to measure program effectiveness. I-P is based on the notion that evaluation must be obtained from the consumer (Guadagnolo, 1985). Rossman (1982) found that the importance of a program is essential and that people were sometimes satisfied with performance aspects of programs that they did not indicate were important to them.

The I-P technique uses a measurement instrument to quantify customer satisfaction with performance by combining importance with satisfaction. Several steps are involved in the process. First, one must determine attributes to measure. These attributes can be discerned through literature review, focus group interviews, and/or the use of managerial judgment. Second, one must develop two sets of questions asking how important an attribute or amenity is to a participant and how satisfied the participant is with the organization's performance regarding that attribute or amenity. Third, data are collected using a Likert scale. Fourth, the responses to those two sets of questions are matched and the means or medians are plotted against one another on a two-way dimensional grid where importance is represented by one axis and performance and/or satisfaction are represented by the other. Finally, the respondents' perceptions are translated into management action through a facilitated interpretation. Figure 2.12(1) shows an example of the I-P grid.

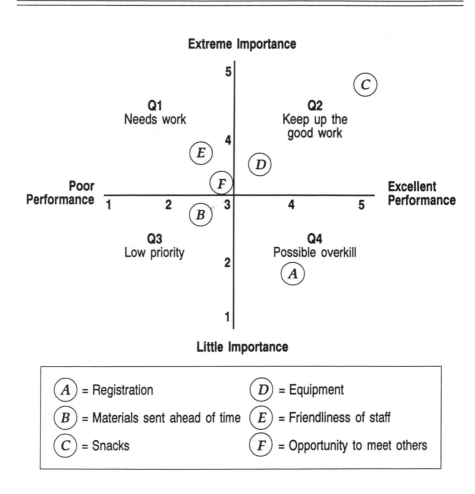

Figure 2.12(1) *Example of Importance-Performance Grid*

Elements in Quadrant (Q) 1 are perceived as high on importance but low on performance, and they represent areas requiring managerial attention (i.e., concentrate here). Q2 is perceived as high on both importance and performance. The status of performance should be maintained (i.e., keep up the good work). Q3 is perceived as low importance but high on performance, suggesting overcommitment of resources in these areas (i.e., possible overkill). Q4 is perceived as low on both importance and performance, which represents those attributes or amenities of low managerial priority.

Many different evaluation uses are possible for the I-P. Richardson (1987) described using it to analyze employees' perceptions of communication effectiveness within a large county parks and recreation department in the Midwest. In this project, the focus was on overall communication flows and sources. Hollenhorst, Olson, and Fortney (1992) used I-P to examine the importance of various attributes of the West Virginia state park cabin experience and to determine visitor satisfaction with these attributes. They examined factors like cleanliness, furniture, reservation systems, appliances, location, kitchenware, linens, bathtub showers, fireplaces, open porch, deck, cathedral ceilings, and telephones. They found that the cabin design and construction did not need to change. Visitors valued basic comforts, current rustic and simple character, seclusion, natural surroundings, and access to water-based recreation.

Guadagnolo (1985) used the I-P with the Pittsburgh Citiparks Department 10K race. He used the instrument to examine such aspects as preregistration, packet pick-up, awards, layout of course, challenge of course, running surfaces, restrooms, starting procedures, crowd control, traffic control, split times given, water stations, first-aid stations, medical care, temperature, adjacent parking, and time of day. He then segmented the runners on certain issues of satisfaction and examined these by groups including males vs. females, and repeat vs. first-time runners.

Bartlett and Einert (1992) evaluated the design features of a newly constructed adult softball complex and found the most acceptable features were the night lighting, perimeter fencing, grassed outfields, and restrooms. They focused on user perceptions as a means for planning designs. Havitz, Twynam, and DeLorenzo (1991) applied I-P to staff evaluations. They found that the same things used to attract customers may be used to attract staff, referred to as internal marketing. Items were measured such as attending training seminars and conferences, conducting training seminars for staff and volunteers, answering the phone (phone etiquette), responding to complaints from the public, giving tours to the public, handling funds and cash, monitoring inventories, initiating requisition requests, and preparing reports. These authors suggested that I-P helped to provide a clear outline for collecting and interpreting data, was tangible and easy-to-do, and allowed for gathering input from a number of employees.

Several tips must be kept in mind when using the I-P. First, one must determine the attributes to measure carefully. Second, be sure to separate importance from performance items on the questionnaire. Finally, as is true in any evaluation, the evaluator must interpret what the data mean after they have been analyzed.

Case Studies

Case studies are used to gather information about individuals or groups including communities, organizations, or institutions. Case studies may be the ultimate form of triangulation in that they require multiple methods and data sources. Case studies are not as "easy" to do as many people think; many aspects must be considered in doing an evaluation case study project.

According to Howe and Keller (1988), a case study is an intensive investigation of a particular unit; an analytical description or construction of a group as it is observed over a given period of time; or the in-depth study of the background, current status, or interactions of a given unit which might be an individual, social group, institution, or community. Case studies are particularly good if an evaluator is examining one situation and does not wish to compare it to another situation, individual, or group. Case studies are both specific and broad as they capture many variables and include descriptions of history and context. They are longitudinal because they tell a story that covers a period of time and usually qualitative because of prose and literary techniques.

The purpose of the case study is to measure how and why something occurs. In a case study, you are not necessarily concerned about generalizing the results to other situations, although case studies often give insight to other situations. You might choose a unique case or a critical case to evaluate such as just one particular team. Further, qualitative and/or quantitative data may be collected. A single case study or several case studies in combination might be done. If multiple cases are used, a similar system and logic should be used in data collection for each. The important aspect in designing a case study evaluation is to determine the unit to be examined whether it is an individual, event, or small group.

Case study techniques are frequently used in therapeutic recreation to analyze a particular client situation. For example, a Case History Review approach has been used in the *Therapeutic Recreation Journal* to provide a basis for examining aspects of therapeutic recreation. Practicing therapeutic recreation specialists write about particular cases and include an assessment, goals and objectives, program planning, implementation, and evaluation as it pertains to a particular person in a situation. The intent of these case studies is to show how the therapeutic recreation process works through treatment.

According to the procedures used for any type of evaluation, the evaluator will need to do the following:

1. identify the focus of the investigation;
2. outline what needs to be studied;
3. select appropriate measurement tools;
4. develop a plan to collect the data considering effectiveness, efficiency, budget and time frame;
5. collate all the data;
6. interpret the data; and,
7. make recommendations from the study.

For case studies, many methods previously discussed might be used to gather relevant data.

Data collected for case studies will vary depending on the situation. Data included might be observations, interviews, parent interviews and other individual interviews, review of documents, archival records, clinical or organizational records, life history profiles, diaries, and reports. Often longitudinal information is collected to provide a historical context. In addition, a multidisciplinary (i.e., using psychological, social, economic, and other information) assessment of the participant, group, or organization is done with an emphasis on precise descriptions. These data are then assembled, organized, and condensed. The analysis for case study data consists of examining, categorizing, tabulating, and recombining evidence, just as is done in other forms of qualitative data collection. Similarly, case studies use pattern making, explanation building, and are conducted over a period of time.

Writing the case study report is ongoing and occurs during the entire process of doing the case study. A final case study narrative is presented which provides a readable, descriptive picture of the unit (person, group, organization, or program) that was examined. It should make accessible to the reader all the information necessary to understand the person or program. A case study may be presented either chronologically or thematically. As a case study is read, you should get a sense that all aspects of a situation have been addressed. The final product should show the patterns that developed, explain what happened, and show information over a period of time. The boundaries of the case study should be clear with alternative perspectives offered along with evidence to support the conclusions that are made. The report should combine descriptive, analytic, interpretive, and evaluative perspectives into the report.

Doing good case studies requires several competencies. The evaluator must be able to ask questions that address the criteria being examined, be a good listener, be adaptive and flexible, be able to put together ideas, and be unbiased. As indicated above, using multiple sources helps in this process. Taking good notes, just as in field observation, is essential. All data sources need to be pulled together in a systematic order. According to Yin (1984), it is essential that multiple sources of evidence are used, a case study data base is created, and that one maintains a chain of evidence concerning the data that is collected.

Case studies have sometimes been criticized for their lack of rigor and lack of generalization and comparisons. Sometimes they appear to be "easy" to do, but generally they require great time and effort. Exemplary case studies are significant, complete, consider alternative perspectives, display sufficient evidence, and engage the reader in an understanding of the case being studied. Case studies may be applied or generalized across settings if a congruity exists between the case and where it will be used. The case study report must be written in such a way that people can see how their situation may or may not be like the case being described. The purpose of case studies is to allow the evaluator to learn the intricate details of how something is working, rather than necessarily to generalize to other situations.

Single-Subject Techniques

A single-subject technique allows you to evaluate the effect of interventions on an individual participant or client. Single-subject techniques use an application of time-series experimental methods with subjects being their own control. Multiple and repeated assessments are used to measure intervention and its effects on an individual. Both qualitative and quantitative information can be provided.

The single-subject technique is similar to the case study except only one person or a very small number of people are used as the sample for the evaluation. According to Dattilo (1988a; 1988b) the single-subject technique offers a way to make informed decisions about the quality of a recreation program and provides a context for understanding behavior dynamics. The technique allows the evaluator to learn the details of how treatment is working for an individual rather than averaging the effects across a number of cases.

The focus of single-subject evaluation is on an individual; a series of measurements or observations occur over a period of time to determine how an individual may be changing as a result of a particular recreation program or as in therapeutic recreation, a particular treatment plan or intervention. Figure 2.12(2) shows an example of the way a single-subject data plot might look. The procedure used is to measure a behavior for an individual before treatment, apply a treatment, and withdraw the treatment and measure. This establishes a baseline (A) over a period of time the treatment will be given and reinforced and then additional measures are taken, after a treatment period (B) is over, follow-up measures (C) will be used to see if and how long the behavior continues.

A single-subject technique will often address the rate and level of attainment of objectives, program strengths and weaknesses, standards of individual performance, validity of innovations and trends, and cost benefits. The technique does not lack precision and sensitivity. As in other situations, however, the results of single-subject analysis can be compromised by inadequate assessment tools,

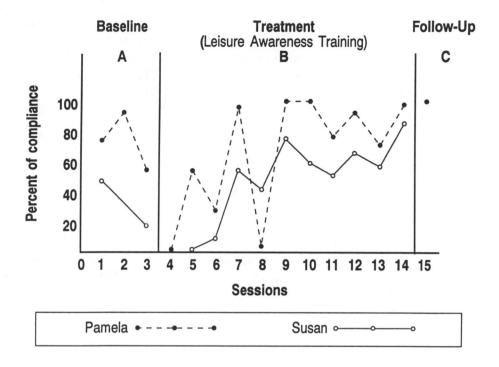

Figure 2.12(2) Example of a Plot for Single-Subject Technique

measurement procedures (Dattilo, 1988a), or observation techniques. Although most of the studies using the single-subject technique in therapeutic recreation have used quantitative data, qualitative data could also be used. The value of single-subject evaluation techniques lies in using patterns identified in baseline and intervention conditions to determine how intervention affects an individual.

Econometric Techniques

The policy/administrative application of evaluation often includes a focus on techniques for economic evaluation. Economic impact and cost-benefit analyses are commonly used techniques and require a great deal more explanation if they are to be applied to park, recreation, tourism, and leisure services organizations. A brief description of some econometric techniques, however, may be useful.

Economic impact evaluations are done to measure the role of a special event on the local economy. Those data are often difficult to gather and expensive to analyze, although standard questionnaire development and analysis can be applied. Economic impact studies attempt to determine both the direct and indirect financial benefits of an activity by gathering expenditure data. For example, if an evaluator wanted to measure the economic impact of a sporting event, she or he would get expenditure data from a sample of visitors and then extrapolate to an entire group. A multiplier is used which refers to the fact that money spent can be spent again and again. An increase in spending will create an indirect effect greater than the original expenditures. A multiplier of 2.0 is a conservative multiplier to use. For every dollar of income spent, two dollars circulate through a community. For example, if someone pays to stay in a hotel, the hotel owner will then pay his or her housekeeping staff who will then go out and buy groceries. The grocer will have money to pay his employees who will then spend their money on clothes for their children and so on. Therefore, the initial money spent will continue to multiply.

Economic impact can be measured along with other data like visitor satisfaction. One can find examples of economic impact studies in the *Journal of Park and Recreation Administration* such as those done by Gitleson, Guadagnolo, and Moore (1988); Loomis (1989); Yardley, MacDonald, and Clark (1990); and Kanters and Botkin (1992).

Little consensus exists concerning the best way to analyze costs and benefits. Costs are not hard to determine but benefits are difficult to measure in either economic or noneconomic terms. In cost-benefit analysis, the evaluator has to determine the benefits in monetary terms. In cost-effectiveness one looks at the cost in relation to some type of outcome that may not be economic. Henderson (1988) has given an example of how cost-effectiveness might be determined in relation to volunteers (Table 2.12). The cost-effectiveness evaluation technique provides additional information from an economic view; however, it does not suffice for evaluating other aspects of volunteers and volunteer programs. An evaluator can do a similar analysis with other leisure service programs to determine how much they cost. One must be careful, however, not to make decisions about programs based solely on costs. Some programs that cost more also have many more benefits that are difficult to measure.

A criticism of cost-benefits approaches is that it is hard to put a price on psychic benefits and the value of lives. The appropriate units of analysis are often difficult to determine. The problems associated with economic analysis should not prevent an evaluator from considering the possibilities in examining policy/administrative aspects of an organization.

Consensus Techniques

The nominal group technique (NGT) and the Delphi technique are examples of consensus strategies that can be used for evaluation. The Air Force, for example, used the nominal group technique to assess future directions (Lankford and

Table 2.12

Cost-Effectiveness Analysis Worksheet
(adapted from Henderson, 1988)

A. Costs

    1. *Direct*
        a. coordinator's salary $ _____
        b. recordkeeping/secretarial   _____
        c. recognition materials   _____
        d. expenses—mileage, meals, etc.   _____
        e. printed materials   _____
        f. office supplies   _____
        g. insurance   _____
        h. other   _____

                                       Total direct $ _____

    2. *Indirect*
        a. overhead   _____
        b. other staff   _____
        c. equipment   _____
        d. other   _____

                                   Total indirect $ _____

                      Total Cost (direct plus indirect) *$*_____ *(A)*

B. Outputs

    1. activity   = # of Vol. x # of hours   x rate/hr. = $ _____
        a. _____   _____ x _____ x ____ = _____
        b. _____   _____ x _____ x ____ = _____
        c. _____   _____ x _____ x ____ = _____
        d. _____   _____ x _____ x ____ = _____
        e. _____   _____ x _____ x ____ = _____
        f. _____   _____ x _____ x ____ = _____
                                           $ _____
             Total (B)   *Total (C)*   *Total (D)*

C. Cost-effectiveness analysis

    Output (D)/Cost (A) = 1: ____ ratio
    For every $1 spent, $X of service are provided

D. Number of participants served by volunteers

E. Other calculations

    Cost (A) # of Volunteer (B) = Cost per volume
    Cost (A) # of Hours Volunteered (C) = Cost per service hour
    Cost (A) # of Participants Served (D) = Cost per client

DeGraaf, 1992). Nominal group technique is a means to identify issues, opportunities, and ways to reach potential participants. This collective decision-making technique can be used for strategic planning, policy development, and goal formation. More structured than brainstorming, the evaluator can obtain consensus on ideas and strategies.

Delbecq, Van de Ven and Gustafson (1975) outlined a six-step process for nominal group technique:

1. introduce topic and explain;
2. participants write down responses on card;
3. all responses are listed;
4. items are clarified;
5. individuals vote on the issues identified; and,
6. votes are tabulated.

You can go through this process twice to get additional information and you can assign value to the tabulated votes.

The most often used consensus method is the Delphi technique. Although the data in a Delphi study are often analyzed quantitatively, they are collected initially using a qualitative process. The Delphi technique is frequently used to establish goals, determine strategies, predict problems, access group preferences, and project needs. Weatherman and Swenson (1974) suggested that the critical characteristics of the Delphi technique are that it relies on the informed judgment of knowledgeable panels concerning a topic that has little reliable objective data. The technique is done anonymously with controlled feedback given to produce a group response.

The first step involved in the technique is to select a panel of "experts" for the topic being addressed. The number of individuals is not as important as the quality of the panel. An open-ended questionnaire is then sent to the panel. The responses to that questionnaire are grouped and tabulated; a second questionnaire is sent asking people to rate on a Likert scale the importance of all the initial responses received. The second questionnaire is tabulated and a final questionnaire is sent to obtain additional ratings and rankings to move toward as much consensus as possible. The final product of the Delphi generally looks like a ranking of the most important issues that the panel uncovers.

Sociometrics

Sociometrics are used to analyze how groups operate by asking how people "get along" with each other. Sociograms are a tool used to identify how members of a subgroup interact and how they function. The sociogram illustrates choices made in a group by plotting them on a matrix. According to Lundegren and Farrell (1985), one merely asks, "Name three people with whom you would most like to work as a partner for the xyz group?" You could ask any question such as, "With whom do you like to play?" (for children), "With whom would you like to go to lunch?" (for adults), or "Who is most supportive of you in the work environment?" This technique is not designed for large groups. It works best with groups of less than twenty.

The evaluator then sets up a matrix with each person's name across the top and down the side. The choices are tallied. You could analyze between sex choices if desirable or any other category that seems appropriate. Figure 2.12(3) shows

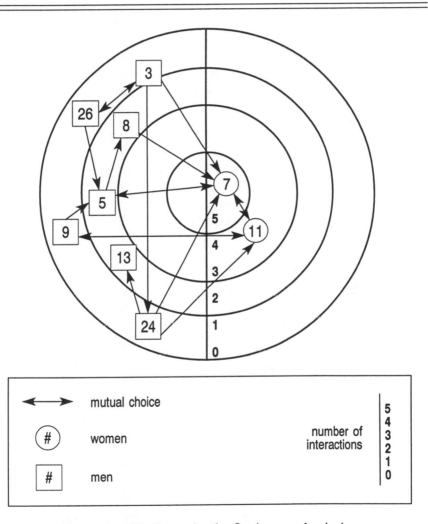

Figure 2.12(3) Example of a Sociogram Analysis

an example of a sociogram analysis (Lundegren and Farrell, 1985). Four concentric circles are then drawn representing the level of choice with the highest in the center. Indicators [circles and squares in Figure 2.12(3)] are labeled and entered onto the diagram. Arrows are drawn for each individual to the symbol of the person chosen. If the choice is reciprocated, a double-headed arrow for mutual choice is used. The process indicates who is most chosen and also shows the isolates. It also tells where pairs are and shows simple choices as well as mutual choices. This technique might be useful for analyzing group cohesiveness or how a group can function better.

Miscellaneous Evaluation Techniques

A number of other techniques have been described in the recreation and leisure services literature that might be of interest to evaluators. We encourage you to check these references if more details about any of the techniques are needed. They provide further examples to consider and will be described briefly.

Nine-Cell Program Planning

O'Sullivan (1988) has written about a nine-cell strategy of program planning and evaluation. This approach examines different programs and assesses them by industry attractiveness (external) and business strength (internal), which she refers to as program potential and organizational capability. The program potential includes the market size, market growth rate, profit margin, competition, cyclicality, seasonality, and scale economies. The organizational capabilities includes the market share, price competitiveness, program quality, knowledge of participant, and sale effectiveness. One can ascertain these ratings by gathering professional staff together and having them numerically rate each category, assign points, average the items, and give a rating to each activity. You also might weight the items within the group. If you think product quality is three times more important than market share, it would calculated that way. Once all activities have been categorized, they are plugged into the cells with either program as high, medium, or low and organizational capacity as strong, average, or weak [see Figure 2.12(4)]. For the three "go" categories, you can allocate resources. In the black categories, programs can be eliminated. You will need to think carefully about grays. The value of the nine-cell approach is that it allows evaluation of several programs by comparing them to each other.

Report Cards

Report cards can be used to focus on indicators of satisfaction. They use items and ask people to rank them as A=excellent, B=better than average, C=average,

Organizational Capability (OC)

	Strong	Average	Weak
High	High PP Strong OC	High PP Average OC	High PP Weak OC
Medium	Medium PP Strong OC	Medium PP Average OC	Medium PP Weak OC
Low	Low PP Strong OC	Low PP Average OC	Low PP Weak OC

Program Potential (PP)

☐ White (go)	☐ Gray (caution)	◼ Black (stop)

Figure 2.12(4) O'Sullivan's Nine-Cell Planning Screen
(adapted from O'Sullivan, 1988)

D=below average, or E=poor. When used in a park, one might ask about first impression, helpfulness of staff, cleanliness of restrooms, information at park, attractiveness at park, safety and security, cleanliness of ground, ease of access, hours of operation, control of pets, and overall satisfaction. You can then use GPA averages to rank services: 4.0 - 3.8 = A, 3.79 - 3.67 = A-, 3.66 - 3.33 = B+, 3.32 - 3.00 = B, 2.99 - 2.67 = B-, 2.66 - 2.33 = C+. The evaluator could look at these grades over a period of time or compare one facility to another. It is usually best to include qualitative summaries with both the letter grades and the numbers.

Service Quality

Service quality is a concept that is being measured frequently these days according to Wright, Duray, and Goodale (1992) and MacKay and Crompton (1990). The premise of service quality evaluation is that consumers are more demanding and an increased competition for customers exists. Five quality dimensions of expectations and perceptions are measured in this approach including tangibles, reliability, responsiveness, assurance, and empathy. The expectations are measured with a statement such as, "Tell us the degree to which you think an excellent recreation center should have the features described in the following statements." A seven-point Likert scale anchored from not at all essential to absolutely essential is used. The perception part asks individuals to "tell us the degree to which you feel Center X has the features described in each statement." A seven-point Likert scale of strongly agree to strongly disagree is used. Features included such aspects as prompt repairs to facilities and equipment, clean and sanitary shower and lockers, good quality healthy food at snack bar, staff interested in patrons, and accurate class descriptions (Wright, Duray, and Goodale, 1992). A service quality score is obtained by subtracting the mean expectation rating from the mean performance rating. Negative results indicate where a "service gap" exists. Zero implied met expectations. In using this approach, adaptations can be made in the item pool for a particular service. Similar to importance-performance, this method is proving to be useful to evaluators in all areas of leisure service management.

From Ideas to Reality

This entire chapter has been an example of how specific approaches using the methods described previously can be applied to evaluation in leisure services. We can learn a great deal from seeing how others have applied methods and developed instruments. In addition to considering some of these possible applications, we encourage you to read journals like the *Journal of Park and Recreation Administration* and *Therapeutic Recreation Journal* to see how others have conducted evaluation projects and to read *Leisure Sciences* and *The Journal of Leisure Research* to learn more about doing research studies.

2.13 Triangulation

Goals for Chapter 2.13:

—To define triangulation;
—To give examples of how triangulation might be used between methods and within methods;
—To identify possible sources of data triangulation; and,
—To describe the problems that may be encountered when triangulating in an evaluation project.

As you know, a variety of method choices and sampling possibilities exist for doing evaluation projects. The use of more than one method, more than one source of data, or more than one evaluator often strengthens an evaluation project. The use of more than one method, source of data, or evaluator is referred to as triangulation. It may be economical to use only one method, source of data, or evaluator, but the possibility for more reliable and valid results obtained from triangulation ought to be considered.

Triangulated Methods

No one method is perfect, so more than one method, referred to as method triangulation, may give additional information to an evaluator. Howe and Keller (1988) suggest that triangulated program evaluation is kindred to the case study. Triangulation is often useful when what is being evaluated is compact (e.g., a given continuing education program), where the subjects are clustered in settings that have definite boundaries in time and location, and when it is desired to know why and how well a program works and how it or similar future programs might be improved. Two types of triangulated methods are frequently used: within method and between method triangulation.

Within method triangulation includes the collection of both qualitative and quantitative data using the same method. Issues of complementariness of qualitative or quantitative are sometimes debated, but it must be kept in mind that methods themselves are neither qualitative nor quantitative as discussed in Chapter 2.01. Depending how a method is used will result in either or both qualitative and quantitative data. Some evaluators feel that combining qualitative and quantitative data is difficult to do from a purist view, but it is not uncommon to ask survey questions that may be both closed-ended (quantitative) and open-ended (qualitative). Different data are received depending on the use of open-ended or close-ended questions.

Between method triangulation is the use of two or more methods to measure the same phenomena. This form of triangulation strengthens the validity of the overall findings. Congruence relates to similarity, consistency, or convergence of results obtained from two or more methods, whereas complementariness refers to one set of results enriching, expanding upon, clarifying, or illustrating the other. An independent assessment of the same phenomena results in complementary results. For example, you might observe an event and also interview a selected group of people that were in attendance at that event. Or you might use participation records from document analysis and then survey a sample of participants to determine their satisfaction with an activity.

Greene and McClintock (1985) suggested that between method triangulation can be differentiated along two dimensions: (a) the degree of independence of the methods used for data collection and (b) the degree to which the implementation of both methods is sequential versus concurrent. The evaluator will need to decide which approach is going to be the best: to have one method follow another or to use two methods at the same time. Evaluators often use qualitative approaches such as focus groups to get information that will then allow them to develop quantitative questionnaires. In addition, sometimes quantitative data are collected and then interviews are used to understand the meaning behind some of the numbers. Nothing is wrong with combining qualitative and quantitative data in these ways and the combination may make for a deeper and more useful project. Howe and Keller (1988) have provided a description of how qualitative and quantitative methods might be used together in Table 2.13.

The biggest problem with mixed method evaluation in leisure services is that few good examples and guidelines exist. The evaluator, however, can make a case for triangulated methods by examining the independence or congruence, as well as the complementariness, of the methods used. Further, triangulated methods can reduce threats to internal and external validity. The evaluator must be aware of the strengths and weaknesses of methods and data when they are used together.

Triangulated Sources of Data

Different participants (sources of data) can provide insight about a topic or issue. An evaluation project often can benefit from more than one data source. For example, if you were interested in the changes that occurred in campers as a result of going to a four-week summer camp, you might talk to campers, but you also might interview counselors and their parents. You would be getting data from different sources that address the same evaluation criteria.

An evaluator might also get data from different periods of time as another example of triangulated sources. For example, before a program begins, you

Table 2.13

Summary of Benefits from Triangulating Methods
(adapted from Howe and Keller, 1988)

Contributions of Qualitative Data to Quantitative Data

Design
Qualitative data can enrich quantitative data by improving:
1. the sampling framework by exploratory interviews and observations to confirm or rationalize the framework.
2. the overall study design by prioritizing information needs and posing the right questions.

Data Collection
Qualitative data collection can enrich quantitative data collection by improving:
1. the instrument package by exploratory interviews and observations of the receptivity, frames of reference, and attention spans of subjects.
2. instrument administration and interpretation by pretesting for validity, reliability, and utility.

Data Analysis
Qualitative data analysis can enrich quantitative data analysis by providing:
1. a conceptual framework to guide the analysis developed from multiple data sources to guide instrumentation, data collection procedures, and analysis.
2. verification of quantitative findings in areas where methods yield an overlap of information.
3. item construction for questionnaires which can be generated from initial observational data.
4. external validation of empirically generated constructs when compared to observational data.
5. case study illustrations of statistically derived models.
6. clarification of quantitative findings by comparing them with field notes covering the same topics.

Contributions of Quantitative Data to Qualitative Data

Design
Quantitative data can enrich qualitative data by identifying:
1. representative cases to serve the goal of generalizability.
2. unrepresentative cases to refine models and theories.

Data Collection
Quantitative data collection can enrich qualitative data collection by providing:
1. leads for later interviews and observations probing specific areas.
2. information about overlooked subjects or less engaged respondents within the sample.
3. correction of the "elite" bias or "gatekeeper" effect of a highly articulate and engaged informant.

Data Analysis
Quantitative methods can contribute to the understanding of qualitative analysis by:
1. correcting the tendency to observe all aspects of a situation as congruent.
2. verifying qualitative interpretations by statistical analysis.
3. casting new light on field observations by yielding unanticipated findings.

might ask about expectations. After it is over you might ask if those expectations were fulfilled. The sources of data would be dependent on the timing of the data collection.

An evaluator might also use the decision makers for an evaluation project as one important additional source of data. For example, you might interview the Board of Directors of an organization as a source of additional data for making decisions. Other sources of data might be program records, program participants, staff delivering programs, family members and other significant relationships to participants, observations made by evaluator, and/or community-level indices. The potential sources of data are numerous for most evaluation projects.

Triangulation Using Multiple Evaluators

Triangulated perspectives are obtained from multiple evaluators. If more than one person is interpreting results, developing instruments, or doing interviews, it is likely that more information will be uncovered. "Two heads are better than one" applies here. Many times evaluation projects are done as a team effort and this teamwork provides the potential for the highest quality because of the variety of perspectives that can be incorporated into a final product.

Cautions in Using Triangulation

Regardless of what form of triangulation is used, the evaluator must report the design and results for all triangulated aspects. Triangulation does not guarantee overcoming all biases. Be careful not just to proliferate methods, sources or evaluators, but to see how they can be integrated. You can compound the error in a poorly designed project that lacks specific criteria if more methods or more sources are added. Problems also arise when data are in conflict due to triangulation. You have to acknowledge that possible situation and try to interpret what is meant by the discrepancies that you may uncover.

From Ideas to Reality

Triangulation is often a great idea, but it can also be expensive in terms of time and money. Most evaluation projects involve limited budgets, short time frames, and political constraints. It is better to use one good method, source of data, or evaluator than a series of poorly implemented methods or sources. If possible, however, triangulated methods, sources, and evaluators can often enhance the reliability, validity, and usability of an evaluation project.

Unit Three—Evidence:
Data Analysis

INTRODUCTION TO DATA ANALYSIS

Once data are collected, the data analysis begins. The exception to this rule is in qualitative interviews and field observations where the data analysis occurs simultaneously with the data collection. Regardless, analysis is a part of the evaluation process pertaining to "evidence" that must be carefully considered. Unit Three will continue the discussion of evidence, but we will specifically address what to do with data and how to manage it so judgments can be made about its meaning.

Data analysis is an aspect of evaluation that scares many people because they associate it with statistics. In fact, when some people think of evaluation, they think about statistics immediately. The math anxiety that some people experience has resulted in fear of doing evaluation projects. This is not to suggest that statistics are easy to comprehend, but neither are they that complex.

This unit will spend considerable time discussing measurement, organizing and coding data, using simple descriptive statistics, and determining the relationships among variables. Data analysis is an exciting aspect of evaluation because it helps evaluators understand what their data mean. We will also talk about how computers make statistical analyses easy in our high-tech society. The adage goes, however, "garbage in, garbage out." An evaluator must know how to get a computer to give the appropriate statistics that will be useful in drawing conclusions and making recommendations.

How to analyze qualitative data is also discussed. Because qualitative data is not mathematical, some people assume that these types of data are easy to analyze. Qualitative analysis is different, but not necessarily easier, than quantitative analysis. When you have completed this unit, you should have a good working knowledge of data analyses that use common statistical procedures and typical qualitative data analysis strategies.

3.01 DATA ACCORDING TO MEASUREMENT

Goals for Chapter 3.01:

—To identify the differences between the levels of data measurement;
—To choose the independent and dependent variables that might be used in a statistical analysis; and,
—To determine whether a univariate, bivariate, or multivariate data analysis would be most appropriate.

Two kinds of data exist in the world: continuous and discrete. Continuous data can be thought of as data that can be measured along a continuum and can take on endless possibilities of intermediate values (Lundegren and Farrell, 1985). Examples of continuous data would be weight, speed, time, and temperature. Values are considered to be approximate because even though the technology applied to measuring instruments might be sophisticated, we can never be exact.

The other kind of data is called discrete data. These data are noncontinuous and finite. There can be no "in-between" numbers as in continuous data. For example, the number of bicyclers to ride a trail on the weekend is a discrete number. With discrete data, we can count "things" that result in an exact number.

Levels of Data Measurement

During the evaluation process, different types of data are collected. In many instances these data are words, observations, or numbers. Measurement is the process of turning the words and observations into numbers that can then be used in statistical analyses. An evaluator must be able to distinguish the level of measurement obtained to make the right choices for statistical procedures. For example, data that are nominal or categorical, like biological sex, will be treated differently from continuous data such as a test score. These levels of data measurement can be divided into four distinct groups: nominal, ordinal, interval, and ratio.

Nominal, or categorical data, are the "lowest" typology because no assumption is made about relationships between values. Each value defines a distinct category with no overlap and serves to label or name a particular group. The numeric values attached to the nominal data are merely identifiers that allow the responses to be counted for later analysis. Examples of nominal data are items such as sex, birthplace, or a yes/no response.

Ordinal data are more sophisticated than nominal data. Each category has a position that is higher or lower than another group, but you do not know how much higher or lower. Although the data are ranked or rated, no distance is measured. Both rankings and ratings use ordinal scales. Ratings generally define points on a scale, and any number of people may be assigned a given point. In rankings, the individuals form a kind of scale with each person having a place in the ordering. Therefore, in rankings, the individuals form the scale, while in ratings, the scale preexists. An example of ordinal data used in a rating would be the classification of employees as leaders, supervisors, or administrators with the ordering based upon responsibility or skills. An example of ranked data could be the list of finishers in a marathon based upon their race times. Although these data are discrete and categorical, they differ from nominal data because they have an order.

More precision is needed when an evaluator wants to add scores or calculate averages. Unlike ordinal data where the distance between categories is not equal, data are needed that have equal intervals. *Interval data* result when the ordered categories have meaningful size differences or distance between values. The interval scale, however, does not have an inherently determined zero point. This type of data allows you to study differences between items, but not their proportionate magnitudes. An example of interval data would be temperature. The difference between 40°F and 41°F is the same as between 80°F and 81°F but 80°F is not twice as hot as 40°F because 0°F by definition is not equal to the absence of heat. Those who have lived in the north know that below zero days are a reality; there is no point at which you can say this is as cold as it can get. Therefore, no inherent zero point exists.

At this point you may be asking yourself, "Where do Likert scales fit?" The definitive answer is, "It depends." Philosophically, many statistical purists believe that Likert scales can only be treated as ordinal data, because they are discrete and categorical data that provide a type of rating scale. Other statisticians believe that these scales can legitimately be viewed as interval data because the ordered categories have meaningful size differences. As will be seen later in the discussion on statistical procedures, defining the data as ordinal limits the analyses available to the less powerful statistics. Many researchers and evaluators will choose to treat Likert scale data as interval data and use a variety of statistical calculations.

The most sophisticated data are *ratio data*. Ratio data have a true zero point as well as all of the ordering and distancing properties of interval data. Height is an example of ratio data because a six-foot tall adult is truly twice as tall as a three-foot tall child.

Evaluators must be aware of the different levels of measurement for data because each statistical procedure requires a specific level. For example, if you wanted to explore the relationship between two types of information that were categorical, or nominal level data (e.g., sex, job title), a chi-square analysis would be appropriate; however, if those data were interval data (e.g., self-esteem scores, age) then a Pearson Correlation analysis might be the best choice.

Describing Variables

In preparing to analyze data, the evaluator will need to define the variables. For example, each separate item on a questionnaire is a variable which, in turn, may become an element that can be analyzed. The initial selection of variables for an evaluation is made when evaluation criteria are selected and the items for a survey are drafted into questions for the respondents to answer, or during the development of an observation checklist. These variables might include demographic information such as age and sex, behavioral aspects such as the type of recreation program in which they participate and frequency of participation, or attitudes including program satisfaction and the importance of facility amenities.

Variables are often classified as dependent or independent. In most cases, variables can be divided into dependent variables (ones that can be influenced), and independent variables (ones that can exert influence). For example, if you were interested in how frequently men and women participated in open swim at a community center, the frequency of swimming may be *dependent* on the sex of the individual (independent variable) completing the questionnaire. Thus, variables like sex, age, and ethnicity are usually independent variables while variables like participation rates, scale scores, and rating scales are often dependent variables.

Types of Analyses

Three types of analyses can be conducted using quantitative data. These analyses depend upon whether you want to examine the characteristics of just one variable, two variables, or more than two variables.

Univariate analysis is the examination of the distribution of cases on only one variable. This type of analysis includes the frequency distribution (the percentage and values) of a particular variable as well as measures of central tendency (mean, median, mode). These analyses are generally used for descriptive purposes. For example, an evaluator may want to know the numbers and percentages of individuals from different ethnic groups that completed a survey about community center programs. A univariate analysis would tell how many people and the percentage of the total that represented these groups.

Bivariate analysis is the evaluation of two variables. Usually one is independent and the other is dependent. This type of analysis is descriptive, but allows you to compare subgroups. For example, an evaluator can now compare the frequency of participation in community center programs by individuals of different ethnic groups, such as African-Americans, Hispanics, European-Americans, and Asian-Americans. With bivariate statistics one can find out if African-Americans participate more than Hispanics, for example.

The third type of analysis, *multivariate analysis*, is just like bivariate except that this analysis uses two or more independent variables and one dependent variable. For example, the frequency of participation could be analyzed by sex and ethnicity; in other words, you could tell if participation rates were different for men and women from different ethnic groups who participated in community center programs. Both bivariate and multivariate analyses are used to explain and compare subgroups.

From Ideas to Reality

Types of analysis options are important. As you will see shortly, a multitude of statistical procedures exist for your use. Evaluators need to determine the type and level of data measurement generated by the evaluation, select and analyze independent and dependent variables, and make the appropriate statistical choices that will best address the evaluation questions. These decisions are not always easy to make, but if you have a solid understanding of the data that you are collecting, the analysis process will be easier to conduct and understand.

3.02 Organizing and Coding Quantitative Data: Getting Your Data Together

```
┌─────────────────────────────────────────────────────────────────┐
│                    Goals for Chapter 3.02:                        │
│                                                                   │
│  —To identify values as they relate to variables within a questionnaire; │
│  —To code data with as much specificity as measured;              │
│  —To write a code book for any given questionnaire;               │
│  —To enter data onto a coding sheet in the appropriate format; and, │
│  —To decide how to handle missing data.                           │
└─────────────────────────────────────────────────────────────────┘
```

A critical step in data analysis involves how the information from an evaluation measurement instrument is organized and coded. The easiest way to think about data organization is to imagine each questionnaire as a case or observation that has a set of variables with values. Each case has only one value for each variable. In other words, each individual has one answer to each question. The case, usually the individual who completes the questionnaire or a specific observation, becomes the basic unit upon which measurements are taken. A case could also be a larger unit such as a park and recreation department, a time period such as the month in which measurements were taken, or a special event.

Once the pilot study is done, the evaluator must decide how to systematically organize and record the information. As soon as the data are collected, the actual recording procedure can begin. Data should be recorded in as much detail as possible. Specific information can always be recoded into larger groups later in the analysis process. For example, age as a value for each case could be recorded as the respondent's actual age and recoded or grouped later into age categories; however, if age is originally recorded as two values such as individuals age 54 and younger and individuals age 55 and older, only these two age categories can *ever* be used in the analyses. By reducing the number of values for a variable, you also have eliminated the possibility of getting specific statistics such as the average age of your respondents. The evaluator can always recode and combine values later, but she or he cannot expand them beyond the values recorded from the original measurement data.

The data from the variables are usually assigned numbers, called values, to represent the responses. This process is known as coding. When just numbers are used, the system is numeric coding. For example, instead of entering "agree" or "disagree" into the computer, the evaluator could code an agree response as a "1" and a disagree response as a "2." When using computers for analysis purposes, this numeric coding makes the process of getting from verbal responses to statistical answers easier.

Since a coding system is often arbitrary, creating a code book is helpful to the evaluator. The code book is like a road map. It tells the evaluator, and anyone else who might be using the data for statistical procedures, how the data are coded. For a very short and simple questionnaire, the code book may not be necessary but it is usually a helpful tool for the evaluator to create. Most code books are simple to put together. Usually the code book will include the variable name, the value labels for each variable, and the corresponding question from the questionnaire. If the data are to be entered into a computer for statistical analysis, the code book can also include additional information such as the location of the data in the record and the number of columns allocated for each variable. Table 3.2(1) is an example of questions from a survey that will generate data and Table 3.2(2) is the corresponding code book.

Table 3.2(1)

Sample Survey Questions

1. Do you feel that women have as many opportunities to advance in the field as men?
   ___ Yes   ___ No   ___ Don't know

2. Please indicate the extent to which you agree or disagree with these statements as they apply to the Park and Recreation field.

	Strongly Disagree	Disagree	Neither Agree nor Disagree	Agree	Strongly Agree
a. Women are often excluded from informal male networks	1	2	3	4	5
b. There is unconscious discrimination based on gender	1	2	3	4	5
c. Women tend to work in areas that are not promotable	1	2	3	4	5
d. Women are less committed to their careers because of family obligations	1	2	3	4	5

3. What is your age? _____ years

Table 3.2(2)

Example of a Code Book

Column #	Variable Name	Variable Label	Questionnaire #
1-3	ID or case number	1-300	(Coded)
4	Opportunities? (OPPORT)	1= Yes 2= No 3= Don't know	#1
5	Excluded (EXCLUDE)	1= Strongly disagree 2= Disagree 3= Neither agree nor disagree 4= Agree 5= Strongly agree	#2a
6	Unconscious Discrimination (UNCONSC)	(same)	#2b
7	Areas not promotable (NONPROM)	(same)	#2c
8	Women less committed (LESSCOM)	(same)	#2d
9-10	Age (AGE)	21- 99	#3

Figure 3.2 (page 228) shows how this same information would appear when coded and entered into a FORTRAN data file for computer analysis. Each line of information is called a record and consists of approximately 72-80 columns of numbers. Only one number is placed in each column, although some software is designed to accept the data without specifying the amount of space needed for the responses. If the questionnaire has many variables, it may take two or three records (or lines) of data per case (respondent). The records are then saved as data files. These data files are usually considered to be rectangular because all cases have the same variables and the same number of records per case. Figure 3.2 also shows how on a program such as MYSTAT, the variable names are used with the coded values listed in column beneath the variable.

Just a word about coding missing data. Almost every evaluator will run into a situation where some data are missing or where the respondent did not understand the directions, resulting in inappropriate responses. Perhaps the respondent filling out the questionnaire did not want to answer a particular question, or maybe she or he decided that two programs needed to be ranked as

FORTRAN Code Sheet:

1	2	3	4	5	6	7	8	9	10	11	12	13	14	15	16	etc.
0	0	1	1	2	4	2	1	2	6							
0	0	2	2	5	4	1	1	4	4							
0	0	3	1	3	2	1	1	3	2							

MYSTAT Data Editor Screen:

	OPPORT	EXCLUDE	UNCONSC	NONPROM	LESSCOM	AGE
1	1	2	4	2	1	26
2	2	5	4	1	1	44
3	1	3	2	1	1	32

Figure 3.2 Sample Code Sheet(s)

number one priorities. Rather than throw out the entire questionnaire just because some information is missing, you can devise a system for handling missing data. You may select a particular code to represent your missing information, or if using a computerized statistical package, a predetermined code may exist in the program. The main point is that you need to be consistent with the missing data and the way you code inappropriate answers. For example, you may have asked respondents to select just one answer. You could make yourself a coding rule and say "if the person chooses more than one answer, the first answer selected will always be used." That way you will not bias the study by selecting answers that you would like to see. Consistency in coding is the key to handling missing data.

From Ideas to Reality

This chapter offers some basic and practical techniques for getting data from a questionnaire into numeric form to be used in computer data analysis. The procedures are specific and must be followed carefully if analysis is to be properly conducted. During this process of the evaluation project, one will need to consider the analyses that will be done and be concerned with accurately coding and entering the data.

3.03 DESCRIPTIVE STATISTICS: OPTIONS AND CHOICES

Goals for Chapter 3.03:

—To explain the most common types of descriptive statistics;

—To calculate and interpret the meaning of frequencies, percentages, mean, median, mode, standard deviation, range, and variance by hand or by using a computer; and,

—To explain the meaning of normal distribution.

After you have coded the quantitative data, you are ready to find the answers to the evaluation criteria you initially established. Some of the answers will be fairly straightforward. For example, univariate statistics such as adding up totals for overall participation rates or figuring percentages of people who participated in different programs is easy to do with descriptive statistics like frequencies and percentages. Sometimes you want to know more complex answers, however, such as: "Are there differences in the satisfaction levels of participants based on their age?" or "Is there any relationship between geographic location of participants and the activities in which they participate?" These types of questions require more sophisticated bivariate and multivariate statistical analyses. To make appropriate choices about which statistics to use, you need to know your options and how to make appropriate choices about the options.

The Basics of Descriptive Statistics

Descriptive statistics are exactly as the name implies; they describe and summarize characteristics of your data (Hudson, 1988). These descriptive statistics are univariate and include frequency counts, individual and cumulative percentages, measures of central tendency, and variations in data characteristics.

Frequency Counts and Percentages

Most evaluators are interested in the actual number of responses they generate for a question. For example, let's say you were interested in the ages of the adolescents that participated in the teen outdoor adventure program. Since one of the questions on the questionnaire instrument asked for age, it is possible to get an actual frequency count of participants who are thirteen, fourteen, fifteen, and so on (see Table 3.3, page 232).

You may also want to know what percentage of the total group of respondents were comprised of thirteen-year-olds. Individual percentages will provide this information. We also can take percentage use a step further with cumulative percentages. These percentages are added together as we move from group to group. As illustrated in Table 3.3, over half of the participants were between the ages of thirteen and fifteen. Also note on the table that N=the total number of respondents for a particular question. When discussing any aspect of univariate statistics, the number of people being described should be noted.

Table 3.3

Age of Participants in the Teen Adventure Program

Age	Frequency	Percent	Cumulative Percent
13-years-old	15	12%	12%
14-years-old	24	20%	32%
15-years-old	28	23%	55%
16-years-old	35	28%	83%
17-years-old	21	17%	100%

N = 123

Central Tendency

Measures of central tendency (mode, median, and mean) are useful for describing the variable under consideration. The *mode* is the most frequently occurring value and is usually indicated by "M." The mode can be used for any level of data but is not generally the preferred measure for interval or ordinal data. For these levels of data, the mode tends to ignore too much other important information. An example of the mode would be the results from asking people to check the month in which they participated the most in community center programs. If the evaluator had coded the answer from 1 to 12 to correspond with the months, and the analysis indicated that July received the highest number of positive responses, then M = 7. In the example illustrated by Table 3.3, the mode is sixteen years old.

The *median* is the value above and below which one half of the observations fall. Statisticians use "m" to mean median. For ordinal data, the median is a good measure of central tendency since it uses ranking information. The median should not be used however, for nominal data since ranking is not possible. In the example in Table 3.3, we could rank the ages of the 123 teenagers, and the 62nd observation would be the age where exactly half of the respondents were above and half below. For this example, m = 15 years.

The third type of central tendency measure is the *mean* ($\overline{X}$= sample mean), also known as the average. The mean is used with interval and ratio data. The mean is the sum of all the values of the observations on that variable divided by the number of observations:

$$\overline{X} = \frac{\Sigma(X)}{N}$$

M = mode $\quad\quad$ N = total number sampled
m = median $\quad\quad$ X = sample variable
$\overline{X}$ = mean (average) Σ = sum of

For example,

$$\overline{X} = \frac{\Sigma(X)}{N}$$

age $\quad$ number of participants

$$= \frac{[13(15) + 14(24) + 15(28) + 16(35) + 17(21)]}{123}$$

total number sampled

$$= \frac{195 + 336 + 420 + 560 + 357}{123}$$

$$= \frac{1,868}{123} = 15.187 = 15.19$$

average age = 15.19

In the age example in Table 3.3, the average age is 15.19 years. The mean might be used when dichotomous variables, such as sex, have been coded as 0 and 1. In this case, the mean is the proportion of cases coded as 1. Finding means for nominal data, however, may not be useful and tells virtually nothing about nominal data that have more than two values.

Several points about measures of central tendency should also be considered. First, these three measures (M, m, $\overline{X}$) need not be the same; in fact, they would not be the same except in a perfect, normal distribution. If the distribution is symmetric, however, the mean, median, and mode are usually close in value. Second, the means are greatly affected by outliers while the median is not. An outlier is a score that is on the extreme end of a scale. A good example of the effect of an outlier can be found in salary information. Often the average salary may be quite a bit higher than the median because the outliers who earn high salaries bring the average up. Thus, the employer might point to the average salary as a way of suggesting that salaries are at an adequate level while the employees may use the median to illustrate that the midpoint salary levels are considerably lower than what management may be implying the mean indicates.

Variations in Data Characteristics

Measures of Dispersion (How Spread Out Are My Data?)

Sometimes, two distributions can have the same mean for central tendency and yet be quite dissimilar. For example, two basketball teams could have their members shoot twenty free throws each. Team A could make 0, 1, 10, 14, and 20. Team B members could make 8, 8, 9, 10, and 10 free throws. Although the mean = 9 for both teams, the teams are obviously dissimilar.

One of the easiest calculations of dissimilarity, or dispersion, is the *range*. The range is the difference between the maximum and minimum observed values. Therefore the range for Team A is 20 and the range for Team B is 2. The range is sensitive to extremes which is useful with ordinal data, but does not take into account the distribution of observations.

Variance is a dispersion measure of variation that is based on all observations and describes the extent to which scores differ from each other (Struening and Guttentag, 1975). In other words, variance tells you how far each score is away from the mean. Many times the amount that the observed scores vary from the mean is critical for understanding the sample. The coach of Team A would likely work on free throw shooting differently than the coach of Team B. The variance (represented as s^2 = variance) is obtained by summing the squared differences from the mean for all observations and then dividing by the number of observations minus 1.

$$s^2 = \frac{\sum(X - \bar{X})^2}{(n - 1)}$$

where s^2 = variance $\bar{X}$ = sample mean
Σ = sum of   (average)
X = observation   n = number of observations

Example Team A:

$$n = 5; X_1 = 0; X_2 = 1; X_3 = 10; X_4 = 14; X_5 = 20$$

$$s^2 = \frac{[(0 - 9)^2 + (1 - 9)^2 + (10 - 9)^2 + (14 - 9)^2 + (20 - 9)^2]}{(5 - 1)}$$

$$= \frac{(-9)^2 + (-8)^2 + (1)^2 + (5)^2 + (11)^2}{4}$$

$$= \frac{81 + 64 + 1 + 25 + 121}{4} = \frac{292}{4} = 73$$

If all of the observations are identical (that is, no variation), then variance is equal to 0. When looking at the distribution curve, the more spread out, the greater the variance. For the basketball team example, the variance for Team A = 73 while the variance for Team B = 1.

The most familiar measure of dispersion is the *standard deviation*. It is the average of the degree to which scores deviate from the mean and has a special relationship to the normal distribution as will be seen in the following discussion on normal distribution. One of the reasons the evaluator pays attention to the standard deviation (represented by SD) is to gain some idea about how scores are dispersed around the mean (Lundegren and Farrell, 1985). The more the scores cluster around the mean, the more you can conclude that everyone is performing at about the same level or is answering questions similarly on an instrument. To derive the standard deviation, take the square root of the variance. This measure is expressed in the same units of measurement as the observations while the variance is in the units squared. Thus, standard deviation is a clearer way to think of variability. In the basketball team example, the standard deviation for Team A would be 8.5, or 8.5 free throws and the SD =1 for Team B.

The Distribution Curve (How Does My Data Look?)

The observations of most variables seem to cluster around the middle of the distribution, and the frequency of observations seems to decrease as you move away from the central concentration. This type of distribution is often called "bell-shaped" or a normal distribution. In society, characteristics such as height, weight, and blood pressure are thought to be approximately normal. Theoretically, if every person's weight were plotted, for example, the results would look like a bell-shaped curve.

The *normal distribution* is the most important theoretical distribution in statistics and serves as a reference point for describing the forms of distributions of quantitative data (Norusis, 1983). For example, let's ask for the weights of the people enrolled in a wellness program at your community center. By plotting the weights of the participants (or calculating them statistically), you can determine if the group is "normal." In other words, does the data fit the bell-shaped distribution?

The normal distribution is symmetric with the three measures of central tendency (i.e., mean, median, and mode) theoretically coinciding at the center with gradually diminishing numbers toward the extremes (Lundegren and Farrell, 1985). In the normal distribution, we would expect to find 68 percent of the observations falling within approximately one standard deviation of the mean and 95 percent of all the observations falling within about two standard deviations of the mean. See Figure 3.3(1), page 236. If an observation is outside the area covered by two standard deviations, an evaluator may want to consider that observation so unusual that it would not fit what is "normally" expected.

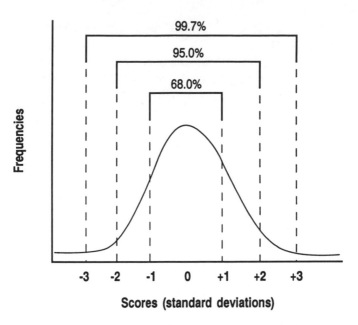

Figure 3.3(1) The Normal Distribution Curve

Other Measures Associated With Distributions

Skewness is a measure used when the distribution is not symmetric, and has a "tail." If the "tail" is toward the larger values, then the distribution is considered to be positively skewed. If the "tail" is toward the smaller values, it is considered to be negatively skewed. If we were to measure the attitudes of parents toward a youth baseball league and found most of the responses were toward positive values, it could be concluded that the responses were positively skewed. In either case, this information would indicate that the distribution of the sample was not normal, because fewer scores are on one side of the mean. Figure 3.3(2) shows an example of a skewed distribution. The issues of central tendency and distribution will be the basis for more advanced statistical procedures discussed later in this book.

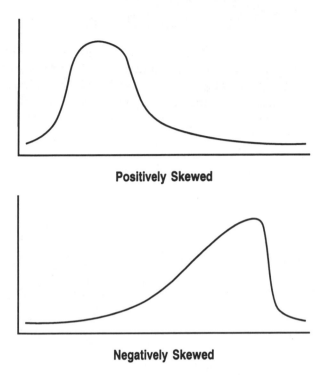

Positively Skewed

Negatively Skewed

Figure 3.3(2) Positively and Negatively Skewed Distributions

From Ideas to Reality

Descriptive statistics are the most basic statistics that an evaluator will use. Many times they are used first in analysis to describe what characteristics the respondents possess and the general responses that have been received from a measurement instrument. They are helpful for what the name means, to describe the information that you have. From these descriptive statistics, many other possibilities exist for data analysis.

3.04 THE WORD ON STATISTICAL SIGNIFICANCE

Goals for Chapter 3.04:

—To define what statistical significance means;
—To describe the difference between Type I and Type II errors; and,
—To apply probability statistics to making conclusions about evaluation criteria.

As you use univariate, bivariate, or multivariate procedures to find answers to address evaluation criteria, you will likely want to know if the differences or relationships in the data are significant. While a discussion of probability theory is beyond the scope of this text, a general understanding of "statistical significance" is important for the evaluator. Statistical significance refers to the unlikeliness that relationships observed in a sample could be attributed to chance alone. In other words, when determining statistical significance, an evaluator wants to be as sure as possible that, indeed, a relationship exists among variables. That relationship may be different or it may be similar.

Before beginning quantitative analysis, an evaluator must decide upon a level at which she or he is willing to say, "If my findings exceed this level, then I am going to consider the findings different from what I would expect due to chance." In the social sciences, statistical significance by convention is generally set at probability (p) < 0.05. In the simplest terms, "p" or the probability of less than 0.05 means that 95 times out of a 100 you would expect to get the same results and 5 out of 100 times the result might be due purely to chance. For example, say you wanted to see if a difference exists between women's and men's participation rates in a free swim at a community center, you select the appropriate statistical test and if the results indicate $p < 0.05$, then it is known that the women and men differ significantly from each other in participation rates. The means of each group will have to be examined to determine whether it is males or females who participate more or less.

There is a caution, however. Tests of significance are based on probability, so $p < 0.05$ is really saying that if this test were to be repeated 100 times, in only five times out of the 100 trials would you be wrong in thinking that the groups were different, when in actuality they were the same. In some fields like medical research, this error rate would be too great, so these researchers may set a significance level of p < 0.001. Thus, a medical researcher who was evaluating a new drug that resulted in statistically significant difference between the experimental, and the control group would be assured that her or his finding was due to chance only one time out of 1,000.

At this point you may be asking yourself, "But what if I do get a wrong answer purely due to chance?" Let's say you are interested in the effect of play in the hospital on the recovery rate of children receiving tonsillectomies, you find through the analysis of your data that the recovery rates of children involved in play were faster and differed significantly at the 0.05 level from the children who weren't in these play sessions. Given the evidence so far, group membership seems to make a difference. Maybe, in reality, that finding was due to chance and little difference existed; an error has been made in assuming that the play opportunity made a difference in recovery. The risk you take in making this type of error, called Type I error, is the same as the level of significance (Salkind, 1991). A significance level of p < 0.05 means that there is a 5 percent chance that you will say the groups are different when in actuality, they are the same, thus committing a Type I error. If using evaluation to determine whether to keep or eliminate a program, you must be careful not to make a Type I error as inappropriate decisions could be made.

Another form of error is called Type II error. This error results when the data suggest that the groups are the same (no significant difference), but in actuality they are different. Ideally, you want to minimize both types of error, but Type II error is not as easy to control as Type I. In Type I situations, the evaluator selects the significance level that she or he is willing to accept. Type II errors are not directly controlled but can be decreased by increasing the sample size. In other words, as the sample size increases, the likeliness that the sample characteristics will more closely match or be representative of the population in a normal distribution also increases, thus reducing the likelihood of Type II error (thinking the groups are the same when they aren't).

If you try to reduce the Type II error rate by increasing the sample size, care must be taken because statistical significance can also be influenced by sample size (Babbie, 1992). For example, a large sample has the power to make everything seem statistically significant and, in reality, little substantive differences may exist. Conversely, an extremely small sample may not show differences that do exist between groups. This weakness points out the importance of always determining whether or not the statistical difference is *meaningful*.

For example, an evaluator may ask all visitors at your parks during the summer to rate on a seven point Likert scale their satisfaction with the available facilities; the sample size at the end of the summer is over 15,000 visitors. A statistical test may indicate that statistical significance exists between tent campers and RV users at the p < 0.05 level, but upon closer examination of the data, we find that the means only differ by three tenths of a point. This example is a good case to illustrate the need to use judgment when determining how meaningful differences really are. In this case, a three tenths of a point difference on a seven point scale is probably not important enough to justify facility changes. Sometimes, statistical procedures exist that will help determine meaningfulness of difference, but often the evaluator is the one who makes a final determination.

Last, statistical significance for a result need not always be found to be meaningful. Sometimes, not finding a difference is extremely important. For example, you know from previous research that adolescent girls generally have lower self-concepts based on self-esteem measures than their male counterparts. A teen adventure club has been established to help teens build self-esteem and experience leadership opportunities. As a part of the summative evaluation it is found that the girls' self-esteem is high and no different than the scores of the boys. The result is important, meaningful, and suggests that perhaps the content of the teen program is contributing to the development of self-esteem among both girls and boys.

Statistical significance is an important concept to be understood, regardless of what statistics are used. For the evaluator, statistical significance is often used as a screening device for making subsequent judgment regarding conclusions and recommendations.

From Ideas to Reality

Statistical significance is one of the most helpful concepts that one will use when doing quantitative data analysis. The probability (p) value tells an evaluator whether or not a statistically significant difference exists between variables. Keep in mind, however, that the meaningfulness is also important. In addition to using what the statistics indicate, one must always examine variables to see if the differences are meaningful and important.

3.05 INFERENTIAL STATISTICS: THE PLOT THICKENS

Goals for Chapter 3.05:

—To explain when parametric and nonparametric statistics would be used;

—Given a situation with the levels of measurement data known, make a decision about which statistical procedure would be best to use; and,

—To use the decision model for choosing appropriate statistical procedures to make decisions about a statistical problem.

Thus far, this text has described ways to calculate and describe characteristics about data. Descriptive statistics provide information about the distribution of data, how varied the data are, and the shape of the data. Of interest now is information related to population parameters: are there relationships or associations within the data? We also may want to know if there are group characteristics within the data that are different from each other. Inferential statistics help evaluators make these determinations and allow them to generalize the results to a larger sample.

Parametric and Nonparametric Statistics

In the world of statistics, distinctions are made in the types of analyses that can be used by the evaluator based on distribution assumptions and the levels of measurement data. For example, parametric statistics are based on the assumption of normal distribution and randomized sampling that results in interval or ratio data. The statistical tests usually determine significance of difference or relationships. These parametric statistical tests commonly include t-tests, Pearson product-moment correlation, and analysis of variance.

Nonparametric statistics are known as distribution-free tests because they are not based on the assumptions of the normal probability curve. Nonparametrics do not specify conditions about parameters of population, but assume randomization and are usually applied to nominal and ordinal data. Several nonparametric tests do exist for interval data, however, when the sample size is so small that the assumption of normal distribution would be violated. The most common forms of nonparametric tests are chi-square analysis, Mann-Whitney U test, the Wilcoxon signed ranks test, Friedman test, sign test, Krurkal-Wallis, and the Spearman rank-order correlation coefficient. These nonparametric tests are generally less powerful tests than the corresponding parametric tests. Table 3.5 provides parametric and nonparametric equivalent tests used for data analysis. The following sections will discuss these types of tests and the appropriate parametric and nonparametric choices.

Table 3.5

Parametric and Nonparametric Tests for Data Analysis
(adapted from Loftus and Loftus, 1982)

Data	Purpose of Test	Parametric	Nonparametric
Single sample	To determine if an association exists between two nominal variables		Chi-square
Single sample	To determine if sample mean or median differs from some hypothetical value	Matched t-test for single sample	Sign test
Two samples, between subjects	To determine if the populations of two independent samples have the same means or median	T-test for independent groups	Mann-Whitney
Two conditions, within subjects	To determine if the populations of two samples have the same mean or median	Within subjects or two-sample t-test	Sign test or Wilcoxon signed ranks test
More than two conditions, between subjects	To determine if the populations of more than two independent samples have the same mean or median	One-way ANOVA	Kruskal-Wallis
More than two conditions, within subjects	To determine if the populations or more than two samples have the same mean or median	Repeated measures ANOVA	Friedman test
Set of items with two measures on each item	To determine if the two measures are associated	Pearson product-moment correlation	Spearman rank

Associations Among Variables

Chi-Square

One of the most common statistical tests of association is the chi-square test. For this test to be used, data must be discrete and at nominal or ordinal levels. During the process of the analysis, the frequency data are arranged in tables that compare the observed distribution (your data) with the expected distributions (what you would expect to find if no difference existed among the values of a given variable or variables). In most computerized statistical packages, this chi-square procedure is called "crosstabulations" or "tables." This statistical procedure is relatively easy to hand calculate as well. The basic chi-square formula is:

$$X^2 = \sum \frac{(O - E)^2}{E}$$

where: X^2 = chi-square
O = observed
E = expected
Σ = sum of

Spearman's and Pearson's Correlations

Sometimes it is necessary to determine relationships between scores. An evaluator has to determine whether the data are appropriate for parametric or nonparametric procedures. This determination is based upon the level of data and sample size. If the sample is small or if the data are ordinal (i.e., rank-order) data, then the most appropriate choice is the nonparametric Spearman's rank order correlation statistic. If the data are thought to be normally distributed and intervally scaled, then the basic test for linear (i.e., straight line) relationships is the parametric Pearson product-moment correlation technique.

The correlation results for Spearman's or Pearson's can fall between +1 and -1. For the parametric Pearson's or nonparametric Spearman's the data are interpreted in the same way even though a different statistical procedure is used. You might think of the data as sitting on a matrix with an x and y axis. A correlation of +1 would mean that the slope of the line would be at 45 degrees upward. A correlation of -1 would be at 45 degrees downward. [See Figure 3.5(1), page 246]. A correlation of 0 would be a horizontal line. The correlation approaching +1 means that as one score increases, the other score increases. A correlation approaching -1 means that as one score increases, the other decreases. A correlation of 0 means no linear relationship exists. In other words, the correlation would be 1 only if the ranks of the x and y values are identical, and -1 only if the ranks of x are the reverse of the ranks of y (Hale, 1990).

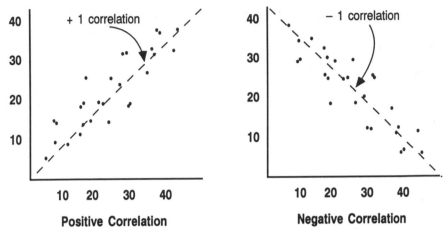

Figure 3.5(1) Examples of Correlation Relationships

For example, if it were found that the correlation between age and number of times someone swam at a community pool was -0.63, it could be concluded that older individuals were less likely to swim at a community pool. Or suppose we wanted to see if a relationship existed between body image scores of adolescent girls and self-esteem scores. If r = 0.89, then we would say a positive relationship was found (i.e., as positive body image scores increased, so did positive self-esteem scores). If r = -0.89, then we would show a negative relationship (i.e., as body image scores increased, self-esteem scores decreased). If r = 0.10, we would say little to no relationship was evident between body image and self-esteem scores. If the score was r = 0.34, then a weak positive relationship exists between body image and self-esteem scores. Anything above r = 0.4 or below r = -0.4 might be considered a medium relationship between two variables. Of course, the closer the correlation is to r = +1 or -1, the stronger the relationship.

Correlations can also be used for determining reliability as was discussed in Chapter 2.03 on trustworthiness. Let's say that an evaluator administered a questionnaire about nutrition habits for the adults in an aerobics class for the purpose of establishing reliability of an instrument. A week later the same test was given again. All of the individuals were ranked based upon the scores for each test, then compared through the Spearman's procedure. If a result of 0.94 was found, then we would feel comfortable with the reliability of the instrument because this finding would indicate that the results were similar from test to retest, that respondents were consistent in their answers. If r = 0.36, then it could be assumed that the instrument had weak reliability because the rankings differed from the first test to the retest.

One caution should be noted in relation to correlations. It cannot be assumed that a correlation implies causation. These correlations should be used only to summarize the strength of a relationship. In the above example where r = 0.89, we can't say that improved body image causes increased self-esteem, because many other variables could be exerting an influence. It can be said, that as body image increases, so does self-esteem and vice versa. Correlations point to the fact that there is, however, some relationship between two variables whether it is negative, nonexistent, or positive.

Tests of Differences Between Groups

Sometimes, you may want to evaluate by comparing two or more groups through some type of bivariate or multivariate procedure. Again, it will be necessary to know the types of data you collected (i.e., continuous or discrete), the levels of measurement data (e.g., nominal, ordinal, interval, ratio), and the dependent and independent variables of interest to analyze.

In parametric analyses, the statistical process for determining difference is usually accomplished by comparing the means of the groups. The most common tests of differences between means are the t-tests and analysis of variance. In nonparametric analyses, the evaluator usually is checking the differences in rankings of her or his groups. For nonparametrics, the most common statistical procedures are the Mann-Whitney U test, the Sign test, the Wilcoxon matched-pairs signed ranks test, and the Friedman analysis of variance test. While these parametric and nonparametric tests can be calculated by hand, they are fairly complicated and a bit tedious, so most evaluators will rely on the computer. Therefore, each test will be described but no hand calculations provided. For individuals interested in the manual calculations, any good statistics book will provide the formulas and necessary steps.

Parametric Choices For Determining Differences

T-Tests

Two types of t-tests are available to the evaluator: the two-sample or independent t-test and the matched or dependent t-test. The independent t-test is used to test the differences between the means of two groups. It is important to remember that the two groups are independent of or not related to each other. For example, you may want to know if youth coaches who attended a workshop performed better on some aspect of teaching than those coaches who didn't attend. In this case, the teaching score is the dependent variable and the two groups of coaches (i.e., attendees and nonattendees) are the independent variable. If the t statistic that results from the t-test has a probability < 0.05, then we know the two groups are different. An evaluator would examine the means for each group and determine which set of coaches had the higher teaching scores.

The dependent t-test, often called the matched paired t-test, is used to show how a group differs during two points in time. The matched t-test is used if the two measurements are related. This test is used if the same group was tested twice or when the two separate groups are matched on some variable. For example, in the previous situation where you were offering a coaching clinic, it may be that you would want to see if participants learned anything at the clinic. You would test a construct such as knowledge of the game before the workshop and then again with the same coaches after the training to see if any difference existed in knowledge gained by the coaches that attended the clinic. If a statistical difference of $p < 0.05$ occurs, you can assume that the workshop made a difference in the knowledge level of the coaches. If the t-test was not significant ($p > 0.05$), the assumption is that the clinic made little difference in the knowledge level of coaches.

Analysis of Variance (ANOVA)

Analysis of variance is used to determine differences among means when there are more than two groups. It is the same concept as the independent t-tests except that you have more than two groups. If there is only one grouping variable consisting of more than two values (a single independent variable), then the procedure is called one-way ANOVA. If there are two independent variables, a two-way ANOVA would be used. The dependent variable is the measured variable and is usually interval or ratio level data. Both one-way and two-way ANOVAs are used to determine if three or more sample means are different from one another (Hale, 1990). For example, a therapeutic recreation specialist may want to know if inappropriate behavior levels of psychiatric patients are affected by the type of therapy used (behavior modification, group counseling, or nondirective). In this example, the measured levels of inappropriate behavior would be the dependent variable while the independent variable would be the type of therapy that is divided into three groups. If a statistically significant difference in the behavior of the patients ($p < 0.05$) was found, the means for the three groups would be compared to determine which therapy was best.

Other types of parametric statistical tests are available for analysis purposes. The t-tests and ANOVA described here are the most frequently used parametric statistics by beginning evaluators.

Nonparametric Choices for Determining Differences

For any of the common parametric statistics, a parallel nonparametric statistic exists in most cases. The use of these statistics depends on the level of measurement data and the sample as is shown in Table 3.5 (page 244). The most common nonparametric statistics used to examine differences include the Mann-Whitney U, Sign test, Wilcoxon signed ranks test, Kruskal-Wallis, and Friedman analysis of variance.

Mann-Whitney U Test

The Mann-Whitney U test is used to test for differences in rankings on some variable between two independent groups when the data are not intervally scaled (Lundegren and Farrell, 1985). For example, you may want to analyze self-concept scores of high fit and low fit women who participated in a weight-training fitness program. A nominal scale form would be administered where respondents rank characteristics as "like me" or "not like me." Thus, this test will allow you to determine the effects of this program on your participants by comparing the two groups and their self-concept scores. This test is equivalent to the independent t-test.

The Sign Test

The Sign test is used when the independent variable is categorical and consists of two levels. The dependent variable is assumed to be continuous but can't be measured on a continuous scale, so a categorical scale is substituted (Hale, 1990). This test becomes the nonparametric equivalent to the dependent or matched t-test. The Sign test is only appropriate if the dependent variable is binary (i.e., takes only two different values). Suppose an evaluator wanted to know if switching from wood to fiber daggerboards on your Sunfish sailboats increases the likelihood of winning regattas. The Sign test will permit this question to be tested by comparing the two daggerboards as the independent variable and the number of races won as the dependent variable.

Wilcoxon Signed Ranks Test

The Wilcoxon test is also a nonparametric alternative to the dependent t-test and is used when the dependent variable has more than two values that are ranked. Positions in a race are a good example of this type of dependent variable. As in the Sign test, the independent variable is categorical and has two levels; for example, to know if a difference exists between runners belonging to a running club and those that do not, in relation to their finish positions in a road race. The results of this analysis indicate the difference in ranks on the dependent variable between the two related groups.

Kruskal-Wallis

The Kruskal-Wallis test is equivalent to the one-way ANOVA. It is used when an evaluator has an independent variable with two or more values that she or he wishes to compare to a dependent variable. This statistic is used to see if the population of more than two independent groups have the same mean or median. Since this procedure is a nonparametric test, the statistic is used when a sample size is small or when you are not sure of the distribution. An example of an application would be to compare the attitudes of counselors at a camp (i.e., the dependent variable) toward three different salary payment plans: weekly, twice a summer, or end of the summer (i.e., independent variable).

Friedman Analysis of Variance

The Friedman Analysis of Variance test is used for repeated measures analysis when you measure a subject two or more times. You must have a categorical independent variable with more than two values and a rank-order dependent variable that is measured more than twice (Hale, 1990). This test is the nonparametric equivalent to repeated measures of analysis of variance (i.e., two-way ANOVA). An example of a situation when this statistical procedure is used would be if you had ranked data from multiple judges. For instance, to experiment with four new turf grasses on four soccer fields, ask your five maintenance workers to rank the grasses on all four fields for durability. These results could be analyzed with the Friedman's procedure.

Making Decisions About Statistics

The decision model for choosing the appropriate type of statistical procedure is found in Figure 3.5(2). This model provides a logical progression of questions about parametric and nonparametric data that will help in the selection of appropriate statistics. Many other forms of statistical measures are possible, but the ones described here will provide the most common forms used in evaluations.

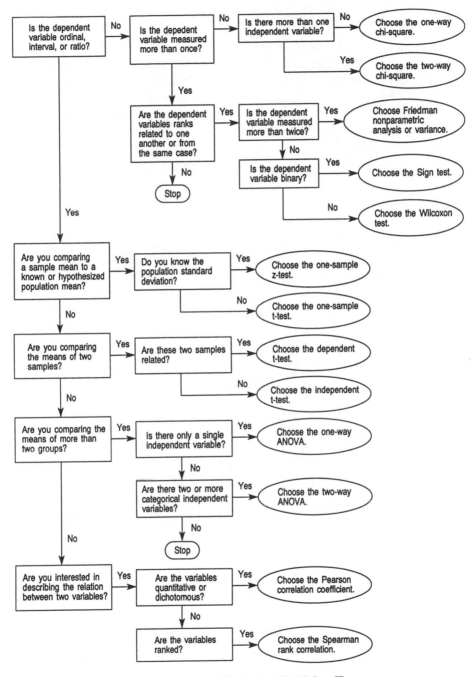

Figure 3.5(2) A Statistical Decision Tree
(adapted from Hall, 1990)

From Ideas to Reality

This chapter is very complex and full of terms that may not be familiar to you. Statistics are often confusing and overwhelming, but as you begin to understand what they mean, they can be extremely helpful. Certainly, one short chapter will not make you an expert on these statistics, but we hope this chapter will at least show you some of the ways that an evaluator can gain valuable information by examining the relationships between and among variables. The more that you use statistical procedures, the more you will understand them. Thank goodness there are computers these days to help conduct these analyses since they save a great amount of time and effort.

3.06 Using Computerized Statistical Packages

Goals for Chapter 3.06:

—To describe the options available for using computers;
—To choose a computer software package that will meet the needs of your evaluation project; and,
—To explain how to interpret whether an analysis is statistically significant.

As was shown in the description of inferential statistics, some calculations can be complicated. As computers have become more prevalent and accessible to leisure service professionals, many statistical packages for computers have been written. An evaluator likely will be faced with the question, "How do I use a computer to help with my data analysis?" She or he will have to examine the available options and decide which statistical packages can help the most.

Many agencies and virtually all universities have statistical software packages that are available on a large computer called a mainframe. These large computers have huge amounts of memory that will allow many people to work at the same time on a variety of applications. These computers use software (i.e., the written programs designed by computer specialists) to do many tasks such as statistical analyses, data processing, graphics, and telecommunications. Sometimes these programs are commercially available and widely used by evaluators and researchers from across the country or world; other times, an agency may have acquired software that has been written specifically for it, so it is unique to the setting. In either case, you will have to learn how to use the program unless the organization has a computer specialist who can run the software for doing statistical analyses.

If a mainframe computer is used, learning the statistical packages will require some investment of the evaluator's time. Programs such as the Statistical Packages for the Social Sciences (SPSS), Statistical Applications Software (SAS), and Biomedical Data Program (BMDP) have a fairly detailed set of procedures and a unique language used to run the statistical packages. Although it is possible to learn about these procedures by reading the manuals, it is usually easier to attend a workshop that will give hands-on experiences that will help you acquire the basics. In addition, you often have to learn the job language used by the mainframe so any request for analysis can be submitted.

The advantages to using existing mainframe programs, however, are often worth the investment of time and energy. An evaluator can do virtually any type of statistical analysis desired with no worries about space limitations or turn-around time. These programs often have built-in graphic options that will allow you to graph results immediately. The beginning evaluator will have a great deal of flexibility in her or his analyses and will be able to do sophisticated computations that result in detailed information. Even if you are doing only descriptive statistics, these computer programs will allow you to work with a large number of cases with almost an infinite number of variables and values.

Many evaluators may not have a large mainframe available for use or may not want to invest the time and energy needed for learning such a system. If so, you probably will have access to smaller computers such as a Macintosh, IBM, or a comparable computer that will allow the use of statistical software. The number of programs available for these personal computers is growing steadily. For example, the personal computers with larger memories (usually a minimum of four megabytes of random-access memory, or RAM) can even run some of the statistical packages like SPSS and SAS used on the mainframes. Acquiring these statistical packages can cost several hundred dollars, but may be worth the money if statistical analysis is an ongoing component of an organization.

More likely, you will be able to purchase a smaller, less sophisticated statistical package that will do the analyses needed to complete the evaluation projects. Most beginning evaluators will be doing basic descriptive and inferential statistics. Some of the programs like Statview, SYSTAT, Excel, and MYSTAT are excellent choices to consider. They are relatively inexpensive, fairly easy to learn, and have good documentation. For illustrative purposes, the Macintosh version of the MYSTAT statistical program will be used in the following overview about some general considerations for computerized statistical packages. It is not within the scope of this book to teach the use of specific statistical packages, but most packages for personal computers are not difficult to learn and use. If you know the variables that you wish to analyze, almost any statistical package will allow the descriptive and inferential calculations that have been discussed in the previous chapters to be done.

An Example of MYSTAT Statistical Program

MYSTAT is an interactive statistics and graphics package that can compute descriptive and inferential statistics on Macintosh, IBM PC-compatibles, and VAX/VMS systems (Hale, 1990). The MYSTAT graphics allow the visualization of one- and two-dimensional data. MYSTAT can handle up to fifty variables and 32,000 cases and currently can be purchased for under $25. This inexpensive program is a scaled-down version of a much larger program called SYSTAT.

MYSTAT has several "windows" from which you perform the basic commands. For example, the Data Editor window allows you to enter and modify your data, the Analysis window displays the results of analysis, and the Graph window allows you to see graphs that you may generate from the data. The program also has a series of menus that allow the user to edit values; sort the data; create, change, or delete variables; analyze data through a variety of statistical procedures; and to get "help" if needed. The program can also accommodate imported text files. To import a text file means that you have the option of entering data on some other system, then bringing these data files to the MYSTAT program.

MYSTAT offers a broad range of statistical procedures through the Analyze menu. The option called STATS provides an array of descriptive statistics; TABLES provides chi-square statistics for frequency and multiway tables; T-TEST provides dependent and independent t-tests; CORR computes the Pearson correlation coefficients; REGRESS computes simple and multiple regression models; and ANOVA will give you full-factorial ANOVAs and ANCOVAs. Lastly, MYSTAT provides selected nonparametric statistics through NPARS that include the sign test, Wilcoxon signed-rank test, and the Friedman nonparametric analysis of variance.

As previously mentioned, MYSTAT also has graphing capabilities. The PLOT option provides scatter plots, bubble plots, and line plots. HIST will give histograms, STEM plots stem-and-leaf diagrams, and SERIES produces time-series plots or case plots.

For all of these procedures, the location of the output can be controlled. For example, while doing the initial analyses, you will likely direct the results to the screen. However, for a "hard copy" of your final results output gathered can be directed to the printer. In some cases, it may be desirable to create new files from the output. The tables and graphics that you produce from MYSTAT can be pasted directly into a word processing file when an evaluation report is written.

Every evaluator analyzing quantitative data will need to use a computer. You can learn how to run the program by reading the documentation and practicing with the data. Learning to use a computer is a lot like learning a foreign language—the more you practice, the better you become. By starting out slowly using descriptive statistics and then moving to more sophisticated analysis, you become more comfortable with the computer and data analysis.

Interpreting Statistics

Each computer program you use will give you a slightly different output as far as how the data will look. In general, however, several examples of how to interpret data will be provided.

Descriptive Statistics. In most computer programs the descriptive statistics will include a list of the frequencies reported for the values of the variables, the mean, median, number of cases, standard deviation, standard error, skewness, and the sum. Most people understand these statistics fairly easily, and usually the evaluator will want to choose those statistics that are most meaningful to discuss. For example, you may have found in an evaluation of a line dancing class that on a five-point Likert scale, 65 percent of the participants rated the instructor as excellent with a 4.3 average on the scale and a 0.68 standard deviation. These descriptive statistics indicate that the leader did a good job and that a great deal of agreement existed concerning the rating of the ability of the instructor.

Correlations. The correlation shows the relationship between two interval variables. Usually, receiving an "r" score indicates correlation. Often if you correlate more than two variables, you will get a matrix with a number of "r" scores so that each variable is compared to every other variable. As indicated earlier, correlations range from -1 to +1, so it will be necessary to look at a score and interpret two aspects: whether it is positive or negative and the strength of that association which is arbitrarily termed as weak or strong. For example, if you found that the correlation between age and physical fitness scores was -0.40, you could conclude that there is a medium to weak relationship between age and fitness in that as one gets older, the fitness scores decrease. If the result had been +0.89 you would conclude that as one ages, one becomes more fit. In this case it could be said that there is a strong positive correlation between age and physical fitness.

T-Tests. If an evaluator wants to see how the means of two groups vary she or he will do an independent t-test. The statistic that the computer will generate is a "t" statistic, which also gives a "p" or "prob" (i.e., probability) statistic. We examine the "p" statistic to see if it is above or below the statistical significance standard set. For example, if the "p" is 0.23 and the standard was set at 0.05, we would conclude that no statistical significance exists between the means of two variables. If, however, we were measuring the matched results of a basketball rules test taken by boys and girls after attending a day-long basketball clinic, we might find that the difference between the two means was significant at 0.008 with higher scores on the posttest. We would conclude that the clinic made a difference in rule knowledge. In that case, the conclusion is that a statistical difference existed between the two means. In most computer printouts, the means and standard deviations for both groups are given along with the "t" and "p" values. You will need to look at the means to determine the location of any significant differences. If you found that boys scored a mean of 18.9 with a SD of 8.3 and girls scored 28.5 with a SD of 10.4, you could conclude that girls learned more about rules as a result of attending the basketball clinic.

Analysis of Variance. Analysis of variance (ANOVA) works the same way that independent t-tests do except that the interest is in determining the differences in means between three or more groups. The statistics given on a printout are the sum of squares, mean-squares, F-ratio, and a "p" value. The F-ratio is the actual ANOVA statistic but the bottom line is the "p" value. You look to the "p" value to see whether it is above or below the standard set, which is usually 0.05. If the "p" value is above, no statistically significant differences occur. If the "p" value is below 0.05 then a difference exists. As in t-tests the evaluator will need to examine the means and standard deviations of the three or more variables to determine where the difference lies. Some computer programs provide a list of the means for each group. In other cases it may be necessary to sort the cases and run descriptive statistics to get the individual means for each group. You will need to know the means to say which of the groups is different from the others.

Chi-Square Statistics. These nonparametric statistics are also referred to as **CROSSTABS** or **TABLES** in different statistical packages. When these types of statistics are run, you will generally get a number of different statistical analyses. The statistic to be most concerned about is the chi-square statistic and the "p" or "prob" statistic. As in the other cases, it can be seen what the "p" value is, and that can be compared to the standard that was set. Most computer programs that run chi-square will give a warning if more than 25 percent of the cells have less than five responses in them. When this occurs, the results are suspect. In chi-square analysis, you will have to "eyeball" the data to determine where the difference exists if you find a statistically significant difference. Since a matrix is provided that shows the number of responses in each cell, you can usually figure out where the difference exists fairly easily.

It is hoped this summary of interpretation will be useful. The data generated from statistical analysis can be rather daunting but will become easier to understand as you work with statistics. Do not hesitate to find someone who understands statistics who can help in the interpretation of the data. The use of inferential statistics supplied by computer programs can contribute greatly to making decisions about the organizations in which we work.

Computer Use With Qualitative Data

The computer can be an effective tool for managing and analyzing qualitative data. A computer is not mandatory for doing qualitative analysis but is often helpful. The computer can help cut down on fatigue, save time, reduce the tedium of clerical tasks like cutting and pasting, and can allow the evaluator to have more time for data interpretation (Henderson, 1991). A number of good software packages exist to help with the analysis of qualitative data like ETHNOGRAPH, QUALOG, Hypercard, and NUDIST. All of these programs prepare a data file through word processing by numbering the lines, identifying the meaningful segments with coding, and sorting the coded segments.

Other Uses for the Computer in Evaluation

The rapid development of computer technology will likely produce many other advancements that will help the evaluator. Telecommunications provides us with access to the most updated resource materials in minutes that used to be difficult and time-consuming to acquire. Word processing and desktop publishing can help produce questionnaires as well as the final reports for an evaluation. Software like Hypercard has been designed to function as stacks of note cards that an evaluator can use for field notes. As previously discussed, data analysis and display are simplified through the use of various computer applications.

During the next few years, other hardware and software discoveries certainly will be produced that will be helpful to an evaluator. Competent evaluators will want to continue to read about changing technology, attend workshops at professional meetings, and talk with colleagues who have discovered new uses for computers. Although using computers may initially seem daunting, they have become an important part of leisure services management. The value and importance for evaluation and other forms of recordkeeping will continue to grow.

From Ideas to Reality

This chapter has been a broad brush approach to examining computer packages and the output that they generate. It is not known what potential packages you will have available for conducting statistical analysis, so it is not useful to teach any particular package. Most packages, however, use similar formats, and if you understand how data are coded, entered, and interpreted, you should be able to read the documentation that comes with the computer package and figure out how to run particular statistics. Once these runs are completed, the easy part is looking to see whether statistical significance exists. For many people, doing the statistical analysis is the fun part after much time has been spent collecting, coding, and entering data.

3.07 Qualitative Data Analysis and Interpretation

Goals for Chapter 3.07:

—To describe the options that are available for analyzing qualitative data;
—To explain the value of being as familiar as possible with data;
—Given a block of qualitative data, analyze it using the enumeration and the constant comparison techniques; and,
—To use content analysis when appropriate.

In evaluations that use qualitative data, we are *not* necessarily concerned with a singular conclusion, but with perspectives. In qualitative data analysis and interpretation the evaluator tries to uncover perspectives that will help her or him understand the criteria being explored in an evaluation project. Further, doing qualitative analysis is a time-consuming task, as the evaluator reads over notes, organizes the data, looks for patterns, checks emergent patterns against the data, validates data sources, and makes linkages. This work is the heart of qualitative analysis and interpretation.

As was described earlier, in-depth interviews and qualitative observations are the most common ways to obtain qualitative data. An evaluator might also ask open-ended questions on a questionnaire that would result in qualitative data. It is particularly important that open-ended questions are asked in such a way that a "yes" or "no" is not possible. One of the difficulties with analyzing qualitative data is that it is easy to get overwhelmed with data. Too much data results in data management problems. Qualitative data can be coded, but not in the same sense as quantitative data. Coding is used as a way to organize data into brief word descriptions. Further, since the qualitative data are not reduced to numbers as in quantitative analysis, the interpretation of data is the evaluator's responsibility. Thus, the evaluator becomes personally involved in the analysis.

Analysis is the process of bringing order to qualitative data and organizing words into patterns, categories, and basic descriptive units. Interpretation involves attaching meaning and significance to the analysis, explaining descriptive patterns, and looking for relationships and linkages within the data. According to Patton (1980b), an interesting and readable evaluation report provides sufficient description to allow the reader to understand the analysis, and sufficient analysis to allow the reader to understand the description. Analysis comes from focusing on the criteria raised at the beginning of a project and then describing how the data evolved into perspectives and conclusions. Qualitative data are often used for formative evaluations but may also be used as summative evaluations and assessments.

Qualitative analyses provide descriptions of what actually happened using word pictures and word summaries. The aim is to get both the "outer" and the "inner" perspectives. The inner perspective is the actual words. The outer perspective is the interpretation of what the words mean. Making sense of the words, however, and not having conclusions appear to be the evaluator's opinions require a rigorous analysis process. When done properly, qualitative data analysis is just as systematic as any quantitative analysis.

Organizing Qualitative Analysis

No magic formulas exist for how to do qualitative analysis. In general, however, the data must be organized into some manageable form which is sometimes referred to as data reduction and data display. Data reduction involves the process of organizing data and developing possible categories for analysis. As soon as field notes are taken or tapes are transcribed, data reduction begins. Additional written procedures are generally used to summarize some of the "raw" data. This data management requires judgment calls and decision rules that each evaluator will develop in summarizing and resummarizing the data.

Write-Ups

Field notes and transcripts can be converted into "write-ups," "memos," or "notes on notes." The write-up indicates the most important content of a study at a particular time. Memos can also be used that describe how the data are evolving with notes about possible patterns and clarifications of concepts. An evaluator also might want to include memos addressing personal emotional reactions as well as any methodological difficulties that might have occurred during data collection. These memos may be "gut reactions" to what is going on, inferences about the quality of the data, new connections made, notes about what to address later, elaborations, or clarifications. Written material should be dated, titled, and anchored to particular places in the field notes or transcripts. The memos require the researcher to "think" rather than to just collect data and ideas.

Qualitative Coding

The evaluator using qualitative data must consider how to organize data so that one can return to it quickly without having to read through reams of material. Coding is data reduction or the process of selecting, focusing, and simplifying. Coding is probably one of the most difficult aspects of analyzing qualitative data.

Much reading and rereading of data is necessary to become completely familiar with the data. After the reading, coding can be done in two ways: by reducing the words to numbers or to descriptions. Evaluators are cautioned about coding to numbers because often the richness of words can be lost when this number coding occurs. Descriptive word codes may be more useful.

The coding for qualitative data may be descriptive, interpretive, or explanatory. These codes are likely to change over time as more data are collected. One way to start the data analysis process is to code the data descriptively according to the evaluation questions or criteria that were originally conceptualized. Codes can then be revised as new ideas emerge and are revised. If possible, it may be useful to have two evaluators code the "raw" data to assure greater reliability. Coding may be done line by line, but is usually done in "chunks." It may be quite general at first and then more focused later. The coding also will help the evaluator become familiar with the nature of the data that are being discovered and may help in focusing future interviews or observations for further broader or deeper information.

Other Organizing Strategies

A filing system can also be developed for organizing data. This system may be developed on the computer for coding chunks of data or by actually physically cutting and pasting notes and putting these edited pages into file folders. Guba and Lincoln (1981) suggested a technique of using note cards to sort ideas into look-alike piles can be used to organize data. The use of cards allows one to visually organize the grouped data and to begin to visualize how data may be categorized.

Some evaluators collecting qualitative data use computers for data organization. A number of good qualitative programs now exist and were discussed in Chapter 3.06. In most of these computer programs, the raw data are entered as word descriptions. The computer can be used to search for certain keywords or group the data according to the coding that you have inserted. The computer can help a great deal in organizing data, but it is still the individual who must make decisions about the way the data are organized and put together.

Displaying the Data

Once the data have been organized, you may then want to develop ways to display them. Data display is the organized assembly of information that permits the drawing of conclusions and the presentation of the respondents' words. Data displays are not required but they may be helpful to the evaluator as she or he begins to make sense of the coded data. A number of ways exist to display data as a means of organizing data for interpretation. Each evaluator will find that certain display strategies work well and others do not, depending on the situation.

In each case, no matter what kind of visual techniques are used to display data, the evaluator will have to make judgments about what data are important and what data are not.

A matrix may also be used after data are coded. A matrix can be easily eyeballed, compared to other matrices, and may use words and phrases. Usually the evaluator will develop categories for the matrix and then fill in the matrix with words or examples from the notes/transcripts that describe the categories. A matrix may be used to outline specific examples that fit particular themes, or it may be used for enumerating the number of responses to particular analysis categories. A number of matrices for a set of data can be developed. Some people prefer to build a matrix on a huge sheet of paper with fifteen to twenty variables (although five to six is usually more manageable).

Visual maps may be used to show the interrelationships that make up behavior. Diagrams are often helpful in organizing ideas and themes as well as patterns and configurations of interaction. The evaluator should also make notes about how she or he, as the evaluator, moved from one idea to another, and how the data displays were refined. Conceptual maps, which may be likened to a flow chart, tie patterns together with arrows and directional lines. They may be useful in stimulating thinking and may be useful to evaluators who like to see analyses visually.

These suggestions for displaying data are tools to be used in interpreting data. Data display is not the end product but is a technique to assist the evaluator. The display techniques are a means to the ultimate ends of providing a rich description and explanation of the meaning of the evaluation data.

Techniques for Data Analysis

Once the data are organized, a number of techniques may be applied to qualitative analysis. For purposes of evaluation research, three overlapping techniques for developing themes/patterns—enumeration, constant comparison, and content analysis—will be discussed. Enumeration refers to the counting of items that are similar. Constant comparison of patterns and themes is a summary of the major ideas that emerge. Content analysis refers to examining the meaning of communication and is similar to constant comparison except that it is usually used with written materials.

In any type of qualitative data analysis, the evaluator is attempting to account for all ideas that are presented, not just the most popular ideas. In other words, the focus is on interpreting conclusions, including pointing out contradictions that exist in the data. Further, the effort of uncovering patterns, themes, and categories is a creative process that requires carefully considered interpretations about what is significant and meaningful in the data.

Enumeration

Enumerative strategies are often used to supplement descriptive data. In this technique the evaluator codes qualitative data and counts it. One may be interested in the number of times certain behaviors occur or the duration of behaviors. Numbers are used in this case to show the intensity and amount of interaction. These numbers may also help the researcher to be analytically honest about how much agreement and disagreement existed about particular conclusions.

In a qualitative project, the evaluator may do some analysis with enumeration, but generally a qualitative evaluator will rely primarily on words and use numbers only as supplementary material. In open-ended questionnaires, however, numbers are frequently used because they are comparable to close-ended questions. For example, you might ask what it was about a program that individuals liked best, provide an enumeration of number counts, and then use the words to explain the meaning of the results. Table 3.7(1) (page 266) provides an example of how enumeration might be used.

Constant Comparison

Constant comparison is a popular systematic analysis technique for recording, coding and analyzing qualitative data. The process of constant comparison includes reading through all data, developing major themes or key conclusions, reading the data again to see that it all fits within the themes, adjusting the themes, and reading again to confirm that the interpretation is valid. (See Table 3.7(2), page 267, for an example of the first part of this process.) Obviously, data analysis takes time. The technique may mean going to others (e.g., colleagues, respondents) to have them confirm that the same themes were uncovered or that interpretations were correct.

The goal of constant comparison is to maximize credibility through the comparison of groups and data. It involves comparisons among data, data sets, documents, and different groups sampled. Different "slices of data" can also be compared. For example, one might triangulate surveys, observations, and anecdotal records and analyze how the results compare to one another. The constant comparison technique is inductive like other forms of qualitative analysis which means the patterns and themes emerge from the data rather than being imposed prior to data collection.

Three stages comprise the constant comparison process. First, the researcher takes "pieces" of data and organizes them by identifying, reducing, coding, and displaying categories of data. The second stage is to integrate the categories and their properties by comparing them to one another and checking them back to the data. In the third stage, the categories are delimited and refined, if necessary, to further focus a "story" about the data and how it fits together with *a priori* or

Table 3.7(1)

Example of Enumeration Coding and Analysis

Background about data: An evaluation was done in a southern university eight months after a four-day workweek was mandated as a measure to try to save energy costs. A questionnaire using both close-ended and open-ended questions was sent to a random sample of faculty and staff who worked at the university. These are some of the responses to a question about attitudes toward the four-day workweek and how they might be coded using strictly a simple enumeration process of indicating whether the attitude is positive, negative, or neutral.

I don't have the physical stamina to hold up to a ten-hour day.   (code=negative)

There are inconveniences such as trying to cram too much into four days.

(code=negative)

What is gained on the "off" day does not compensate for the stress on the other four days.

(code=negative)

It causes hardships at home with trying to take care of kids when they aren't in school early in the morning and in the afternoon.   (code=negative)

It's great. It would be hard to adjust to going back.   (code=positive)

I can be home on Fridays with my four-year-old son and I like it a lot.

(code=positive)

I am able to spend time on Fridays with friends, relatives, and I enjoy doing these things.

(code=positive)

I don't feel I'm getting as much done during the week as I did before.

(code=negative)

It's not good for morale because it squeezes too many expectations into too little time.

(code=negative)

The week goes by quickly and it gives me a chance to catch up on my personal projects on Friday.   (code=positive)

It makes sense.   (code=positive)

I like it a lot but my older colleagues are not coping very well with it.

(code=neutral)

Total = 6 negative, 5 positive, 1 neutral, 12 total. The data would be reported as numbers to show the relative amount of agreement concerning however the data were coded. Percentages should not be used as they may be confusing to the reader who is accustomed to seeing percentages related to quantitative statistics.

Table 3.7(2)

Example of Constant Comparison Technique

These are some of the same responses to a question about attitudes toward the four-day workweek and how they might be coded using an initial constant comparison approach.

I don't have the physical stamina to hold up to a ten-hour day. (code=tired)

There are inconveniences such as trying to cram too much into four days.
(code=inconveniences, but they are not identified)

What is gained on the "off" day does not compensate for the stress on the other four days.
(code=stress)

It causes hardships at home with trying to take care of kids when they aren't in school early in the morning and in the afternoon. (code=inconveniences with children)

It's great. It would be hard to adjust to going back. (code=like, but no reason)

I can be home on Fridays with my four-year-old son and I like it a lot.
(code=time to spend with people)

I am able to spend time on Fridays with friends, relatives, and I enjoy doing these things.
(code=time to spend with people)

I don't feel I'm getting as much done during the week as I did before.
(code=time problems)

It's not good for morale because it squeezes too many expectations into too little time.
(code=time problems)

The week goes by quickly and it gives me a chance to catch up on my personal projects on Friday. (code=personal time)

It makes sense. (code=logic)

I like it a lot but my older colleagues are not coping very well with it.
(code=concern for others)

This is a preliminary coding. You would go through all the data and work with them until you saw themes emerging. For examine, time is both a negative and a positive factor concerning the attitudes toward the four-day workweek. It opens time up for some people on the weekends, but the time also creates stress and a feeling of lack of production in some people.

---

emerging evaluation criteria. The evaluator wants to make sure that no other themes or categories might be included or that any important data are being excluded. If new themes are discovered, then the researcher must go back through the data, compare them to the new categories, and go through the analysis process once again.

The constant comparison technique causes one to look continually for diversity. It allows the assurance of accurate evidence, establishes generality of a fact, specifies concepts, verifies theory, or generates theory. According to Glaser and Strauss (1967), constant comparison does not generate a perfect theory or perfect conclusions, but rather perspectives and conclusions that are relevant to the context in which the data were observed or recorded.

Content Analysis

Content analysis is the process used to analyze documents, records, transcribed conversations, letters, or any document in a textual form. Content analysis and its many forms relate to a process of ascertaining meaning about a written phenomena being studied. In this sense, the strategy is more analytic than oriented toward data collection. Further, content analysis generally uses the basic process of qualitative constant comparison and has many similarities to those procedures.

Like unobtrusive techniques, this method may be used with a project that stands alone or may be used in triangulation with other data analysis strategies. Field evaluators frequently use document analysis as a form of content analysis to obtain historical information about a setting or situation being evaluated. The fundamental aspects of the content analysis strategy are that it is nonreactive, unobtrusive, and uses words and/or numbers to describe particular phenomena.

Content analysis is a process for making inferences by systematically identifying characteristics of messages. It may be done in words, phrases, sentences, paragraphs, sections, chapters, pictures, books, or any relevant context. Content analysis may be inductive or deductive. In the inductive form, the themes and patterns will emerge from analyzing the data rather than using a predetermined code such as described in the constant comparison process. In the deductive form, usually an elaborate numerical coding system is used to break down the meaning of the words. These numbers may then be analyzed quantitatively with statistical procedures and are treated just as you would treat any quantitative data. The deductive analysis of qualitative data results in reducing qualitative data to quantitative data for statistical purposes. Both inductive and deductive forms may be useful for the evaluator depending upon the criteria that are being examined.

Making Interpretations

Drawing conclusions to make interpretations about qualitative data occurs throughout the evaluation process. It is usually, but not always, an interactive cyclical process that is ongoing as data are collected and as they are organized. As you read data to organize it for enumeration or constant comparison, you are continually reexamining the data. "Negative evidence," which means you will be trying to make sure everything fits your categories, will be sought. If all the data do not fit the themes or categories, the evaluator will either have to explain contradictions or make new categories.

You will also be looking for multiple sources of evidence to draw conclusions. Sample systematically and widely and try to avoid becoming too attached to initial themes and patterns. An important strategy concerning data analysis is, therefore, not to stop the interpretation process too soon. Although an evaluator often is focusing on the end product, you must make sure not to reach the end too soon or become locked too quickly into a pattern of analysis that misses other possible meanings. The emergent nature of qualitative data must be allowed to happen. Documenting feelings throughout the data collection/analysis process is useful as these attitudes and feelings may give insights about the data and its context.

The complete qualitative data analysis process generally includes the simultaneous techniques of collecting, coding and organizing data, and interpreting data in its context. As indicated earlier, interpretation involves attaching meaning and significance to the data. With the voluminous amount of data collected in qualitative projects, beginning the analysis during data collection helps to organize the data and make it less overwhelming. Data interpretation and the development of conclusions should, therefore, begin as soon as possible after data collection.

Another key strategy to emphasize is that interpretations in qualitative projects come from being intimately familiar with the data. Therefore, one of the important tasks the evaluator does is to read the data over and over. The interpretation of meaning is not a task that can be assigned to someone else like one might hire someone to enter data into a computer or to run the statistics and give the evaluator the printout. Only through interaction with the data will you become familiar enough to see the emerging patterns and themes.

When all data are collected and analyzed, however, you will need to draw conclusions and make recommendations regarding the evaluation project. During the final stage of data analysis, you will also note what data you will use to support or exemplify the conclusions. The data will be used to illustrate how the conclusions were drawn. Two important aspects will be evident in the conclusions. Examples of *emic*, or ideas expressed by the respondents, as well as *etic*, or data expressed in the evaluator's language. As you begin to draw conclusions, you will make statements, called "thick description" (Geertz, 1983), based on both the emic and etic that is uncovered in the analysis. Table 3.7(3) (page 270) shows an example of a write-up that might be used.

The evaluator using qualitative data will actually use quotes and anecdotes to tell the story from the data. These descriptions and quotations are essential and should not be trivial or mundane. The evaluator will want to use a balance of description with the analysis and interpretation. The conclusions from qualitative data can be fairly lengthy but you should try to condense them to hit upon the important points. The written conclusions let the reader know what happened in the organization, what it was like from the participant's view, and how the events were experienced. The description will depend to a great extent on the evaluation criteria being addressed. In drawing conclusions and making interpretations, however, you must acknowledge that a fine line exists between description and causes. Causes can be described but cannot always say the direct relationship that might exist among variables or themes. The application of this caveat will depend to a great extent on the nature of the data analyzed.

Table 3.7(3)

Sample of a Few Lines of a Qualitative Evaluation Write-Up

The women with disabilities interviewed in this project defined leisure as free time or having time to do the things they wanted to do. They also talked about "having fun," "relaxing," "doing nothing," and "doing things at your own will and pace" as their definitions of leisure. A general distinction was made between recreation and leisure as indicated by the 41-year-old married woman with chronic fatigue syndrome:

> To me, recreation is doing something physical. Playing
> softball with your child or riding a bike or something along
> that line. And leisure can be just doing something quietly
> like reading a book or even playing a game, but something
> that's quiet. So to me that's the difference.

Among the examples of leisure and recreation activities that the women with disabilities said they enjoyed doing were: dancing, eating out, shopping, painting pictures, writing poetry, gardening, listening to music, sewing, swimming, photography, walking, church activities, watching TV, and playing games. No single activity or even group of activities were common for all women with disabilities who were interviewed. Overall, the women interviewed suggested that solitary and more passive activities were done at home while going into public places to participate in a more active recreation generally required some type of assistance or companionship....

From Ideas to Reality

The last section of this chapter has addressed the judgment part of the trilogy of evaluation. As indicated throughout this text, however, it is difficult to separate the processes involved with analyzing qualitative data into distinct steps. Thus, data collection, data analysis and drawing conclusions/recommendations go hand-in-hand. You should have all the information you need from this chapter to work with the qualitative data that you might collect. Evaluators will find, however, that handling qualitative data effectively requires practice. You can learn best by actually working with such data.

Unit Four—Judgment:
Data Reporting

INTRODUCTION TO JUDGMENT

An evaluation project isn't over until the judgment is made. The really intensive work part of evaluation is done by determining the criteria and getting evidence through data collection and analysis. But the third part of the trilogy, the judgment phase, is often the real thinking part. An evaluator, has to try to make sense of the findings that she or he analyzed. By its very definition, evaluation requires that you determine the worth or make judgments. Thus, if judgments are not made, the evaluation may have little value.

Unit Four will discuss how to report the evaluations by developing conclusions and recommendations. Using visuals to display data and how to write and present reports also will be discussed. We will focus on the most important part of all—using evaluations! Finally, evaluation systems and projects also need to be evaluated, so some of the common problems that occur in conducting projects and how you can do a self-assessment of your own work will be discussed.

When you have completed this—last unit of this textbook, you should be fairly familiar with how evaluations are supposed to work. You will not be an expert, but at least you will have a working knowledge of how to proceed with an evaluation project and how to justify the use of evaluations within an organization.

4.01 THE USE OF VISUALS FOR SHOWING DATA

Goals for Chapter 4.01:

—To explain the differences between different types of graphics;
—To prepare an appropriate graphic given data results; and,
—To evaluate a well-presented graphic from one that is not done well.

One of the most important steps in the evaluation process is the transmittal of the information that has been gathered to people who will use it in decision making. Sometimes this process is simplified through the visual representation of the data findings in tables and graphs. These visuals are usually incorporated into reports and presentations but also offer a way to organize the findings so that judgments through conclusions and recommendations can be made.

The old adage, "a picture is worth a thousand words," is true in evaluation, especially when handling complex quantitative data. A good rule of thumb is to use a visual when you find yourself visualizing something as you write, or if there are several sets of numbers to compare (Robinson, 1985). An evaluator should know not only when to use visuals but the best type to use (i.e., drawings, charts, tables, graphs, or photos).

When designing effective visuals, consider several general points. The visual should be appropriate to the audience and as simple as possible. No matter how "glitzy" you make the visuals, they will be totally useless unless the reader or audience understands them. Each part of the visual should be clearly labeled and visually pleasing with neat spacing, plenty of white space, and easy-to-read type.

Further, the visuals and the text should work together to provide integral documentation and support for the findings discussed in the narrative part of your report. You should always refer to a table in the appropriate place in the text. For example, if you included a table showing the participation in various recreation centers based on race, you might show this in two ways. You might say, "As can be seen in Table A, some recreation centers are predominated by a single racial group," or you might say, "Some recreation centers are predominated by a single racial group (see Table A)." The following sections will address specific information about making tables and figures.

Tables

Tables are the most common form of visual used for showing data. One of the primary advantages to tables is that the "number clutter" in the text can be drastically reduced. For example, instead of reading a tedious list of means used to compare two groups of participants, this data can be displayed in a table. A second advantage is that comparisons are shown more clearly in tables than with words. Tables also allow you to display data in a concise form. Tables, however, should not be included if all the information on a table can be more easily included in the narrative. Tables supplement the text, but should not duplicate it.

An evaluator always refers to the specific table number in the text and places the full table as close as possible after its reference in the text. If the table does not follow immediately after it is referenced, place it as soon as you can on the next full page. Try not to divide a table between two pages unless it is too long. A table that covers more than a page, however, may be better placed in the appendix rather than in the body of the report.

Most publication manuals provide guidelines for the specific information and format of tables. For example, the *Publication Manual of the American Psychological Association (APA)* (1983) has explicit instructions for authors on the correct format to be used with tables. Several general guidelines for tables should be kept in mind:

1. Put table number (in Arabic numbers) and title at the top of the table.
2. The title should be as descriptive as possible but not overly wordy.
3. Indicate on the table itself (either at the bottom or with the title) the source of the data if it is not directly from your evaluation data.
4. Include units of measure in the headings or entries to avoid confusion.
5. Arrange data that are to be directly compared in vertical columns.
6. Arrange data in logical order, preferably by the most important characteristic.
7. Align on the decimal point columns of numbers representing the same units of measure. Rounded off numbers to the nearest whole, tenth or one-hundredth are easier to read than long decimal numbers.
8. If independent/dependent variables are to be presented, independent variables should be in the row and dependent variables should be in the columns.
9. Use notes in the form of superscript letters if you need to explain anything further. You can put a superscript letter next to a heading and then explain its meaning under the table. Asterisks (*) are usually used on tables to note statistical significance.
10. For tables that have data cases, always include the number of respondents at the bottom of the table by indicating N=(the number).

Tables are usually quantitative but can be used with qualitative data or examples of written material. Sometimes a table with words or phrases can help a reader understand a concept more easily than reading through paragraphs of information. Whether qualitative or quantitative data are displayed, you should be able to see the significance of a table at a glance. It is usually best to use lines to separate tables and to separate related information within tables. A number of examples of tables, as well as figures, that follow the APA format can be found throughout this book.

Figures

Any type of illustration other than a table is usually called a figure. A figure can be a chart, graph, photograph, drawing, or some other graphic depiction. Just as with tables, you must carefully consider how to use a figure. A well-prepared figure can show a great deal of information. Figures do take time, however, to produce. As with tables, you must make sure that a figure supplements the text and does not simply duplicate it. Further, you need to consider what type of figure ought to be included and how elaborate it ought to be. The figure should convey essential facts, be easily read, be easily understood, and be carefully prepared. Several guidelines that pertain to tables also pertain to figures:

1. Put figure number (in Arabic numbers) and title at the bottom of the figure.
2. Indicate on the figure itself (either at the bottom or with the title) the source of the data if it is not directly from the evaluation data.
3. Use notes in the form of superscript letters if there is a need to explain anything further. A superscript letter can be put next to a heading, and its meaning under the figure explained.
4. For figures that have data cases, always include the number of respondents at the bottom of the table by indicating N=(the number).

Graphs are a popular way to display visual data. Graphs show data in pictorial form, but also have the advantage of showing relationships. The most commonly used are line graphs, bar graphs (also called column graphs), and pie graphs or charts.

Line Graphs

Line graphs are the most useful for showing trends in relationships between two variables; generally the shape of the curve is more important than the precise value of any given point. The following guidelines suggested by Robinson (1985) are useful when constructing line graphs:

1. Use a full grid only if you must for precision (hash marks on the axes usually work best).

2. Label both axes in direction of increase with the independent variable on the horizontal axis and the dependent variable on the vertical axis.
3. Avoid using a legend or key if possible; label the curve directly.
4. Adjust scale for ease of reading. If the graph is too big when zero is used at the intersection of the vertical and horizontal axis, you can use a double slash mark to show how numbers were skipped for a large interval on either of the axes.
5. Make data curves easy to identify.

Figure 4.1(1) shows an example of a basic line graph.

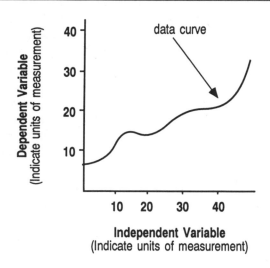

Figure 4.1(1) Example of a Basic Line Graph Design

Bar Graphs

Bar graphs, and a variation called histograms, are used to show quantitative relationships. Technically speaking, if the bars are vertical, they may be called column graphs; if they are horizontal, they are usually called bar graphs. An example of data appropriate for a bar graph would be the number of participants in six different recreation programs in one year. Robinson (1985) has suggested the following guidelines for bar graphs:

1. Be sure to make it easy to distinguish the bars by using width or shading;

2. Label the graph clearly; and,
3. Choose between vertical or horizontal bars logically. For example, use vertical bars for quantities we think of vertically, i.e. temperature, and horizontal bars for ones we think of horizontally, i.e., distance.

Figure 4.1(2) provides an example of a generic bar graph.

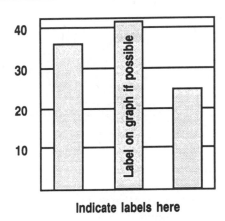

Indicate labels here

Figure 4.1(2) Example of a Generic Bar Graph Design

Pie Graphs

Pie graphs or pie charts are useful for showing the relative proportions to the whole. They are sometimes called 100 percent graphs because they show how 100 percent of something is distributed. Expenditures for budgets are often shown pictorially in pie charts. Sometimes the precise quantities are difficult to see when displayed as a pie graph so it is best to use five or fewer categories. Shading or using color also makes the graphs easier to understand. The following suggestions are useful when constructing pie graphs (Robinson, 1985):

1. Arrange the segments clockwise in order of size with the largest at twelve o'clock;
2. Place labels within the segments if possible;
3. Avoid making the reader rotate the page; and,
4. Include percent for each segment, if space permits.

Figure 4.1(3) (page 280) shows an example of a generic pie chart.

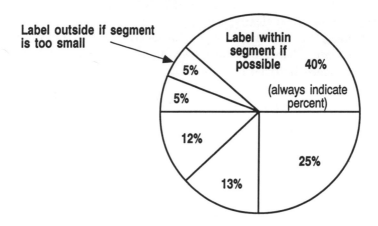

Figure 4.1(3) Example of a Generic Pie Graph

Other Types of Figures

Graphs are the major type of figures that will likely be used in evaluation reports, but also drawings or pictures might be considered depending upon the topic that is being addressed. The "rules" for these types of figures are the same as for other figures and tables. They must be necessary, simple, and easy to read. They should be labeled appropriately and should be keyed to the text. All figures should be numbered consecutively. You should also consider how easily drawings and photographs will reproduce if more than one copy of a report is needed.

Further Considerations

For any of these graphics, remember that the actual construction of a visual may be enhanced through the use of computer graphics programs. Programs such as Cricket Graph for the Macintosh allow you flexibility in designing your visuals. Other statistical packages also offer graphics possibilities such as in MYSTAT. The finished product from computers can be high in professional quality. We would suggest, however, that no matter how tables and figures are produced, manually or with the help of a computer, that you remember to make them simple, uncluttered, and easily understood.

From Ideas to Reality

Some people find the development of tables to be interesting work especially after the data have been collected and analyzed. Graphics, including tables and figures, offer an opportunity for the evaluator to be creative, providing many possibilities to convey visually exciting ideas and data. As people read a report, some will find that the tables and figures are the most interesting part of the report because they allow the reader to make interpretations about the data. Whatever the case, the evaluator should consider the possibility of using tables and figures when they are appropriate in an evaluation report. They can add greatly to the readability of the findings section of the report.

4.02 Developing Conclusions and Recommendations: The Grand Finale

---

Goals for Chapter 4.02:

—To describe the differences between conclusions and recommendations; and,

—To write conclusions and the subsequent recommendations from project findings.

Drawing conclusions is ongoing throughout an evaluation project, but a point comes when the conclusions and recommendations must be finalized and written. For qualitative data, the process of analysis is the process of drawing conclusions. For quantitative data, however, statistics and probabilities are only numbers until the evaluator interprets them in the form of conclusions.

Evaluation does not occur if judgments are not made. The evaluator's responsibility is to base judgments on the data that are available. Judgment occurs in the form of conclusions and recommendations. Although some conclusions may result in self-evident recommendations, the good evaluator will explicate the recommendations that evolve from conclusions. Sometimes recommendations are made to keep the program, policy, or whatever is being evaluated the same, while other times they result in specific suggestions about improvement, change, or even termination. Whatever the case, the evaluator needs to have confidence in what is being concluded and offered as recommendations.

How easy or how difficult conclusions and recommendations are to write will depend to a great extent on the type of project and the desires of the stakeholders in the evaluation process. Mobily and Iso-Ahola (1980) suggested that as the amount of data available increases, so does the number of alternatives that can be addressed in conclusions and recommendations. This statement, however, assumes that the data are reliable and valid. If you have followed the appropriate procedures for data collection and analysis, the trustworthiness of the conclusions and recommendations should not be a problem. The criteria established and the evidence collected should result in a framework for developing conclusions and offering the best course of action.

The Relationship Between Findings/Results and Conclusions/Recommendations

An evaluator will need to organize the data to discuss her or his findings. Developing visual presentations is a good way to organize the data, but she or he will also need to discuss it in a narrative form in the report. Using the narrative and various visuals will tell the story. You will report statistics and tell "p" values in the findings, and will show qualitative data by actually using quotes and anecdotes to interpret the results. In other words, findings or results are the data summaries portrayed either through narrative and tables/figures if the data are quantitative, or are the etic summaries of descriptive and anecdotal material from qualitative data. From the findings, then, it will be necessary to develop the "bottom line" which is essentially what the overall conclusions are and what action needs to be taken to address those conclusions.

Writing Conclusions

Conclusions follow directly from the findings and are used to summarize what has been learned as a result of the evaluation project. The conclusions should relate *directly* to the criteria or objectives of the project. In a report, which will be discussed in more detail in Chapter 4.03, the conclusions section follows immediately after the findings or results section. No new evidence or findings are presented in the conclusions that have not been presented previously.

Several aspects should be considered when writing conclusions. Some of the important qualities are: conciseness, accuracy, relevancy, and reflection of the purposes and findings. Smith (1989) suggested several key points to keep in mind. First of all, be sure to make conclusions. One cannot expect the reader to make judgments based on the findings in an evaluation project. Conclusions are an essential part of the evaluation process. It is also useful to involve others in an organization in writing conclusions so that they understand what the data say and from where conclusions came.

Second, present conclusions with the best possible justification for why they were made. Conclusions should be drawn from evidence and recommendations made from conclusions, but do not overextend either. No conclusion should ever exist that does not have explicit data as the basis for it. Although often difficult, try to keep personal biases out of the conclusions. The conclusions should be a summary of what the findings that have already been presented mean.

Finally, it should be kept in mind that conclusions are not difficult to make if the criteria are clear, the evaluation questions are explicitly stated, and the data is reliable and valid. If the study has not been adequately designed, conclusions are difficult to make in actuality and may raise ethical issues.

Making Recommendations

Recommendations are the proposed courses of action to be followed based on the conclusions. The recommendations and conclusions should be closely linked such that the recommendations appear as an inevitable outcome of the conclusions. They are the finale to the project and follow from the study's findings and conclusions. Many evaluators often stop short of making recommendations even though the purpose of evaluations is to determine the worth or value of something so that action can be taken. Although the findings should speak for themselves, a good evaluator will need to interpret the data and make specific judgments in the form of recommendations.

Several aspects should be kept in mind when writing recommendations. Recommendations must relate directly to the criteria and the conclusions. Do not stray off to tangentially related topics in developing recommendations. While keeping in mind the purpose of the project, judgments should be made based on the best information available even though sometimes this information is not perfect. Indeterminacy always exists in any evaluation project, but the evaluator simply has to acknowledge anything that might be less than ideal for a given situation. People are continually making judgments anyway, so they might as well be stated formally as recommendations so that they are less likely to be misunderstood. Not to make a recommendation or a judgment is to suggest that everything is fine concerning whatever aspect of an organization that is being evaluated.

Some people have a hard time differentiating between conclusions and recommendations. Conclusions state an interpretation of the findings whereas recommendations are specific tactical proposals for action that eliminate, replace, or augment current actions to steer a program, person, policy, place, or participant into preferred directions. Recommendations may provide examples, call for further evaluation and more information, suggest an allocation of resources, advocate offering the same services to others, propose reordered priorities or changes in policy or program, or may rank program strengths or deficiencies according to their importance or seriousness. As can be seen, recommendations may take a number of directions. Table 4.2 (page 286) shows an example of conclusions and recommendations resulting from conducting an evaluation project.

The evaluator, as well as the user or stakeholders, should keep in mind that recommendations are not surefire prescriptions for success (Sadler, 1984). They are suggestions based on what the evaluator saw in conducting the evaluation project. The use of recommendations is another issue that must be considered by those who have the power to make changes and this use will be discussed further in Chapter 4.05. Not all recommendations can be addressed, but stakeholders

Table 4.2

Example of Conclusions and Recommendations

(material adapted from evaluation report of Lara Pietrafesa, Kim Boyette and Tonya Bryan)

This project was an evaluation of satisfaction with Student Recreation Center Aerobics Program at the University of North Carolina in Chapel Hill. Data were collected using the triangulated methods of questionnaires to participants, interviews with instructors, and observations of randomly selected classes.

Conclusions:
1. Participants and instructors were generally satisfied with the aerobics program as indicated by the high marks given to the facilities and equipment.
2. Participants had high satisfaction with the instruction and the total workouts that they were able to achieve.
3. Instructors were satisfied with the management of the classes and the teaching schedules that they were assigned.
4. Concern was expressed by both participants and instructors concerning the large class sizes, the number of classes offered, and the scheduling of the classes.

Recommendations:
1. The Student Recreation Center should continue to maintain the high quality of the facilities and equipment and the communication that exists between management and the instructors.
2. More classes need to be offered at different times during the day. No classes are offered in midafternoon or after 8:30 p.m., so these times might be appropriate to consider as new class times. Offering more classes should cut down on the classes that are presently overcrowded and make the offerings more convenient to student schedules.

---

should at least know the possibilities for changes that are offered through recommendations.

The evaluator might wish to consider who should be involved in making recommendations. It is generally best to involve others who will be affected by possible recommendations. If, for example, the evaluator talks to program staff who may know parts of an organization better than her or him, these staff may be most helpful. If staff are involved at every step of the evaluation and especially in drawing up recommendations, they are more likely to become invested and use the evaluation results.

In making recommendations, the evaluator should also consider the organization's willingness and/or ability to make changes. Recommendations that are impossible to carry out because of insufficient resources may cast doubt on the ability of the evaluator to do his or her job. If you only have hunches about possibilities for changes, make sure you say those ideas are hunches rather than presenting them as specific recommendations. In other words, the recommendations ought to be realistic and practical for implementation possibilities.

The end result is that conclusions and recommendations offer judgments about gathering more data, making a change, raising an issue, leaving things as they are, or a combination of these possibilities. In making recommendations, the evaluator must have confidence that the evaluation was well-done and that judgments were based on sound data.

From Ideas to Reality

Writing conclusions and recommendations is the final process in interpreting the data and making judgments within an evaluation project. These conclusions and recommendations are usually brief, concise, and to the point. When the evaluator has reached the point of writing conclusions and recommendations and is able to address the criteria that have been used throughout the project, the "bottom line" of the evaluation has been reached. Sometimes conclusions and recommendations are easy to write; other times you will have to work to figure out what the findings/results mean. If the evaluator has done a good job of planning the project and collecting data, the conclusions and recommendations should become obvious once the data are analyzed.

4.03 WRITING REPORTS: SAVING A PAPER TRAIL

```
┌─────────────────────────────────────────────────────────┐
│                                                          │
│              Goals for Chapter 4.03:                     │
│                                                          │
│  —To outline the components that comprise an evaluation report; │
│  —Given a report, write an executive summary for the report; and │
│  —To assemble a report as a result of having developed criteria, collected │
│    data, and interpreted the findings.                   │
│                                                          │
└─────────────────────────────────────────────────────────┘
```

Evaluation projects ought to result in written reports. A situation might occur when an evaluator would conduct a project, and she or he or a very small group of people, would be using the results directly, so a report would not be written. Most of the time, however, you will want to have written material as a record of what was done and what was learned. Without something written, in time, it will be difficult to remember what was done and the recommendations that were made. Even regular activities like staff evaluations should have a summary written that can be placed in an individual's personnel file.

The report may vary from a full report to a *Reader's Digest* condensed version. The report length and type will depend upon the agency, the extent of the project, and how the information will be shared. The extent of the report needs to be negotiated between the evaluator and agency at the beginning of the project. Regardless of the extent or nature of the report, as an evaluator you will want to strive for technical detail and excellence. As Hudson (1988) suggested, reports should be comprehensive, organized, and clearly written. Regardless of the temporal, financial and physical resources, an evaluator should not shortcut the preparation of the final report.

The report should provide a clear picture of the evaluation process and answer the questions or criteria posed. It should tell who, what, when, why, where, and how, just as was done when the project was planned. In the final report, however, these responses should be precise and concise. And, of course, the report must contain judgments in the form of conclusions and recommendations. The formal report consists of several components which will be discussed in detail: cover; executive summary; table of contents; the body of the report that includes introduction, methods, findings, conclusions and recommendations; and appendices.

Cover

The cover is not necessarily the most important aspect from the evaluator's standpoint, but it is the first thing that the evaluation report reader will see. The cover should be designed with special consideration because it speaks first giving the first impression. It need not be fancy, but should include the title of the evaluation project, who was evaluated, names of evaluators, for whom the report was prepared, dates of the evaluation, and date of the report.

Depending on the relationship of the evaluator to the agency, the report might be sent under a cover letter or a cover letter might be one of the first pages. The cover letter simply transmits the report from the evaluator to the organization. The cover letter states that the report is completed and offers any other general information that ought to be considered by the agency or the reader.

Executive Summary (Abstract)

Evaluation reports typically include an executive summary, sometimes called simply a summary or an abstract. The summary includes in a page, or less than 500 words, the most important points of the entire project. Most people will read the executive summary and then decide whether to read the rest of the report. In other cases, the summary may be the only part read as some people will simply not have time to read an entire report.

The summary almost always appears before the main text. It includes a statement of the purpose, how the project was conducted, and the main conclusions and recommendations.

The executive summary is written in nontechnical terms. It is usually written to be accessible to a wide audience. In many cases, the full evaluation report will not be distributed widely within an organization, but the executive summary might be shared with a number of people who can then get the full report if they want further details.

Ironically, even though the executive summary goes first, it must be written carefully *after* the rest of the report is written. Nothing should appear in the executive summary that is not carefully described in the main part of the report. The executive summary is the condensed version of the most important aspects of the report. Table 4.3(1) shows an example of an executive summary.

Table of Contents

Depending on the length of the report, a table of contents may or may not be needed. Often these tables are helpful to the reader in finding a particular topic. If a number of subheadings are used, these should be listed in the table of contents and indented appropriately to show the level of the headings. If a number of tables

Table 4.3(1)

Example of an Executive Summary

(adapted from the work of students Cathy Mitchell, Tonya Sampson, and Charlene Hardin)

The Qualifying Tournament at the University of North Carolina at Chapel Hill (UNC-CH) for the Intramural Big Four Tournament was the focus of this evaluation. The purpose of the evaluation was to improve the qualifying tournament at UNC-CH with a specific focus on determining the reason for low participation and analyzing the currently used methods of advertising. Three methods were used for data collection: captains of teams that participated in the qualifying tournament received a questionnaire during the tournament, captains of regular season teams that did not participate received a telephone interview, and the directors of the intramural programs at the Big Four universities involved (i.e., Wake Forest, Duke, North Carolina State University, and University of North Carolina-Chapel Hill) were personally interviewed. Two major conclusions were drawn. First, the majority of regular season captains did not know about the qualifying tournament, or they would have considered participating. Second, very little advertising was done at UNC-CH to inform potential participants of the qualifying tournament. The evaluators recommend that the following methods of advertising be considered in the future: use the student newspaper to make announcements, put banners around campus, send flyers to residence halls and fraternities/sororities as well as post them on campus, and set up a table in the "pit" to provide information to interested persons. The evaluators also suggest that the organizers of the Big Four Tournament consider automatically sending regular season champions for each activity to the tournament. In the event that a team or individual cannot attend, then a qualifying tournament should be held.

and figures are used, the evaluator may want to list the tables and figures by title and page number immediately following the table of contents as was done for this textbook. Obviously, the table of contents like the executive summary, cannot be completed until the main body of the report is written, even though it is placed up front in the report.

Introduction

The introduction is the first of the four sections that are typically included in the body of the evaluation report. Each of these sections should begin with a brief introduction about the project and what will be covered in that section. In any of the sections, subheadings should be used liberally as they help the reader to follow the report. Subheadings, however, are meant as crutches and should not preclude the writer's using transition sentences between subheading topics.

The introduction to the main report sets the scene, tells the purpose of the project evaluation, and describes the characteristics of the agency or the units being evaluated. Depending on the criteria, the introduction might refer to an organizational chart to show information about the organization and may explicate the purpose or mission of the organization. Program goals and objectives might be presented as well as a bit of history if the reader is unfamiliar with the background of a project.

The introduction will also describe the design procedures including the model for evaluation used, the timing, and a justification for why a study was undertaken. The evaluator should describe any limitations and restrictions that were imposed or encountered in doing the project. It is also good to state the evaluation process briefly and provide a general time line.

The specific criteria that were examined and the evaluation questions that you addressed are the most important aspects of the introduction. If these questions are made specific at the beginning, the conclusions can be addressed as answers later in the report and the reader will be able to understand why the evaluation project was undertaken.

Methods

The methods section contains details about the procedures used for data collection and analysis, the development or selection of instruments, and the details of sampling including composition, size, and time periods. The methods should relate directly to the criteria identified. The connections between the method(s) chosen and the evaluation questions should be evident. Any examples of questionnaires, checklists, or interview schedules should be put into the appendix with a note in the narrative saying that "In Appendix A is an example of the questionnaire used."

Any limitations or problems that existed in data collection or analysis should be noted in this methods section. The methods should be specific enough that those who want to do a similar evaluation project could read the methods section and be able to replicate the project. The strengths and weaknesses of methods used should also be justified and noted briefly.

Findings

The findings section is where the results are presented. In most reports, this section is the longest section. The findings may include qualitative or quantitative analyses. If triangulated methods or data sources are used, all results from the methods or sources should be mentioned in this section.

A description of the respondents usually is presented first in the findings section of an evaluation report. This information provides the reader with background about who or what comprised the sample. Organizing this section in relation to the specific criteria, or the evaluation questions raised is often useful. In the case of a goal-free evaluation, the findings section should provide a structure for organizing the results that will evolve as data are collected. The use of tables and figures, described in Chapter 4.01, are usually helpful in presenting the findings. In addition, the analysis of patterns, themes, tendencies, trends, and categories should be made clear in this section. All the data should be presented here that are relevant to the project. No additional data should be introduced outside of this section.

Conclusions and Recommendations

The conclusions and the recommendations are the final section of the body of the report and should naturally link to the criteria identified and the findings. The conclusions will show the relationships of the findings to the evaluation criteria. The recommendations address the strengths and weaknesses of the findings about the area being evaluated and propose courses for action. Possible and/or desired recommendations for change or improvement should be stated along with possible suggestions for future evaluations. A summary of how to write conclusions and recommendations was presented in Chapter 4.02.

Appendices

The appendices will include any material that is too detailed or technical to be considered in the regular report. Examples that might be in the appendices include: organizational charts, instruments, instructions to subjects, tables of data if too large for the findings section, and copies of correspondence. Few people ever read appendices, but they will look at them if any questions arise, so this information needs to be included.

Sometimes additional information is included in an appendix such as the cost of a project or a detailed summary of evaluation procedures. Do not, however, include anything in the appendices that has not been referred to in the text. The text should indicate why and where each appendix exists. Similarly, the appendices should be given page numbers and are often labeled with A, B, C, and so on to enable the reader to find them easily and not be confused by the Arabic numbering of tables and figures within the report.

Table 4.3(2) gives a summary outline of the order that information should appear in an evaluation report.

Table 4.3(2)

Outline for a Written Report

Cover
Cover Letter (optional)
Executive Summary
Table of Contents including list of Appendices
Table of Figures/Tables (optional)
Introduction
    Purpose
    Setting
    Models/Design
    Criteria Measured
Methods
    Procedure
    Sampling
    Statistics or Analysis Used
Findings
    Results of Analysis
    Tables and Figures
Conclusions
Recommendations
Appendices

General Observations about Report Writing

The evaluation project report should be readable and free of academic jargon. You may know a lot about evaluation, methods and statistics, but your audience may not. Therefore, the report should be made as simple and as straightforward as possible with clear explanations if they are needed. The data in an evaluation project should do the impressing, not a fancy writing style. Do not write to impress—write to communicate.

People write in different ways. Some people find a detailed outline to be helpful. Others like to start with lead sentences, or to develop tables and figures first. Some people like to write the findings first, and then fill in the other parts.

It doesn't matter where you start writing a report. The important thing is that final product tells the evaluation story.

For some people, writing the report is a delightful experience once all the other hard work is done. Other people will struggle with writing. As stated before, the better the project is done, the easier it will be to write about it. Writing, however, requires a fair amount of effort. You will likely have to write several drafts before the report is complete. Some people find it helpful to write for awhile and then set the report aside and come back to it in a couple of days with fresh eyes. Writing is a personal experience so you have to decide what way is best, making sure, however, to give yourself adequate time to write the report. It is not something that is always easy to organize and complete at the last minute.

Keep in mind that you can't include everything in the report. You will have to think carefully about what to address and what data to supply. A fine line exists between too little and too much data in an evaluation report, but it is necessary to try to find that compromise. Having others in an organization look at the report before it is finalized to get their reactions to the information that is included may be useful. It is paramount, however, to keep your criteria in front of you as you write so as to avoid going into any unnecessary tangents.

Sometimes rather than writing a full report, an evaluator may want to use a summary sheet for a particular project. The executive summary may be a basis for the summary sheet, but it may be desirable to go into a bit more detail concerning the conclusions drawn.

If a short summary is used instead of a full report, it should include: name of activity and/or event, place of activity and/or event, participants (characteristics and number), strengths of program, weaknesses of program, and recommended changes. A series of these short reports would provide a good paper trail that may help in planning future evaluation projects.

From Ideas to Reality

The final report is the composite of all one's work on an evaluation project, so it should be made readable and usable. As outlined in this chapter, standard components are usually found in an evaluation report, but one can be creative within that report as long as the information is communicated clearly. Variations may exist in a report. Before a project is begun, it should be determined what the final report will resemble, and then work should be done on the components of the report as one moves along. Writing the report can be exciting and fun because it is the tangible evidence that documents all the hard work that you have done on a project.

4.04 ORAL PRESENTATIONS: TELLING THE TALE

Goals for Chapter 4.04:

—To give a presentation that describes the results of an evaluation project;

—To evaluate another presentation in terms of its strengths and weaknesses; and,

—To choose visuals that will be appropriate for the presentation that you are giving.

Along with a written report for an evaluation project, sometimes an oral report or presentation is also given. In the long run, the oral report may be the most effective way to get the information to people. Many people will not take the time to read an entire written report, but they will listen to a presentation if it is interesting.

The oral report will vary greatly and may be long or short, formal or informal, and addressed to technical or general audiences. Many of the same principles of the written report pertain to oral presentations regarding the format. A written or oral report will have an introduction, methods, findings, and conclusions and recommendations sections. Many times in an oral report, however, you will not have much time so you must be selective with the material presented.

Several basic principles govern any type of oral presentation. First, material should be presented in terms of your purpose and audience. Second, important points should stand out. Third, the points should be stated as simply as possible.

As you begin to develop an oral presentation you will need to ask questions like: "What sort of people will make up the audience?" "What will be their primary concerns?" and "Should I focus on the whole picture or just a portion of it?" Keep in mind that for most people, listening carefully is harder than reading carefully. As a listener, if a person misses a point in a speech, she or he cannot go back to it as is possible with reading. Therefore, a speaker must be careful to catch and hold the audience.

In writing a report, an evaluator can write an executive summary for the nontechnical audience, but in a speech one cannot give a two-part speech and ask some people not to listen to portions of the presentation. Thus, care must be taken to carefully consider what will be discussed. The presentation should be kept at the general audience level. You must figure out the target audience and write the speech aimed at them. How much does the audience know now? How technically sophisticated are they about the content of the evaluation as well as evaluation procedures? What will they do with the information given to them?

Most speeches either inform or persuade. In an evaluation report, you are presenting a summary with recommendations so the attempt is to both inform and persuade. You are, in a sense, selling ideas. You want to present the material carefully, honestly, and as truthfully as you analyzed it. If an evaluator believes in the trustworthiness of her or his evaluation project, it will be difficult to present the material in any other way.

Planning the Oral Presentation

The evaluator needs to know if the audience members will have the report in front of them or whether they will have read it previously. She or he will need to think about what two or three questions would be uppermost in their minds. From this information, one can begin to prepare the presentation by writing an outline. Like the written report, an oral report is a matter of selecting and organizing information on the basis of the project's purpose and the analysis of the audience. Keep in mind that you have to think of your time limits. The presentation speech needs to have a beginning, middle, and end. The presentation should always inform the audience members by saying what it is they will be told, telling them, and then summarizing what was told.

Time limits are important. For every minute a speaker runs over her or his allotted time, the more hostile the audience often gets. People talk too long for two reasons: they haven't planned their presentation and/or they do not realize how long it takes to cover a point. Good organization is even more important in an oral report than a written one. Everything cannot be covered. The presentation should be planned, however, so it can be shortened if needed, or more detailed if time allows.

A mode of delivery will need to be chosen. Speaking from memory is not recommended. Speaking from the actual written report can result in not talking to the audience. Speaking from notes is the best way to assure a conversation with the audience. Also, always keep in mind that the audience is listening, not reading.

The introduction, which includes the purpose and process (methods), sets the stage. Most audiences will listen carefully for 60 seconds at the beginning of a talk. Then they decide what to do next. If the topic and/or presentation is interesting, they will continue to "tune in." The bottom line is to get their attention.

The body has the substance of the talk and usually includes a brief description of the procedures used and some of the major evaluation findings. The conclusion of the presentation will include the recommendations or calls for action.

When preparing an oral presentation, keep it simple. Concentrate on the overall picture and stick to the basics. Just as you would use subheadings, make it clear to the audience the pattern of what is said. Use words like "for example" and highlight the conclusions and/or recommendations with numbers like first, second, third. It is usually best to limit the use of math and numbers in a speech, or else explain what is being done. Visual aids such as slides and transparencies can also help get the message across.

Using Visual Aids

Visual aids might be helpful; in a short presentation, however, do not use too many. For fifteen minutes about three or four visual aids are enough. The aids must be seen easily by the audience.

The speaker may want to use flip charts which are portable, require no special equipment, do not require a dark room, and allow for spontaneity. Flip charts, however, are usually not good for large audiences because they cannot be seen easily from the back of a room.

A chalkboard can be used spontaneously, but writing takes time and attention away from speech. Slides are permanent, portable, and versatile and can include photos, graphs, and charts. Slides, however, take advanced preparation, require a darkened room, and can provide a distraction when the room is darkened.

Overhead transparencies are easy to make and can be effective with large audiences. They are, however, easy to abuse by relying on them too much during a presentation. To avoid a common mistake, the transparencies must have *large* print and be simple.

Handouts are useful for detailed or complex material, especially statistical examples. They can also be used to cover content you may not be able to get across in a speech. If your speech would benefit, distribute pertinent handouts before speaking; however, detailed handouts may present a temptation for the audience to read rather than listen to the speaker. If handouts are a backup, they should be give out at the end of the presentation. Use different colored paper for each handout if there is more than one handout for people to examine during the presentation.

Props can be effective attention-getters, but they must be large enough to be seen by the entire audience. Passing an item around is not a good substitute for a large prop.

The bottom line is to make visual aids big, simple, and clear so their meaning can be grasped quickly. When people are looking at the visual aid, they are not listening to what is being said. Try to keep distraction of visual aids to a minimum by practicing with the aids. Practice using them when practicing your speech. Try to get the audience to shift its attention naturally. Be sure the audience can see the aids. Point to and emphasize major aspects on the screen or overhead. And of course, know how to operate equipment.

Giving the Presentation

The delivery of an oral presentation takes practice. Do not expect to do it perfectly the first time. Learn from your mistakes. With competence comes a feeling of being in control of the situation. When you feel in control, you will feel more comfortable in the situation. Practice ahead of time, preferably with someone else or with a videotape, but at least practice out loud. Evaluate the presentation and work to improve it. Do not practice until the speech sounds canned, but do go over it two or three times.

When giving the actual presentation, dress appropriately for the setting. Avoid anything flamboyant or extreme that would detract your audience's attention. The four most common voice errors made are talking too softly, too fast, without expression, or using vocalized pauses (e.g., uh, ok, now, you know, I mean). Practice avoiding these errors. Maintaining frequent eye contact is essential to a good speech—the audience will tell you how the presentation is.

Ninety percent of the audience's perception of how good the presentation is will be determined by the attitude you project. You need to project an attitude of competence and confidence. Remember that you are the expert on this topic. Show interest in the evaluation project. Treat the audience with respect and courtesy, and its members will respond in kind. Be aware of time limits. Use a watch.

After a presentation, time is usually allowed for questions. In answering questions, the question should be repeated so all can hear. This repeating of the question will also give the speaker a moment to gather her or his thoughts. If the answer isn't known, it is alright to say so. Unexpected questions often offer interesting perspectives. Do not get into a long argument with one member of the audience. Other people will get bored. Invite that person to talk further with you afterward.

Presenting an oral report after an evaluation project is the frosting on the cake. After all the work you have done, you will want to share the results with an audience who is interested. It will be up to you, however, to make sure that the presentation is as interesting as your project conclusions.

From Ideas to Reality

It isn't possible to include a videotape along with this book to show an example of a good presentation, but most evaluators have had numerous experiences listening to presentations. The advice suggested in this chapter should be useful to consider, but it is also important to draw on personal experience with other presentations. We can learn a great deal by observing others and adopting the strengths of their modes of communication. The prerequisite for a good presentation, however, will always be having something important to say which is a result of all the hard work that was put into developing the criteria, evidence, and judgment for an evaluation project.

4.05 USING EVALUATIONS FOR ENLIGHTENED DECISION MAKING

Goals for Chapter 4.05:

—To explain the value of involving potential users in all phases of the evaluation process; and,

—To describe the ways that recommendations might be used in an organization.

The best evaluation criteria and data collection will be useless unless the conclusions and recommendations are used in some way for decision making. The purpose of any evaluation is to get information for action. Depending whether you are an internal or external evaluator, you may have a different stake in what action occurs. Nevertheless, if an evaluation is to be done as more than just an application of research methods, it needs to be used. An evaluator can use several strategies to make sure that the evaluation is used. These strategies are not just done at the end of the project, but must be considered throughout the project.

Several authors (Chenery and Russell, 1987; Guba and Lincoln, 1989; Patton, 1978) have discussed the value of utilization-focused evaluation. Patton (1978) described the active-reactive-adaptive approach to evaluation that starts by keying the decision makers and information users, and then determining what relevant evaluation questions should be asked or what criteria should be examined. When offering suggestions for changes in an organization, those people (e.g., staff, participants) directly affected by the changes should be consulted and should be involved in making recommendations. This involvement is not always possible, but should be considered.

The proposed recommendations are a starting point for action. This action can be applied to any of the five Ps. Several types of actions can be suggested: evaluate some more, change something, take no further action, or terminate something. An agency also has the prerogative to ignore the recommendations, but hopefully this does not occur unless the benefits and consequences of the recommendations have been carefully considered. For any evaluation project, the potential exists for implementing findings, considering the findings for implementation, implementing changes which are different from but related to findings, or accepting the findings but taking no action. You might ask if an evaluation project is successful if recommendations are:

  • implemented in total?
  • implemented in part?
  • considered but rejected?
  • not implemented but other changes made?
  • not implemented but other unrelated changes made?
  • not implemented, no changes made?
  • not implemented and evaluation findings challenged or rejected?

No specific answers exist to these questions, but an evaluator must consider what they imply. According to Farrell and Lundegren (1987), evaluators may experience some resistance to recommendations if the organization is more fixated on survival rather than change. Some organizations do not want to rock the boat, have hidden political issues, ingrained staff conventions, and/or staff with inadequate skills and competencies to make necessary changes. An evaluator can do little about some of these factors except know that they exist and try to design the evaluation project with those considerations in mind.

In general, a successful evaluation might be defined in many ways. Utilization might be defined as serious consideration of the results in making decisions whether the actual recommendations are actually instituted. Utilization also occurs when the results are actually applied to a situation. An evaluator who has spent much time and effort working on an evaluation would hope that at least some of the recommendations are used and/or implemented.

Conducting Projects to Influence Their Use

Theobald (1979) says evaluations run two major risks: (1) a technical failure in research design, and (2) political barriers in terms of how a study will be received. This textbook has dealt with designing technically appropriate and trustworthy evaluations. Sometimes recommendations are not used because the evaluation project is done poorly or in a mediocre fashion and the findings do not seem trustworthy.

Addressing potential political barriers is often more difficult to do. Potential users of evaluations should be identified early, and the evaluator should find out what they want to get from a project. Administrators need to be informed and involved in the process because these individuals generally will be responsible for providing resources for implementing the recommendations. The prompt completion and early release of results is often another way to encourage use.

An evaluator should not undertake an evaluation project if she or he is sure the results will have no effect on decisions, or if it is believed an organization is not interested in change. Don't undertake an evaluation project unless a high probability of producing valid, precise, and applicable information exists and the results can be made conceptually clear to program administrators, managers, and practitioners. Otherwise, an evaluation project is a waste of time and resources.

Although writing reports has already been discussed at length, the use or value of an evaluation may be dependent on how a report is written. Effective methods of presentation of findings and dissemination of information using clarity and attractiveness, spelled out recommendations, summary sheets, and evaluators who are strong advocates of the recommendations will be essential if evaluations are to be used. The report, however, can be written in a variety of styles. For example, a research study was done by Brown, Braskamp, and Newman (1978); they developed four reports that were called jargon-loaded objective, jargon-loaded subjective, jargon-free objective, and jargon-free subjective. Jargon referred to words that conveyed a concept to a professional audience. Objective included local and national survey results and said "75 percent said...." Subjective utilized phrases like "I believe, I think." After reading the four reports, teachers and school administrators were asked to indicate how much they agreed with the recommendations. The authors concluded that the style of report did affect the audience. Jargon-loaded were perceived as more technical. The jargon-free subjective was the easiest to read. The style, however, did not affect the acceptance or believability of the recommendations.

Encouraging Evaluation Utilization

Once the evaluation project is completed and reported, several plans might be offered to communicate the recommendations both inside and outside the organization. First, it may help to call a staff meeting and discuss the recommendations and their implications. Meeting with staff one-on-one to discuss the results may also be useful and appropriate.

Second, participants might be consulted. Sometimes the program participants can make sure that their recommendations are considered as can colleagues and co-workers who understand the importance of conducting the evaluation.

Third, the organization's decision makers will need to reevaluate their goals and objectives to see if they are realistic in light of the evaluation recommendations. The Board of Directors or Recreation Commission may be the appropriate people to involve. Once possible recommendations to address are determined, a list of priorities must be set and a timeline for making changes developed. Often more recommendations are made than can be handled at any one time. Some of the less expensive and less complex items can be addressed immediately, while others may take more planning. Budgets and other resources may also need to be tied into the plans for using the information.

Fourth, the evaluator must not expect that *all* recommendations for change can be made. Sometimes it is a matter of priority or identifying the relative importance of different recommendations. Time lag may also result with recommendations. Some take a few weeks or months to implement while others may take years. Sometimes evaluators must impress upon people the value of moving slowly toward some kinds of change. Further, sometimes the recommendations may result in greater change or more changes than an organization actually wants. Thus, in making recommendations that have the potential for use, the evaluator may find it is better when only moderate changes are suggested and only a few important suggestions are made rather than extensive recommendations.

Fifth, keep in mind that in some situations, the conclusions from a project may be negative. It is important to consider carefully what negative evaluations mean. One of the problems with some evaluation methods, like experiments, is they don't tell why something happened. The evaluator must carefully examine what results mean before offering recommendations to terminate a program. The same is true with evaluations that show no difference occurred or show mixed results. As was discussed earlier, no difference may not be sufficient reason to eliminate a program, but it may mean that the recommendation is for further evaluation using a different method. If the results of an evaluation are unclear, you may want to do further evaluation.

Finally, additional suggestions to encourage the implementation of evaluation recommendations include encouraging positive attitudes about evaluations in staff and decision makers. The focus of evaluations should be on what they tell us that can improve the delivery of leisure services, rather than just a summary of good news/bad news. Evaluators will need to help people see the connections between findings of evaluations and what is going on in an organization. Helping staff and decision makers develop positive attitudes about evaluation, however, should not occur only at the end of the project, but throughout the design, data collection, and judgment phases.

From Ideas to Reality

The most likely way that evaluations will be used is if a trustworthy evaluation has been done and if the evaluator has drawn specific conclusions and recommendations that can be feasibly implemented. Evaluations are sometimes not used because the evaluator is afraid to go out on a limb and draw conclusions or make unpopular recommendations. In this case, a gap exists between evaluation findings and clear courses for future action. The implications of making changes, however, are not always obvious. If the evaluator does not make judgments in the form of conclusions and recommendations, decision makers in agencies may not realize the ways that evaluations can help them improve. We have offered a number of ways to think about how evaluations can be used, but it must be emphasized that utilization is a process that has its origins when a project is first designed. You will need to set the stage for using the recommendations from an evaluation project at the very beginning and then strive to conduct the best project and communicate the results as effectively as possible.

4.06 EVALUATING THE EVALUATION: PITFALLS AND PROBLEMS

Goals for Chapter 4.06

—To summarize how to avoid problems in conducting an evaluation study; and,

—To evaluate your own studies as well as those of others to make sure they are trustworthy.

The process of evaluating an evaluation system or project is ongoing. Now that we have covered the major topics of criteria, data (evidence), and judgment related to conducting evaluation projects, a few words of summary about how to evaluate evaluation systems and projects may be appropriate. For any undertaking, a professional should always consider what she or he did well and what could have been improved. This final chapter will offer some notes on what to consider in evaluating an evaluation project, whether it is your own or someone else's. Also identified are several common pitfalls that may be encountered doing evaluations. This summary will likely sound familiar as most of these points have been addressed elsewhere in the text, but we would like to pull together the underlying themes one last time.

Evaluating anything is not always easy, especially when it is approached in a formal, systematic way. You must be confident, first of all, that an evaluation system or project can make a difference in an organization. Many people are fearful of evaluations, so you must make sure that receptivity to what you are doing exists. Some people are afraid of criticism and evaluation has the potential for offering criticism, but hopefully in a constructive way. Some people have little faith in evaluations because they have been through them before, and they did little good, or the recommendations were never carried out.

Further, political pressures exist. Fears and biases can affect an evaluation project and the evaluator ought to know that they may exist. You should make sure to be in agreement with the stakeholders and decision makers about what is to be evaluated. For example, if the Park and Recreation Commission thinks that the youth basketball program ought to be evaluated and as Athletic Director, you think the entire youth sports program needs to be examined, you will have to do some negotiation concerning what the evaluation will entail. If you are not aware of the political pressures, you may become discouraged during the course of the evaluation process. All of these skepticisms need to be taken into account in evaluating the success of an evaluation project.

The evaluator needs to go into an evaluation project with all good intentions and with her or his mind open. Each evaluation will be different so you cannot use the same old method or the same instrument in every case. Organizations that have good objectives or standards to follow will likely be able to do evaluations easier than those organizations that do not. Where objectives do not exist, it will be necessary to write your own or rely on other models. The evaluator will also need to work with the resource and time constraints that are often built into evaluation projects. Sometimes nothing can be done about time and money constraints, but in some cases doing no evaluation is better than doing one that is poorly designed or that collects the wrong data. Even though determining criteria, using models, and determining types of data are not very exciting, these design steps are crucial in setting up a good evaluation.

For an evaluation to be successful, good evaluation methods and measurement tools must be selected. Sometimes it is difficult to measure some evaluation criteria. You must be aware of this possibility in undertaking an evaluation project and not promise more than can be delivered. A lack of assessment tools exists in leisure services; in many cases, an evaluator will have to develop instruments to address the criteria for particular projects. Developing instruments is not a bad situation, but it will take an additional amount of effort. A lack of standardized instruments exists in the field of leisure services because most professionals have not been particularly oriented toward measurement and statistics. Sophisticated statistics do not have to be used in evaluation projects, but it is necessary to know what statistics are appropriate given particular situations.

Gremlins to Avoid

In conducting an evaluation project, problems will always exist. Table 4.6 (page 313) provides some guidelines to assist in developing evaluation systems as well as individual evaluation projects. The evaluator can also be aware of some of the downfalls or gremlins that commonly occur in doing evaluations:

- Make sure you have the skills and knowledge necessary to do the type of evaluation needed. If not, get help or get someone else to do the evaluation.

- Be clear about the purpose of the evaluation. Make sure stakeholders are also clear about those purposes as well.

- From an administrative point of view, make sure the expense of an evaluation in terms of time and effort is comparable to the value received from doing the evaluation. This cost-benefit may be difficult to measure, but the concept should be kept in mind.

- For an evaluation system in an organization, consider how both internal and external evaluators can be used from time to time. Using only one or the other has some drawbacks. In setting up a system, consider how you might use both.

- Remember that evaluation does not only occur at the end of something (summative) but may occur as an assessment or as a formative evaluation.

- Try not to allow bias, prejudice, preconceived perceptions, or friendship influence the evaluation outcomes. Further, do not let the whims of the administration prevent you from doing the type of evaluation that you think needs to be done.

- Make sure you go into an evaluation thoroughly understanding the organization and its limitations. This suggestion may pertain more if you are an external evaluator, but it should be considered in all situations and contexts.

- Select and use evaluation research methods and measurement instruments that are specifically related to the criteria. To avoid this gremlin you must spend time at the beginning of a project carefully planning what you will do.

- In conducting evaluation projects, think about the logical timing of the project. Keep in mind when it can best be done within an agency and when people involved are most likely to be receptive to data collection as well as the reporting of conclusions and recommendations.

- Continually think about how the criteria, evidence, and judgment phases of the project fit together. Each succeeding component should be a natural outgrowth of what has gone before.

- Collect data carefully. Careless collection of data results when the wrong instrument and poorly written questions that are inappropriate to respondents are used.

- Although we have already covered much about instrument design, keep in mind that a well-written questionnaire is necessary to avoid pitfalls related to reliability and validity. In addition, consider the reading level of a questionnaire so you do not bias the sample toward higher educated groups.

- When doing any evaluation using quantitative data, keep in mind issues related to randomization, maturation, and history.

- Consider sample selection carefully so that you are not biased. In addition, think carefully how you will motivate people to participate. Before you begin to collect data think about the size of the sample, its representativeness, and the desired response rate.

- When doing evaluation be aware of the possibility of the Hawthorne effect whereby people will act different just because they are glad you are paying attention to them.

- Data analysis should be considered before a project is begun. The statistics or qualitative analysis to be used need to be determined early on.

- In using statistics where you will address statistical significance, you must be able to determine how much difference makes a difference. Small differences may be statistically significant with a large population but they may not mean anything. As an evaluator, you must be able to decide what the statistics mean.

- Make conclusions and recommendations based only on the data that you collect from the project. Do not claim more than you have evidence to support.

- Make sure you address all the results from an evaluation, not just those aspects that are positive. You may have to handle negative results carefully, but you also may have an ethical responsibility to make sure they are addressed. Be careful that you do not discount any findings.

- Be open to finding unexpected results as you conduct an evaluation project. The real value of some evaluation projects is what you learn that you did not expect.

- Write a concise, complete, well-planned evaluation report. Unless you are able to communicate the results of a study, it will do little good. This report also requires that you write specific recommendations.

- Get results disseminated as soon as possible after an evaluation project is completed. Nothing kills the enthusiasm for an evaluation like having it drag on for months, or even years.

Not all these issues will occur in all projects but they are worth considering as you embark on doing evaluations that are usable and that will result in enlightened decision making. Successful evaluations will require careful planning and hard work, but the rewards and benefits will be there for those professionals who understand the value of evaluations in all areas of leisure services.

Table 4.6

Guidelines for Evaluation Systems and Projects

Systems:
Make data appropriate to criteria
Rebut evaluation fears
Get receptivity within the organization
Use both external or internal evaluators
Institute a systematic process
Be aware of political pressures
Counter possible measurement problems

Projects:
Reflect conclusions and recommendations from data
Determine evaluation criteria carefully
Check trustworthiness of instruments
Collect data carefully
Have a clear evaluation purpose
Develop the necessary competencies to be an evaluator
Write a clear, concise evaluation report
Make the evaluation project timely and complete it on time
Use sound instrument design
Select an appropriate sample
Use statistics and data analysis properly

From Ideas to Reality

Many topics have been covered in this textbook. As we discussed early in the book, you will not become an expert by reading this book. Any single chapter discussed here will lead to numerous books and articles written about that given topic. To become an expert in evaluation will require much deeper study and further information in evaluation on all these topics. But, hopefully you have a foundation and a beginning point for exploring and applying evaluation processes further. If some of the suggestions offered in this chapter and throughout this book are needed, you should be able to make evaluation not just an idea but a reality in your professional life. As indicated in the very beginning, becoming a good evaluator requires education, training, practice, and a healthy dose of common sense. We hope this book has provided some education and training. The practice and common sense is up to you. Best wishes.

Selected References

American Camping Association. (1992). *Standards for day and resident camps.* Martinsville, IN: American Camping Association, Inc.

American Camping Association. (1993). *Standards for conference and retreat centers.* Martinsville, IN: American Camping Association, Inc.

American Psychological Association. (1983). *Publication manual of the American Psychological Association (3rd ed.).* Washington, DC: American Psychological Association.

Armstrong, J. B. (1989). An evaluation management model for environmental education programs. *Dissertation Abstracts International, 51/02A,* p. 486.

Babbie, E. (1992) *The practice of social research (5th ed.).* Belmont, CA: Wadsworth Publishing Co.

Bartlett, P. and Einert, A. E. (1992). Analysis of the design function of an adult softball complex in a new public recreation park. *Journal of Park and Recreation Administration, 10*(1), pp. 71-81.

Bennett, C. F. (1982). *Reflective appraisal of program (RAP): An approach to studying clientele-perceived results of Cooperative Extension programs.* Ithaca, NY: Cornell University Press.

Brown, R. D., Braskamp, L.A., and Newman, D.L. (1978). Evaluator credibility as a function of report style: Do jargon and data make a difference? *Evaluation Quarterly, 2*(2), pp. 331-341.

Bullock, C. C. (1982). Interactionist evaluators look for "what is" not "what should be." *Parks & Recreation, 17*(2), pp. 37-39.

Bullock, C. C. and Coffey, F. (1980). Triangulation applied to the evaluative process. *Journal of Physical Education and Recreation, 50*(10), pp. 50-52.

Bullock, C. C., Mahon, M. J., and Welch, L. K. (1992). Easter Seals' progressive mainstreaming model: Option and choices in camping and leisure services for children and adults with disabilities. *Therapeutic Recreation Journal, 26*(4), pp. 61-70.

Burros Mental Measurements Yearbook. Lincoln, NB: Burros Mental Measurements.

Campbell D., and Stanley, J. (1963). *Experimental and quasi-experimental designs for research.* Chicago, IL: Rand McNally.

Chenery, M. F. (1991). *I am Somebody: The messages and methods of organized camping for youth development.* Martinsville, IN: American Camping Association, Inc.

Chenery, M. F. and Russell, R. V. (1987). Responsive evaluation: An application of naturalistic inquiry to recreation evaluation. *Journal of Park and Recreation Administration, 5*(4), pp. 30-38.

Connolly, P. (1982). Evaluation's critical role in agency accountability. *Parks & Recreation, 17*(2), pp. 34-36.

Coyne, P. A. and Turpel, L. T. (1984). Peer program review: A model for implementation of standards. *Therapeutic Recreation Journal, 23*(2), pp. 7-13.

Crompton, J. L. (1979, October) Recreation programs have life cycles, too. *Parks & Recreation,* pp. 52-57, 69.

Crompton, J. L. (1985). *Needs assessment: Taking the pulse of the public recreation client.* College Station, TX: Texas A&M University Press.

Crompton, J. L. and Lamb, C. W. (1986). *Marketing government and social services.* New York, NY: John Wiley & Sons.

Dattilo, J. (1988a, March). *Single-subject methodology.* Paper presented to the 1988 SPRE Institute on Research at Saratoga Springs, NY.

Dattilo, J. (1988b). Assessing music preferences of persons with severe disabilities. *Therapeutic Recreation Journal, 22*(2), pp. 12-23.

Delbecq, A., Van deVen, A., and Gustafson, D. H. (1975). *Group techniques for program planning: A guide to nominal group and Delphi processes.* Glenview, IL: Scott Foresman & Co.

Denzin, N. K. (1978). *The research act: A theoretical introduction to sociological methods (2nd ed).* New York, NY: McGraw-Hill Publishing Co.

Dillman, D. A. (1978). *Mail and telephone surveys: The total design method.* New York, NY: John Wiley & Sons.

Driver, B. L., Brown, P. J., and Peterson, G. L. (Eds.) (1991). *Benefits of leisure.* State College, PA: Venture Publishing, Inc.

Dunn, J. K. (1987). Establishing reliability and validity in evaluation instruments. *Journal of Park and Recreation Administration, 5*(4), pp. 61-70.

Dunn, J. K. (1989). Guidelines for using published assessment procedures. *Therapeutic Recreation Journal, 23*(2), pp. 59-69.

Ellis, G. D. and Williams, D. R. (1987). The impending renaissance in leisure service evaluation. *Journal of Park and Recreation Administration, 5*(4), pp. 17-29.

Ellis, G. and Witt, P. (1982). Evaluation by design. *Parks & Recreation, 17*(2), pp. 40-43.

Ellis, G. D. and Witt, P. A. (1986). The Leisure Diagnostic Battery: Past, present, and future. *Therapeutic Recreation Journal, 20*(4), pp. 31-47.

Ewert, A. (1990). Decision-making techniques for establishing research agendas in park and recreation systems. *Journal of Park and Recreation Administration, 8*(2), pp. 1-13.

Farrell, P. and Lundegren, H. N. (1987). Designing and objectives-oriented evaluation and translating results into action. *Journal of Park and Recreation Administration, 5*(4), pp. 84-93.

Ferber, R., Sheatsley, P., Turner, A., and Waksberg, J. (n.d.) What is a survey? Washington, DC: American Statistical Association.

Ferguson, D. D. (1983). Assessment interviewing techniques: A useful tool in developing individual program plans. *Therapeutic Recreation Journal, 17*(2), pp. 16-22.

Fetterman, D. M. (Ed.). (1988). *Qualitative approaches to evaluation in education.* New York, NY: Praeger Publishers.

Fielding, N. G. and Fielding, J. L. (1986). *Linking data.* Newbury Park, CA: Sage Publications, Inc.

Franklin, J. L. and Thrasher, J. H. (1980). *An introduction to program evaluation.* New York, NY: John Wiley & Sons.

Gardner, D. E. (1977). Five evaluation framework. *Journal of Higher Education, 48*(5), pp. 571-592.

Geertz, C. (1983). Thick description: Toward an interpretive theory of culture. In R. M. Emerson (Ed.). *Contemporary field research* (pp. 37-59). Boston, MA: Little, Brown and Co.

Gitelson, R. F., Guadagnolo, F., and Moore, R. (1988). Economic impact analysis of a community-sponsored ten kilometer road race. *Journal of Park and Recreation Administration, 6*(4), pp. 9-17.

Glaser, B. G. and Strauss, A. L. (1967). *The discovering of grounded theory: Strategies for qualitative research.* Hawthorne, NY: Aldine.

Glover, R. B. and Glover, J. (1981, November). Appraising performance—Some alternatives to the sandwich approach. *Parks & Recreation*, pp. 27-28.

Greene, J. and McClintock, C. (1985). Triangulation in evaluation. *Evaluation Review, 9*(5), pp. 523-545.

Guadagnolo, F. (1985). The importance-performance analysis: An evaluation and marketing tool. *Journal of Park and Recreation Administration, 3*(2), pp. 13-22.

Guba, E. G. and Lincoln, Y. S. (1981). *Effective evaluation.* San Francisco, CA: Jossey-Bass Inc., Publishers.

Guba, E. G. and Lincoln, Y. S. (1989). *Fourth generation evaluation.* Newbury Park, CA: Sage Publications, Inc.

Halberg, K. J. and Olsson, R. H. (1989). Automated versus manual leisure assessment: A comparison. *Therapeutic Recreation Journal, 23*(4), pp. 73-79.

Hale, R. (1990). *MYSTAT: Statistical applications.* Cambridge, MA: Course Technology, Inc.

Halle, J. W., Boyer, T. E., and Ashton-Shaeffer, C. (1991). Social validation as a program evaluation measure. *Therapeutic Recreation Journal, 25*(3), pp. 29-43.

Havitz, M. E., Twynam, G. D., and DeLorenzo, J. M. (1991). Important-performance analysis as a staff evaluation tool. *Journal of Park and Recreation Administration, 9*(1), pp. 43-54.

Henderson, K. A. (1988). Questionnaire development: Fun or frustration? *Camping Magazine, 60*(7), pp. 32-33.

Henderson, K. A. (1988). Are volunteers worth their weight in gold? *Parks & Recreation, 23*(11), pp. 40-43.

Henderson, K. A. (1991). *Dimensions of choice: A qualitative approach to recreation, parks, and leisure research.* State College, PA: Venture Publishing, Inc.

Henderson, K. A. (1992). Camper surveys: A tool for program planning and marketing. *Camping Magazine, 64*(3), pp. 42-43.

Henderson, K. A. and Zabielski, D. (1992, February). *Theory application and development in recreation, parks, and leisure research: An examination of the literature from 1981-1990.* Paper presented to the Southeast Recreation Research Conference, Asheville, NC.

Hollenhorst, S., Olson, D., and Fortney, R. (1992). Use of importance-performance analysis to evaluate state park cabins: The case of the West Virginia State Park System. *Journal of Park and Recreation Administration, 10*(1), pp. 1-11.

Howe, C. Z. (1980). Models of evaluating public recreation programs: What the literature shows. *Leisure Today/Journal of Physical Education and Recreation, 50*(10), pp. 36-38.

Howe, C. Z. and Carpenter, G. M. (1985) *Programming leisure experiences: A cyclical approach.* Englewood Cliffs, NJ: Prentice-Hall.

Howe, C. Z. and Keller, M. J. (1988). The use of triangulation as an evaluation technique: Illustrations from regional symposia in therapeutic recreation. *Therapeutic Recreation Journal, 22*(1), pp. 36-45.

Hudson, S. (1988). *How to conduct community needs assessment surveys in public parks and recreation.* Worthington, OH: Publishing Horizons, Inc.

Hunter, I. R. (1983). Methodological issues in therapeutic recreation research. *Therapeutic Recreation Journal, 17*(2), pp. 23-32.

Iso-Ahola, S. (1982). Intrinsic motivation—An overlooked basis for evaluation. *Parks and Recreation, 17*(2), pp. 32-33, 58.

Kanters, M. A. and Botkin, M. R. (1992). The economic impact of public leisure services in Illinois. *Journal of Park and Recreation Administration, 10*(3), pp. 1-16.

Kaufman, R. and Thomas, S. (1980). *Evaluation without fear.* New York, NY: New Viewpoints.

Krathwohl, D. R. (1956). *Taxonomy of educational objectives, Handbook I: Cognitive domain.* New York, NY: David McKay Co.

Krathwohl, D. R. (1964). *Taxonomy of educational objectives, Handbook II: Affective domain.* New York, NY: David McKay Co.

Krejcie, R. V. and Morgan, D. W. (1970). Determing sample size for research activities. *Educational and Psychological Measurement, 30,* pp. 607-610.

Kraus, R. and Allen, L. (1987). *Research and evaluation in recreation, parks, and leisure studies.* Columbus, OH: Publishing Horizons, Inc.

Krueger, R. A. (1988). *Focus groups.* Beverly Hills, CA: Sage Publications, Inc.

Lankford, S. and DeGraaf, D. (1992). Strengths, weaknesses, opportunities, and threats in morale, welfare, and recreation organizations: Challenges of the 1990s. *Journal of Park and Recreation Administration, 10*(1), pp. 31-45.

Lincoln, Y. S. and Guba, E. G. (1985). *Naturalistic inquiry.* Newbury Park, CA: Sage Publications, Inc.

Loftus, G. R., and Loftus, E. F. (1982). *Essence of statistics.* Monterey, CA: Brooks/Cole Publishing Co.

Loomis, J. B. (1990). Estimating the economic activity and value from public parks and outdoor recreation areas in California. *Journal of Park and Recreation Administration, 7*(1), pp. 56-65.

Lundegren, H. M. and Farrell, P. (1985). *Evaluation for leisure service managers.* Philadelphia, PA: W. B. Saunders Co.

MacKay, K. J. and Crompton, J. L. (1990). Measuring the quality of recreation services. *Journal of Park and Recreation Administration, 8*(3), pp. 47-56.

Malik, P. B., Ashton-Shaeffer, C., and Kleiber, D. A. (1991). Interviewing young adults with mental retardation: A seldom used research method. *Therapeutic Recreation Journal, 25*(1), pp. 60-73.

Michigan State University. (1976). *Survey research for community recreation services. Research Report 291.* East Lansing, MI: Michigan State University Agricultural Experiment Station.

Mills, A. S., Um, S., McWilliams, E. G., and Hodgson, R. W. (1987). The importance of random sampling when conducting visitor surveys. *Journal of Park and Recreation Administration, 5*(2), pp. 47-56.

Mobily, K. and Iso-Ahola, S. (1980). Mastery evaluation techniques for the undergraduate major. *Leisure Today/Journal of Physical Education and Recreation, 50*(10), pp. 39-40.

Mohr, L. B. (1988). *Impact analysis for program evaluation.* Chicago, IL: The Dorsey Press.

Moursund, J. P. (1973). *Evaluation: An introduction to research design.* Monterey, CA: Brooks/Cole Publishing Co.

Norusis, M. J. (1983). *Introductory statistics guide.* Chicago, IL: SPSS, Inc.

Okey, J. R., Shrum, J. W., and Yeany, R. H. (1977, Fall). A flowchart for selecting research and evaluation designs. *CEDR Quarterly,* pp. 16-21.

Olson, E. G. (1980). Program portrayal: A qualitative approach to recreation program evaluation. *Leisure Today/Journal of Physical Education and Recreation, 50*(10), pp. 41-42.

Orthner, D. K., Smith, S., and Wright, D. (1986). Measuring program needs. *Evaluation and Program Planning, 9,* pp. 199-207.

O'Sullivan, E. L. (1988). Formulating strategic program decisions utilizing the nine-cell approach. *Journal of Park and Recreation Administration, 6*(2), pp. 25-33.

Patton, M. Q. (1978). *Utilization-focused evaluation.* Newbury Park, CA: Sage Publications, Inc.

Patton, M. Q. (1980a). Making methods choices. *Evaluation and Program Planning, 3,* pp. 219-228.

Patton, M. Q. (1980b). *Qualitative evaluation methods.* Newbury Park, CA: Sage Publications, Inc.

Posavac, E. J. and Carey, R. G. (1992). *Program evaluation: Methods and case studies.* Englewood Cliffs, NJ: Prentice Hall.

Richardson, S. L. (1987). The importance-performance approach to evaluation communication effectiveness. *Journal of Park and Recreation Administration, 5*(4), pp. 71-83.

Riley, B. and Wright, S. (1990). Establishing quality assurance monitors for the evaluation of therapeutic recreation service. *Therapeutic Recreation Journal, 24*(2), pp. 25-39.

Robinson, P. A. (1985) *Fundamentals of technical writing.* Boston, MA: Houghton Mifflin Co.

Rossi, P. H. and Freeman, H. E. (1993). *Evaluation: A systematic approach. (5th ed.).* Newbury Park, CA: Sage Publications Inc.

Rossman, J. R. (1980). Theoretical deficiencies: A brief review of selected evaluation models. *Leisure Today/Journal of Physical Education and Recreation, 50*(10), pp. 43-45.

Rossman, J. R. (1981, October). *Development of a leisure program evaluation instrument.* Paper presented at the NRPA Leisure Research Symposium, Minneapolis, MN.

Rossman, J. R. (1982, June). Evaluate programs by measuring participant satisfactions. *Parks & Recreation,* pp. 33-35.

Sadler, D. R. (1984). Evaluation and the logic of recommendations. *Evaluation Review, 8*(2), pp. 261-268.

Salkind, N. J. (1991). *Exploring research.* New York, NY: Macmillan Publishing Co.

Schneider, A. L. and Darcy, R. E. (1984). Policy implications of using significance tests in evaluation research. *Evaluation Review, 8*(4), pp. 573-582.

Scriven, M. (1967). The methodology of evaluation. In R.W. Tyler, R.M. Gagne, and M. Scriven, *Perspectives of curriculum evaluation,* (pp. 39-83). Chicago, IL: Rand McNally.

Shafer, R. L. and Moeller, G. (1987). Know how to word your questionnaire. *Parks & Recreation, 22*(10), pp. 48-52.

Smith, M. F. (1989). *Evaluability assessment: A practical approach.* Boston, MA: Kluwer Academic Publishers.

Struening, E. L. and Guttentag, M. (1975). *Handbook of evaluation research.* Newbury Park, CA: Sage Publications Inc.

Stumbo, N. J. (1983). Systematic observation as a research tool for assessing client behavior. *Therapeutic Recreation Journal, 17*(4), pp. 53-63.

Stumbo, N. J. (1991). Selected assessment resources: A review of instruments and references. *Annual in Therapeutic Recreation, 2,* pp. 8-24.

Taylor, S. J. and Bogdan, R. (1984). *Introduction to qualitative research methods: The search for meaning (2nd ed.).* New York, NY: John Wiley & Sons.

Tinsley, H. E. A. (1984). Limitations, explanations, aspirations: A confession of fallibility and a promise to strive for perfection. *Journal of Leisure Research, 16*(2), pp. 93-98.

Theobald, W. (1979). *Evaluation of recreation and park programs.* New York, NY: John Wiley & Sons.

Theobald, W. (1987). Historical antecedents of evaluation in leisure programs and services. *Journal of Park and Recreation Administration, 5*(4), pp. 1-9.

Toppel, A. H., Beach, B. A., and Hutchinson-Troyer, L. (1991). Standards: A tool for accountability, the CARF process. *Annual in Therapeutic Recreation, 2,* pp. 96-99.

Touchstone, W. A. (1984). A personalized approach to goal planning and evaluation in clinical settings. *Therapeutic Recreation Journal, 18*(2), pp. 25-31.

Twardzik, L. (1987). Accreditation: A method for evaluating public park and recreation systems. *Parks & Recreation, 22*(3), pp. 60-64.

van der Smissen, B. (1978). *Evaluation and self-study of public recreation and park agencies.* Arlington, VA: National Recreation and Park Association.

Vaske, J. J., Donnelly, M. P., and Williamson, B. N. (1991). Monitoring for quality control in state park management. *Journal of Park and Recreation Administration, 9*(2), pp. 59-72.

Weatherman, R. and Swenson, K. (1974). Delphi techniques. In S. H. Hedley and J. R. Yates (Eds.), *Futurism in education* (pp. 97-114). Berkeley, CA: McCutchan Publishing Corp.

Webb, E. J., Campbell, D. T., Schwartz, R. D., and Sechrest, L. (1966). *Unobtrusive measures: Nonreactive research in the social sciences.* Chicago, IL: Rand McNally.

Weiss, C. H. (1972). *Evaluation research.* Englewood Cliffs, NJ: Prentice-Hall.

Weiss, C. H. (1975). Interviewing in evaluation research. In E. L. Struening and M. Guttentag (Eds.), *Handbook of evaluation research.* Newbury Park, CA: Sage Publications Inc.

Wright, B. A., Duray, N., and Goodale, T. L. (1992). Assessing perceptions of recreation center service quality: An application of recent advancements in service quality research. *Journal of Park and Recreation Administration, 10*(3), pp. 33-47.

Yardley, J. K., MacDonald, J. H., and Clarke, B. D. (1990). The economic impact of a small, short-term recreation event on a local community. *Journal of Park and Recreation Administration, 8*(4), pp. 71-82.

Yin, R. K. (1984). *Case study research: Design and methods.* Newbury Park, CA: Sage Publications Inc.

GLOSSARY

A priori—the determination ahead of time of processes or procedures.

Ability Tests—tests to measure what an individual is capable of doing.

Accountability—a relative term that describes the capability of a leisure service delivery system to justify or explain the activities and services it provides.

Accreditation—the process of assuring that an organization has met specific standards set by a professional or an accrediting body.

Achievement Tests—tests to show what an individual has learned.

American Camping Association (ACA)—the organization that sets standards for organized camping in the United States.

American Psychological Association (APA)—an organization that provides among many aspects, guidelines for writing reports.

Analysis of Variance (ANOVA)—parametric statistic used to measure the differences between three or more group means.

Anonymity—no one knows the identity of the participants.

Appendices—the supportive material included with an evaluation report that includes more information about the sample, instrument, and analyses.

Archives—records or documents that exist.

Assessment—the examination of some type of need that provides the foundation for further planning.

Attitude Tests—tests that measure the opinions or beliefs of the testtaker about an object, person, or event. They usually refer to some internal state of mind or set of beliefs that are stable over time.

Audit Trail—the process of documenting how data were collected and analyzed in a qualitative study.

Between Method Triangulation—the use of two or more methods to measure the same phenomena.

Bivariate—the examination of the relationship of two variables.

Black Box Model—the goal-free approach to evaluation.

Body—the major part of an evaluation report that includes the introduction, methods, findings, and conclusions/recommendations.

Case Study—an intensive investigation of a unit that might be an individual, a group, or an organization.

Case—the individual who participates in doing a survey.

Central Tendency—the measures of mean, median, and mode.

Chi-Square—a nonparametric statistical analysis of two categorical variables.

Closed-Quantitative Questions—questions asked that provide specific options for answers.

Code Numbers—the numbers used to identify individuals for purposes of keeping track of who responded and did not respond to a survey.

Codebook—the written information that tells how coding has been done.

Codesheet—a compilation of all of the data or records for the cases examined in a study.

Coding—the numeric assignment of a value to a variable.

Commission on Accreditation of Rehabilitation Facilities (CARF)—the national accrediting body for rehabilitation programs.

Competencies—the abilities one has to undertake a task.

Conclusions—a summary of the major points learned in an evaluation project.

Concurrent or Criterion-Related Validity—a form of internal reliability that asks whether the scores on a particular instrument correlate with scores on another instrument.

Confidentiality—the identity of the participants is known by the evaluator but she or he does not share that information.

Consensus—overall agreement.

Constant Comparison—a systematic method for recording, coding, and analyzing qualitative data that includes comparisons among cases, groups, and themes.

Content Analysis—a process used in analyzing documents, records, transcribed conversations, letters, or anything in a textual form.

Content Validity—the contents of the theoretical expectations that one wishes to measure.

Continuous Data—data that can be measured along a continuum and have an infinite number of possible values.

Control Group—the group in an experimental design that does not receive an intervention or a treatment.

Conversational Guide (also called an **Unstructured Interview**)—an interview form in which no questions are predetermined but they emerge as the interviewer and interviewee begin to converse.

Correlation—measures of association.

Cost-Benefit Analysis—relating the costs of a program or an operation to the benefits realized as expressed in dollar figures.

Cost-Effectiveness Analysis—a ratio of the costs of a program or service to the revenue generated.

Cover Sheet—the letter sent with a questionnaire or with a final report to explain what the enclosure is about.

Cover—the physical paper that surrounds an evaluation report and gives the information about the title, authors, and organization.

Covert—when something is hidden or not known.

Credibility—a quality measure of the internal validity or how well something measures what it is supposed to measure.

Criteria—the standards or the ideals upon which something is being evaluated.

Criterion-Referenced Evaluations—measurement based on a level of performance.

Data Display—a form of data reduction where information is assembled to aid in interpreting themes that emerge from qualitative data; or, the presentation of qualitative data so that it can be analyzed.

Data Reduction—the process of organizing data to interpret themes that emerge from qualitative data.

Debriefing—the process of discussing and informing participants of the results of a project.

Deductive Analysis—examining something by going from broad ideas to specific applications.

Delphi Studies—a technique that seeks to draw conclusions based on the consensus established from experts about a particular topic.

Demographics—characteristics of an individual.

Dependability—the consistency of an instrument to measure the same results time after time.

Dependent Variable—the variable that is assumed to have been caused by another variable usually referred to as the independent variable.

Descriptive Designs—investigative methods used to gather factual data.

Descriptive Statistics—measures used to characterize data.

Discrete Data—noncontinuous finite numbers that have no in between measurements.

Econometrics—any process that involves an analysis of how economic aspects affect an organization.

Economic Impact—the amount of revenue activity generated in an area due to a particular event such as a festival or due to tourist trades.

Effectiveness—the end results or the impact on individuals.

Efficiency—the relationship between inputs and outputs.

Emic—ideas expressed by the respondents that are shown as quotes or anecdotes.

Empirical Data—data that can be observed.

Enlightened Decision Making—using systematic evaluations to make the best and most informed decisions concerning the value or worth of programs.

Enumeration—a qualitative data analysis procedure that counts the number of occurrences.

Ethics—the philosophical basis for determining right and wrong.

Etic—interpretations of the researcher concerning how respondents expressed their ideas.

Evaluation—the systematic collection and analysis of data to address some criteria to make judgments about the worth or improvement of something; making decisions based on identified criteria and supporting evidence.

Evaluation Process—the steps undertaken in doing an evaluation project that include broadly the establishing of criteria, the collection of data, and the judgment of the results.

Evaluation Project—the specific study undertaken to determine the worth or value of some aspect of the five Ps.

Evaluation Report—the written or oral report that summarizes the evaluation project.

Evaluation Research—the process used to collect and analyze data or evidence.

Evaluation System—a process for determining and addressing the evaluation needs of an organization related to the five Ps of program, participants, personnel, policy, and place.

Evaluator—the individual or individuals conducting the evaluation. It may be a student, professional, or an outside consultant.

Evidence—the data that is collected and analyzed in an evaluation project.

Executive Summary—the abstract that says in 200 to 300 words what has been found in a project.

Experimental Designs—investigative methods used to assure control in the collection of data.

Expert Judgment—the use of professionals who have expertise or training to enable them to make evaluation judgments.

External Evaluator—someone who evaluates from the outside and is not employed regularly by the organization.

External Validity—how well the results of a measurement can be generalized to similar situations.

Face Validity—a common term used to describe whether an instrument measures the contents it is supposed to measure.

Five Ps—the components that might be evaluated within a leisure service organization (i.e., program, participants, personnel, policy, and place).

Focus Groups—a particular form of group interviews where individuals within a group are asked to respond and discuss particular criteria or issues.

Follow-Up Contact—a second or third encounter with an individual, usually in the form of a phone call or postcard/letter to request that they respond to a survey.

Follow-Up Questions—similar to probes. They are asked in an interview to try to encourage people to give additional information.

Formal Evaluation—the systematic evaluation undertaken where specific criteria are set, data are collected, and judgments made.

Formative Evaluation—the systematic examination of the steps in the development and implementation of some aspect of the five Ps. It is usually related to some aspect of the process and occurs during an activity.

Frequency Counts—the number of times a behavior occurs.

Friedman's Analysis of Variance—a nonparametric test used for repeated measures.

Full Participant—an individual who participates fully in a group but is also doing an observation as a method of evaluation.

Goal-Attainment—a model of evaluation where preestablished goals and objectives are used to measure outcomes.

Goal-Free—a model of evaluation of something irrespective of the goals and objectives.

Goal—general statement about an organization and its programs that evolves from the organization's purpose or mission.

Hawthorne Effect—a term used to describe how the presence of evaluators may affect responses.

Hypothesis—the questions or hunches, based on theory, derived concerning the possible outcomes of a research project.

Impact Evaluation—another term for program evaluation that refers to whether interventions produced the intended effects.

Importance-Performance—a research technique that is used to quantify customer satisfaction by combining measures of importance with satisfaction.

Independent Variable—a variable whose values are given and which may cause an independent variable.

In-depth Interviews—personal interviews that cover a range of topics in which the interviewee is asked to talk.

Inductive Analysis—examining something by going from specific examples to broad ideas.

Inferential Statistics—measures used to compare variables or to predict future behavior.

Informal Evaluation—intuitive unstructured approaches to making decisions.

Informed Consent—a person's permission to participate in a project.

Inputs—the resources available and expended in an organization.

Inter-Observer Reliability (also known as **Inter-Rater Reliability**)—a measure of the consistency of agreement from rater and rater.

Inter-Rater Reliability (also known as **Inter-Observer Reliability**)—a measure of the consistency of agreement from rater and rater.

Internal Evaluator—someone who evaluates some aspect of the five Ps from within the organization.

Internal Validity—how well an instrument measures what it is supposed to measure for a particular project.

Interpretation—the process of analyzing data to determine what they mean.

Interpretive—a worldview that suggests the world can be viewed from multiple perspectives and truths.

Interval Data—data put into ordered categories that have meaningful size differences.

Interval Sampling—choosing predesignated periods of time for doing sampling.

Interview Guide (also called a **Semistructured Interview**)—a list of the topics to be covered in an interview. They include no particular sequence or specific wording.

Interview Schedule—the list of questions asked in an interview.

Interviewer Bias—the potential prejudice, inadvertent leading, or unconscious judgment that may exist in conducting an interview.

Intuition—the internal sense that one has about something.

Intuitive Judgment—a pseudo-model of evaluation that allows an individual to evaluate based on gut-level feelings about some aspect of the five Ps.

Joint Commission on Accreditation of Healthcare Organizations (JCAHO)—the organization that sets standards of evaluation and accreditation for hospitals.

Judgment—the determination of the value or worth of something based on the evidence collected from previously determined criteria. It is the outcome of data collection.

KASA—a level of program evaluation that includes the measurement of Knowledge, Attitudes, Skills, and Aspirations.

Key Informants—people who provide more in-depth information than regular respondents.

Kruskal-Wallis—a nonparametric test used to examine the differences in means between two or more groups.

Latency Recording—a measure of the time elapsed between a cue and when a behavior occurs.

Leisure Programming Cycle—the process of conducting needs assessments, setting objectives, planning programs, implementing programs, evaluating, and making revisions.

Leisure Services or Delivery System—human service organizations and enterprises that provide recreation, leisure, and/or educational services to improve the quality of life of individuals within the society. These may be therapeutic, private, not-for-profit, public, or commercial organizations.

Likert Scales—a particular kind of close-ended question that uses a scaling system usually going from strongly disagree to strongly agree.

Mann Whitney—a nonparametric statistic used to determine differences in rankings on some variable.

Mean—the average for a variable.

Measurement Instrument—the tools, usually in the form of a survey, used to gather data.

Measurement—the collection of information or the gathering of data, usually quantitative.

Median—a descriptive statistic of the point at which half the scores lie above and half lie below.

Methods—the established procedures used to collect data.

Missing Data—information that is not reported by an individual on a questionnaire. The missing data may be due to an oversight or because the individual did not want to answer a question.

Mode—the most common response to a variable.

Multiplier—a number used in econometric studies to show the potential that a dollar has to be spent and respent in a community

Multivariate—the examination of the relationship of more than two variables.

MYSTAT—a specific computer program, modeled after SYSTAT that can be used for statistical analysis.

National Recreation and Park Association (NRPA)—the professional association of individuals employed in leisure service delivery systems.

Negative Evidence—qualitative data that is opposite or contradictory to the major points that are being uncovered.

Nominal Data—categorical data that defines a distinct group.

Nominal Group Technique (NGT)—a collective decision-making technique used to do assessments and strategic planning.

Nonparametric—statistics based on assumptions of a nonnormal distribution that usually includes smaller sample sizes.

Nonprobability Sampling—the sampling strategy used to select people in some way that is not based on an equal potential for being selected.

Nonreactive—unobtrusive observation by not interacting with people.

Nonrespondents—those individuals who are asked but fail to respond to a survey.

Nonresponse Bias—the error that might exist in a survey because some people responded and those that did not might be different.

Nonsampling Error—the biases that exist due to who responds to a survey.

Norm-Referenced Evaluations—measurement based on the relative position of a person or things in relation to each other using the same measuring tool.

Normal Distribution—the way that scores occur.

Open-Ended Questions—questions asked that do not provide options for answers.

Oral Histories—in-depth interviews conducted that explore the entire life of an individual.

Ordered Responses—responses to a question that have a logical order associated with the way that the responses are listed.

Ordinal Data—data that is ranked and shows how each measure relates to another measure.

Outcomes—the results or impact or effect of something.

Outlier—responses that occur way outside the normal distribution.

Overt—when something is known.

Paper/Pencil Tests—measurements that are given for an individual to administer to the self.

Paradigm—a world view that describes how one thinks about evaluation.

Parametric—statistics based on the assumption of normal distribution and randomized groups.

Partially Close-Ended Questions—questions asked that provide fixed responses but allow the respondent to add her or his additional responses if they are not appropriate.

Participant—the individual who receives the services of a leisure service delivery system. These may be clients, consumers, players, or anyone otherwise involved in programs and activities in communities, organizations, or in institutions.

Pearson's Correlation—a parametric statistic used to measure the relationship between two variables.

Peer Program Review—a process used in therapeutic recreation where professionals review and evaluate one another's programs.

People Involvement—the number and characteristics of individuals who participate in a program.

Performance Appraisal—the process of personnel evaluation.

Personality Tests—tests that relate to a variety of characteristics of an individual.

Personnel Evaluation (also referred to as **Performance Appraisal**)—the evaluation of staff.

Personnel—all staff that work for pay or without pay within a leisure service organization.

Physical Evidence—traces from the past that provide information.

Pilot Study—a "practice" run for an instrument or a project that gives the evaluator preliminary information about measurement instruments, sampling procedures, or method administration issues.

Politics—the personal and collective beliefs that exist.

Population—all the people who might comprise a delineated group.

Positivism—a worldview that suggests facts and truths can be found and articulated.

Posttest—the measurement given to an individual or group after some intervention is done.

Practice Change—the personal adoption and application of new ideas.

Predictive Validity—the ability of an instrument to predict some behavior.

Preordinate—preestablished goals and objectives are used to measure outcomes.

Pretest—the measurement given to an individual or group before some intervention is done.

Probability Sampling—the sampling strategy that allows everyone within a group to have an equal opportunity of being selected.

Probes—the questions asked in interviews to encourage people to give additional information. These include questions like "Can you give me an example?" "Can you tell me more?" or "How did you feel?"

Professional Judgment—a model of evaluation using expert opinions to determine the worth or value of a program.

Program Audit—an accountability term used to quantify the amount of services rendered and the identity of program participants.

Program—all of the activities, instruction, competition, and events that are planned by a leisure service organization.

Qualitative—data that appears in the form of words.

Quality Assurance (QA)—the process used in healthcare organizations as well as other organizations to assure that certain standards are being met.

Quality Control—assuring that the highest standards of practice are maintained.

Quantitative—data that appears in the form of numbers.

Quasi-Experiments—those methods that do not meet the strict requirement of an experiment including using random samples, control groups, and pretesting.

Random Digit Dialing—a sampling method used for phone interviews where prefixes and numbers are randomly dialed to get respondents for a study.

Randomization—the process of assigning people randomly to groups when an experimental design is used.

Range—the difference between the highest and lowest scores.

Rapport—establishing a trusting relationship between two individuals or between an individual and a group.

Ratio Data—the most sophisticated level of data in which a true zero point is calculated.

Reactions—the degree of interest, likes and dislikes, satisfactions, motivations, appeal, and perceived benefits that people attribute to a program.

Recode—to change a code by collapsing data.

Recommendations—the proposed courses of action to be followed based upon the conclusions drawn.

Record—the listing of all the information from an individual or a case.

Reliability Correlation or **Coefficient**—a statistic that tells how likely an instrument is to measure consistently.

Reliability—the determination of whether a measure consistently conveys the same meaning. Also called *stability* or *dependability*.

Research—the systematic collection of data to answer a theoretical question.

Response Rate (also called **Return Rate**)—the percentage of responses to a survey based upon the actual number returned divided by the number sent.

Responsive Evaluation (also referred to as **Utilization-Focus Evaluation**)—paying attention to the use of the evaluation by addressing the evaluation needs and interests of stakeholders such as administrators, boards, funding agencies, staff, or participants.

Return Rate (also called **Response Rate**)—the percentage of responses to a survey based upon the actual number returned divided by the number sent.

Sample—a representation of a total population.

Sampling Error—the amount of statistical error that might exist because you cannot always sample correctly.

Sampling—the process of drawing a representative selection of respondents from the population.

Scientific Method—the formal process used in research whereby research questions/hypotheses are generated, data collected, and results related back to original questions/theories.

Self-Check—the process of examining oneself in relation to making evaluation decisions.

Semantic Differentials—a particular kind of close-ended question that includes a list of bipolar adjectives that the respondent chooses.

Semi-Structured Interview (also called an **Interview Guide**)—a list of the topics to be covered in an interview. They include no particular sequence or specific wording but are all covered at some point in the interview.

Service Quality—a technique used to measure the dimensions of consumer expectations and perceptions.

Sign Test—a nonparametric statistic used to determine differences when the data is categorical.

Single Subject Technique—a way to evaluate the effect of interventions on an individual participant or client.

Skewness—a measure of the symmetry of a distribution.

Snowball Sampling—using an initial sample of people and then getting those individuals to suggest others who might fit the criteria for the sample.

Social Desirability—the possibility that a respondent may answer a questionnaire based on what she or he perceives to be the socially acceptable answer or the "right" answer.

Sociometrics—a technique used to analyze how individuals within groups relate to one another.

Spearman Correlation—a nonparametric statistic used to measure the relationship between two variables.

Staged Questions—questions asked in such a way that one must respond to one question in order to know which question to answer next.

Standard Deviation—the measure of dispersion or how closely data groups around a mean.

Standardized Interview (also called a **Structured Interview**)—an interview form that includes the exact wording and sequencing of questions as they are asked to each individual participating in a study or project.

Standardized Tests—tests designed and modified by a process that results in specified instructions for administration and interpreting the results.

Standards—predetermined criteria used to evaluate how an organization functions.

Statistical Packages—software developed to assist in statistical analysis.

Statistical Significance—the unlikeliness that differences between groups are a result of chance.

Structured Interview (also called a **Standardized Interview**)—An interview form that includes the exact wording and sequencing of questions as they are asked to each individual participating in a study or project.

Summative Evaluation—the systematic terminal examination of the impact and effectiveness of a program. It usually occurs at the end of something.

Surveys—the category of methods that asks people directly about some criteria. Surveys may be done using questionnaires or interviews.

Symbolic Interactionism—a process of analysis where meanings are associated with the words expressed by people.

Systems Approach—a model of evaluation that focuses on determining whether an organization is successful under a given set of conditions.

T-Tests—parametric statistic used to measure the difference between two group means.

Theoretical Sampling—a sampling strategy used to collect qualitative data where people are interviewed/observed based on the data gathered until a saturation point is reached when no further new data are being uncovered.

Theory—a systematic structure for giving order and insight to what has been observed.

Thick Description—a way of writing qualitative data that includes both the evaluator's and the respondents' perspective.

Time Sampling—spot checking based on a plan for doing observations.

Transferability—the qualitative equivalent to external validity or how well the results of a measurement can be generalized to other situations.

Triangulation—collecting data for an evaluation project by using more than one method, source of data, or evaluator.

Trilogy—three of something. The focus of evaluation is on the trilogy of criteria, evidence, and judgment.

Trustworthiness—the quality of the data collected that assures that errors do not exist. The term is usually used to refer to qualitative data but may be appropriate for quantitative as well.

Type I Error—a belief that two groups are different when in fact they are the same.

Type II Error—a belief that two groups are the same when in fact they are different.

Univariate—the examination of the distribution of cases on only one variable.

Unobtrusive Methods—observing, recording, and analyzing human behavior in a situation where interaction with people generally does not occur and where people are unaware that their behavior is being observed or recorded.

Unordered Responses—responses that have no specific order related to the way they are portrayed.

Unstructured Interview (also called **Conversational Guide**)—an interview form in which no questions are predetermined but they emerge as the interviewer and interviewee begin to converse.

Usability—how easy an instrument is to administer and analyze.

Utilization-Focused Evaluation (also called **Responsive Evaluation**)—the active approach to evaluation that starts by finding out what the key decision makers expect from an evaluation and then determining how to conduct the evaluation.

Validity—the determination of whether a measure does what it says it does.

Variable—logical groupings of characteristics.

Variance—a dispersion measure that describes the extent to which scores differ from one another.

Visual Maps—a method of graphically showing the relationship of concepts in qualitative analysis.

Wilcoxon—a nonparametric test used to determine the relationship when the dependent variable has more than two values ranked.

Within Method Triangulation—the collection of both qualitative and quantitative data using the same method.

Worldview—the philosophy from which each of us views the world. This is also referred to as a paradigm.

APPENDIX—TABLE OF RANDOM NUMBERS

```
10480 15011 01536 02011 81647 91646 69179 14194 62590 36207 20969 99570 91292 90700
22368 46573 25595 58393 30995 89198 27982 53402 93965 34095 52666 19174 39615 99505
24130 48360 22527 97265 76393 64809 15179 24830 49340 32081 30680 19655 63348 58629
42167 93093 06243 61680 07853 16376 39440 53537 71341 57004 00849 74917 97758 16379
37570 39975 18137 16656 06121 91782 60468 81305 49684 60672 14110 06927 01263 54613

77921 06907 11008 42751 27756 53498 18602 70659 90655 15053 21916 81825 44394 42880
99562 72905 56420 69994 98872 31016 71194 18738 44013 48840 63213 21069 10634 12952
96301 91977 05463 07972 18876 20922 94595 56869 69014 60045 18425 84903 42508 32307
89579 14342 63661 10281 17453 18103 57740 84378 25331 12566 58678 44947 05585 56941
85475 36857 53342 53988 53060 59533 38867 62300 08158 17983 16439 11458 18593 64952

28918 69578 88231 33276 70997 79936 56865 05859 90106 31595 01547 85590 91610 78188
63553 40961 48265 03427 49626 69445 18663 72695 52180 20847 12234 90511 33703 90322
09429 93969 52636 92737 88974 33488 36320 17617 30015 08272 84115 27156 30613 74952
10365 61129 87529 85689 48237 52267 67689 93394 01511 26358 85104 20285 29975 89868
07119 97336 71048 08178 77233 13916 47564 81056 97735 85977 29372 74461 28551 90707

51085 12765 51821 51259 77452 16308 60756 92144 49442 53900 70960 63990 75601 40719
02368 21382 52404 60268 89398 19885 55322 44819 01188 65255 64835 44919 05944 55157
01011 54092 33362 94904 31273 04146 18594 29852 71585 85030 51132 01915 92747 64951
52162 53916 46369 58586 23216 14513 83149 98736 23495 63250 93738 17752 35156 35749
07056 97628 33787 09998 42698 06691 76988 13602 51851 46104 89916 19509 25625 58104

48663 91245 85828 14346 09172 30168 90229 04734 59193 22178 30421 61666 99904 32812
54164 58492 22421 74103 47070 25306 76468 26384 58151 06646 21524 15227 96909 44592
32639 32363 05597 24200 13363 38005 94342 28728 35806 06912 17012 64161 18296 22851
29334 27001 87637 87308 58731 00256 45834 15398 46557 41135 10367 07684 36188 18510
02488 33062 28834 07351 19731 92420 60952 61280 50001 67658 32586 86679 50720 94953

81525 72295 04839 96423 24878 82651 66566 14778 76797 14780 13300 87074 79666 95725
29676 20591 68086 26432 46901 20829 89768 81536 86645 12659 92259 57102 80428 25280
00742 57392 39064 66432 84683 40027 32832 61362 98947 96067 64760 64584 96096 98253
05366 04213 25669 26422 44407 44048 37937 63904 45766 66134 75470 66520 34693 90449
91921 26418 64117 94305 26766 25940 39972 22209 71500 64568 91402 42416 07844 69618

00582 04711 87917 77341 42206 35126 74087 99547 81817 42607 43808 76655 62028 76630
00725 69884 62797 56170 86324 88072 76222 36086 84637 93161 76038 65855 77919 88006
69011 65795 95876 55293 18988 27354 26585 08615 40801 59920 29841 80150 12777 48501
25976 57948 29888 88604 67917 48708 18912 82271 65424 69774 33611 54262 85963 03547
09763 83473 73577 12908 30883 18317 28290 35797 05998 41688 34952 37888 38917 88050

91567 42595 27958 30134 04024 86385 29880 99730 55536 84855 29080 09250 79656 73211
17955 56349 90999 49127 20044 59931 06115 20542 18059 02008 73708 83517 36103 42791
46503 18584 18845 49618 02304 51038 20655 58727 28168 15475 56942 53389 20562 87338
92157 89634 94824 78171 84610 82834 09922 25417 44137 48413 25555 21246 35509 20468
14577 62765 35605 81263 39667 47358 56873 56307 61607 49518 89656 20103 77490 18062

98427 07523 33362 64270 01638 92477 66969 98420 04880 45585 46565 04102 46880 45709
34914 63976 88720 82765 34476 17032 87589 40836 32427 70002 70663 88863 77775 69348
70060 28277 39475 46473 23219 53416 94970 25832 69975 94884 19661 72828 00102 66794
53976 54914 06990 67245 68350 82948 11398 42878 80287 88267 47363 46634 06541 97809
76072 29515 40980 07391 58745 25774 22987 80059 39911 96189 41151 14222 60697 59583
```

INDEX

Leisure Education: Program Materials for Persons with Developmental Disabilities
>   by Kenneth F. Joswiak

Leisure Education Program Planning: A Systematic Approach
>   by John Dattilo and William D. Murphy

Leisure in Your Life: An Exploration, Fourth Edition
>   by Geoffrey Godbey

A Leisure of One's Own: A Feminist Perspective on Women's Leisure
>   by Karla Henderson, M. Deborah Bialeschki, Susan M. Shaw and Valeria J. Freysinger

Leisure Services in Canada: An Introduction
>   by Mark S. Searle and Russell E. Brayley

Marketing for Parks, Recreation, and Leisure
>   by Ellen L. O'Sullivan

Outdoor Recreation Management: Theory and Application, Third Edition
>   by Alan Jubenville and Ben Twight

Planning Parks for People
>   by John Hultsman, Richard L. Cottrell and Wendy Zales Hultsman

Private and Commercial Recreation
>   edited by Arlin Epperson

The Process of Recreation Programming Theory and Technique, Third Edition
>   by Patricia Farrell and Herberta M. Lundegren

Protocols for Recreation Therapy Programs
>   edited by Jill Kelland, along with the Recreation Therapy Staff at Alberta Hospital—Edmonton

Quality Management: Applications for Therapeutic Recreation
>   edited by Bob Riley

Recreation and Leisure: Issues in an Era of Change, Third Edition
>   edited by Thomas Goodale and Peter A. Witt

Recreation Economic Decisions: Comparing Benefits and Costs
>   by Richard G. Walsh

Recreation Programming and Activities for Older Adults
>   by Jerold E. Elliott and Judith A. Sorg-Elliott

Reference Manual for Writing Rehabilitation Therapy Treatment Plans
>   by Penny Hogberg and Mary Johnson

Research in Therapeutic Recreation: Concepts and Methods
>   edited by Marjorie J. Malkin and Christine Z. Howe

Risk Management in Therapeutic Recreation: A Component of Quality Assurance
>   by Judith Voelkl

A Social History of Leisure Since 1600
>   by Gary Cross

The Sociology of Leisure
>   by John R. Kelly and Geoffrey Godbey

A Study Guide for National Certification in Therapeutic Recreation
>   by Gerald O'Morrow and Ron Reynolds

Therapeutic Recreation: Cases and Exercises
>   by Barbara C. Wilhite and M. Jean Keller

Therapeutic Recreation Protocol for Treatment of Substance Addictions
>   by Rozanne W. Faulkner

A Training Manual for Americans With Disabilities Act Compliance in Parks and Recreation Settings
>   by Carol Stensrud

Understanding Leisure and Recreation: Mapping the Past, Charting the Future
>   edited by Edgar L. Jackson and Thomas L. Burton

Venture Publishing, Inc., 1999 Cato Avenue, State College, PA 16801